Following the Color Line

AMERICAN NEGRO CITIZENSHIP
IN THE PROGRESSIVE ERA

hARPER ✝ ɔORChBOOKS

EDITORS' NOTE: *A check-list of Harper Torchbooks, classified by subjects, is printed at the end of this volume.*

AMERICAN PERSPECTIVES

EDITED BY BERNARD WISHY AND
WILLIAM E. LEUCHTENBURG

ADAMS, JOHN & DANIEL LEONARD: *The American Colonial Crisis: *The John Adams–Daniel Leonard Letters to the Press, 1774–1775,* edited by Bernard Mason

ARNOLD, MATTHEW: *Civilisation in the United States and Other Writings, edited by Warren Susman

BAKER, RAY STANNARD: Following the Color Line: *American Negro Citizenship in the Progressive Era,* edited by Dewey W. Grantham, Jr. TB/3053

BERMAN, HYMAN (ed.): *The Rise of American Labor: *A Reader*

BOURNE, RANDOLPH S.: War and the Intellectuals: *Collected Essays, 1915–1919,* edited by Carl Resek. TB/3043

BRANDEIS, LOUIS D.: Other People's Money, edited by Richard M. Abrams. TB/3081

BROOKS, VAN WYCK: Van Wyck Brooks: *The Early Years; A Selection from His Works, 1908–1921,* edited by Claire Sprague. TB/3082

CAIRNES, J. E.: *The Slave Power, edited by Harold Woodman

FREEHLING, WILLIAM W. (ed.): The Nullification Era: *A Documentary Record.* TB/3079

GILMAN, CHARLOTTE PERKINS: Women and Economics: *A Study of the Economic Relation Between Men and Women as a Factor in Social Evolution,* edited by Carl N. Degler. TB/3073

HAMILTON, ALEXANDER: The Reports of Alexander Hamilton, edited by Jacob E. Cooke. TB/3060

HUNTER, ROBERT: Poverty: *Social Conscience in the Progressive Era,* edited by Peter d'A. Jones. TB/3065

HUTCHISON, WILLIAM R. (ed.): American Protestant Thought: *The Liberal Era.* TB/1385

JACKSON, HELEN HUNT: A Century of Dishonor: *The Early Crusade for Indian Reform,* edited by Andrew F. Rolle. TB/3063

JEFFERSON, THOMAS: Notes on the State of Virginia, edited by Thomas P. Abernethy. TB/3052

LIBBY, O. G.: *The Geographical Distribution of the Vote of the Thirteen States on the Federal Constitution: 1787–1788, edited by Lee Benson

MCLOUGHLIN, WILLIAM G. (ed.): The American Evangelicals, 1800–1900. TB/1382

OSOFSKY, GILBERT (ed.): *Three Slave Narratives

PARTON, JAMES: The Presidency of Andrew Jackson, from the "Life of Jackson," edited by Robert V. Remini. TB/3080

PIKE, JAMES S.: The Prostrate State: *South Carolina under Negro Government,* edited by Robert F. Durden. TB/3085

RAUSCHENBUSCH, WALTER: Christianity and the Social Crisis, edited by Robert D. Cross. TB/3059

REID, WHITELAW: After the War: *A Tour of the Southern States, 1865–1866,* edited by C. Vann Woodward. TB/3066

RHODES, JAMES FORD: *The Coming of the Civil War (Vol. I); The Civil War (Vol. II). An abridgment of "The History of the United States from the Compromise of 1850," edited by Grady McWhiney

RIIS, JACOB: The Making of an American, edited by Roy Lubove. TB/3070

SHINN, CHARLES HOWARD: Mining Camps: *A Study in American Frontier Government,* edited by Rodman Paul. TB/3062

SMITH, JOHN: Captain John Smith's America: *Selections from His Writings,* edited by John Lankford. TB/3078

STEFFENS, LINCOLN: *The Struggle for Self-Government, edited by Joel A. Tarr

TARBELL, IDA M.: The History of the Standard Oil Company: *Briefer Version,* edited by David M. Chalmers. TB/3071

TINDALL, GEORGE B. (ed.): A Populist Reader. TB/3069

TOURGÉE, ALBION W.: A Fool's Errand: *A Novel of the South during Reconstruction,* edited by George M. Fredrickson. TB/3074

* *in preparation*
5/68

Following the Color Line

AMERICAN NEGRO CITIZENSHIP
IN THE PROGRESSIVE ERA

BY

RAY STANNARD BAKER

Illustrated

INTRODUCTION AND NOTES TO THE TORCHBOOK EDITION BY
DEWEY W. GRANTHAM, JR.

HARPER TORCHBOOKS
THE UNIVERSITY LIBRARY

HARPER & ROW, PUBLISHERS
NEW YORK, EVANSTON, AND LONDON

"I AM OBLIGED TO CONFESS THAT I DO NOT REGARD THE
ABOLITION OF SLAVERY AS A MEANS OF PUTTING OFF THE
STRUGGLE BETWEEN THE TWO RACES IN THE SOUTHERN STATES."

—*De Tocqueville, "Democracy in America"* (1835)

FOLLOWING THE COLOR LINE

Introduction to the Torchbook edition copyright
© 1964 by Dewey W. Grantham, Jr.

Printed in the United States of America.

This book was originally published in 1908 by Doubleday, Page & Company.

First HARPER TORCHBOOK edition published 1964 by
Harper & Row, Publishers, Incorporated
49 East 33rd Street
New York 16, N.Y.

INTRODUCTION TO THE TORCHBOOK EDITION

BY DEWEY W. GRANTHAM, JR.

Ray Stannard Baker had already gained an eminent reputation as a magazine reporter before he retired from journalism following the First World War and turned his attention to the writing of his many volumes on Woodrow Wilson. One of the writers discovered by Samuel S. McClure, he became a practitioner of the new journalism and a member of the famous muckraking team that wrote for *McClure's Magazine.* Baker investigated a variety of social problems in early twentieth-century America, and his articles on labor organizations and on the railroad question brought him praise from experts in those fields and something of the status of a public servant at large. On occasion the effervescent Theodore Roosevelt invited him to the White House to sound him out before forming public policy. In the fall of 1906, the serious and energetic young Midwesterner turned to a new subject: the Negro in American life. The result was *Following the Color Line,* his most notable achievement as a journalist.

Shortly before Baker began his investigation of the Negro question he had joined with several other leading staff members of *McClure's* in the purchase of *The American Magazine.* The new venture desperately needed the kind of articles that Baker and Lincoln Steffens and Ida M. Tarbell had formerly written for *McClure's.* Baker's search for material that would help make the new magazine an "assured success" brought him to the race problem, a topic of growing national interest in an era marked by the completion of the Negro's political proscription in the South, the erection of an elaborate structure of Jim Crow legislation in the region below the Potomac, and the perpetuation and even worsening of a pattern of violence and brutality in the treatment of southern Negroes. Baker had long been interested in the problem of lawlessness and mob violence, and in earlier years he had made a few excursions into Negro folklore. He had traveled to Georgia to interview Joel Chandler Harris and with the help of "Uncle Remus" had talked with some of the "ancient Negroes" who remembered the old stories. In the fall of 1904 he visited the scene of four widely-publicized lynchings—in Georgia, Alabama, Ohio, and Illinois—while preparing two articles on lynching for the January and February, 1905, numbers of *McClure's*. During the next two years the reporter's earlier interest in the Negro and lawlessness was reinforced.

By the early years of the twentieth century the capitulation of the South to extreme racism was virtually complete, in part because of the steady erosion of indigenous restraints during the period since Reconstruction and in part because of the acquiescence of northern liberalism as expressed in the press, the courts, and national politics. The terrible toll of mob violence against Negroes in the South was producing a growing harvest of bitterness and fear; Negro migration and racial conflict also led to race riots in several northern cities; and the country as a whole seemed to be awakening to the realization that it faced "a new Negro problem." What *should* be the status of the Negro in American life? In announcing the forthcoming appearance of Baker's articles, the editors of *The American* answered one rhetorical question with another: "Could there be anything more necessary—North or South—than light and information and publicity?"

At the outset Baker considered the possibility of confining his investigation to one southern state, perhaps South Carolina, but he quickly abandoned that idea for one treating the question in a national setting. Once the journalist settled on a subject, he could absorb himself in it completely. Reading, traveling, interviewing, collecting statistics, and filling his notebooks with information and impressions, he accumulated a mass of material from which he fashioned more than a dozen substantial magazine articles. After he had spent several weeks in the field gathering material, he would retire to his home in East Lansing, Michigan, to think and write. From the time he began his research in late October, 1906, until the appearance of his last article in the September, 1908, issue of

The American, the Negro in America was Baker's major preoccupation as a journalist.

Baker began his intensive work in Atlanta on November 1, 1906, only a few weeks after a terrible race riot occurred in that city. That event became the subject of his first article and set the stage for the rest of the series. From Atlanta Baker moved on to the black belt of Alabama and Georgia, visiting such places as Tuskegee and the plantation of J. Pope Brown. Eventually he visited most of the southern states. He also followed the color line in half a dozen or more of the great northern cities, as well as in some smaller towns and communities north of the Ohio River. The subject grew more complicated and more difficult as he got into it. Wherever he went he talked with public officials, leading spokesmen of the two races, and students of the race question. Among those he interviewed or corresponded with were Booker T. Washington, William E. B. Du Bois, Edwin A. Alderman, William E. Dodd, Edwin Mims, Alfred Holt Stone, Oswald Garrison Villard, Albert Bushnell Hart, and Mary White Ovington. His project attracted so much attention, particularly in the South, that people sent him unsolicited information and sought him out in person to offer help or advice. Baker drove himself, sometimes working sixteen hours a day, but he became increasingly excited over the prospects of his series. "I believe," he wrote his father on November 22, 1906, "I am going to be able to do a real public service with these articles. . . ."

The first article, profusely illustrated with photographs, appeared in the April, 1907, number of *The American.* It was followed during successive months by four more pieces on the Negro in the South, after which, to the delight of the southern press, Baker shifted his attention to race relations in the North. The first article in this group appeared in the February, 1908, issue and the series continued until September of that year with monthly installments devoted to the Negro in the North and race relations in the United States generally. The articles were an immediate success and interest in them increased as they were published. The February and March, 1908, numbers of *The American* were completely sold out. Newspaper comment was generally favorable, especially in the North, and the author observed to one correspondent that while some southern journals had given him "the anticipated fits" others had been "unexpectedly appreciative." Southern liberals and moderates applauded the series. Alexander J. McKelway, a North Carolina progressive, described the articles as "eminently fair." A northern liberal, Oswald Garrison Villard, who was later to be one of the founders of the National Association for the Advancement of Colored People, termed the first article "very successful indeed." Booker T. Washington and W. E. B. Du Bois were both complimentary in their evaluation of the series, although Du Bois had reservations about a few of Baker's points. There were a few astringent notes: some of the more militant Negro spokesmen were critical of an interpretation that seemed to stress the duty of Negroes to the neglect of their rights.

While the magazine articles were still appearing, Baker reached an agreement with Walter Hines Page to have them brought out as a book by Doubleday, Page & Company. The articles were arranged in *Following the Color Line* in the order of their appearance in *The American Magazine*, except for the inclusion of the two articles on lynching from *McClure's*, which were combined as Chapter IX of the book. Few revisions were made in the articles for book publication. As a book the work is somewhat episodic and lacks clear unity. Yet it is a comprehensive account, possessing a balance and objectivity unusual for its time. The style is characteristically readable and lively, and the narrative reveals Baker's insatiable curiosity about the human condition. The book's publication evoked the enthusiasm of scholarly as well as popular critics. The reviewer for the *American Journal of Sociology,* for example, described it as "remarkable for its objectivity and psychological insight." It was, students of Ray Stannard Baker agree, the most significant of his publications prior to his biography of Woodrow Wilson.[1]

[1] See John Erwin Semonche, "Progressive Journalist: Ray Stannard Baker, 1870-1914" (Ph.D. dissertation, Northwestern University, 1962), p. 173. I am indebted to this careful study of Baker's career as a journalist not only for the author's discussion of the writing of *Following the Color Line* but also for his perceptive treatment of Baker's broader role during the years 1892-1914.

Baker, as he said, was trying "to get at the *facts*," trying to picture conditions as they actually existed during the first decade of the twentieth century. He was an indefatigable and a talented newspaperman—keen, observant, and imaginative. He took pains to express all views on the question and his frequent use of the phrase "South or North" provides a clue to his determined search for balance. Although he eschewed the role of sociologist or historian, his constant effort to understand the data he had collected and the observations of his own eyes gave his essays a dimension lacking in most journalism. These qualities were most important, perhaps, in making his account authentic and comprehensible to the average reader. The work does not always probe deeply, but it has much to commend it: the analysis of race relations in a national context, the description of concrete social situations from which racial strife arose, the graphic portrayal of the lynching mob in action, the appraisal of Negro migration, the realistic account of Negro town life, the interpretation of the opposing parties among Negro leaders, the recognition of the "wide and deep" chasm developing between the best elements of the two races, and the insight into the nature of racial prejudice and discrimination in South and North.

Following the Color Line was a moderate and in many respects even a conservative appraisal of the problem it surveyed. To some extent this was a tactical decision of *The American Magazine*. As John S. Phillips, one of the magazine's editors, reminded Baker in April, 1907: "For the sake of effect we must keep the interest and friendliness of Southern readers. After all, they are the people whom we wish to reach and enlighten." One observer suggested that Baker was "rubbing it in" just enough to make the Southerners "face the situation." Yet, fundamentally, the journalist expressed his honest convictions. They were not essentially radical in character. Baker's associations in the South tended to be with well-meaning moderates, men who joined with northern philanthropists in the annual Conferences for Southern Education during this period, and his interpretation reflects the paternalism and optimism associated with the current vogue of the Booker T. Washington school.

Southern white readers of whatever disposition on the race question could find much to please them in Baker's book. His interpretation of Reconstruction as a time of chaos and corruption was favorable to the southern white leaders. He agreed that for the time being some segregation was necessary and he frankly said that Negroes "as a class are to-day far inferior in education, intelligence, and efficiency to the white people as a class." While he asserted that both the approach of Booker T. Washington and that of W. E. B. Du Bois were valuable, he obviously preferred the Tuskegee idea of education for service over Du Bois' more aggressive program. As a backward race Negroes would have to go forward primarily under the tutelage of white men. Genuine progress would come only with "time, growth, education, religion, thought." Baker also held other assumptions that were common during the period of his investigation. At times he fell into the familiar southern habit of categorizing the Negro as a race in various particulars. When he used the word "Southerner," he meant *white* Southerner; he did not include the Negro. It was this assumption, accepted naturally and perhaps even unconsciously by Baker, that led Du Bois to remark to him in April, 1907:

> Of course, as I have said to you personally, the great trouble with anyone coming from the outside to study the Negro problem is that they do not know the Negro as a human being, as a feeling, thinking man; that they do know the Southerners have met them in their homes and have been intimate with them and the result is that while they speak of the Southerner in the second person, they continually regard the Negro as in the third person, a sort of outside and unknown personality.[2]

Although Ray Stannard Baker thought of himself as the objective reporter, he was intensely interested in educating his readers, in being a "maker of understandings." ":The best thing," he wrote a few months before beginning his exploration of the color line, "seems to be more publicity, more information, more preaching in the wilderness." Like many other progressives, Baker had a profound faith in the possibility of awakening and regenerating the individual citizen, "his intelligence, his unselfishness, his social re-

[2] Du Bois to Baker, April 3, 1907, Ray Stannard Baker Papers (Manuscript Division, Library of Congress). It might be noted that even Du Bois used the word "Southerners" to mean southern whites.

sponsibility." Yet during the years he was working on *Follownig the Color Line* Baker was becoming increasingly convinced of the necessity of a collectivist approach to social action, and his book presented a class analysis of historical movements.[3] Clearly there was some contradiction in the journalist's acceptance of a Washingtonian philosophy of improvement by individual effort and his class interpretation of history. The contradiction is never reconciled in *Follownig the Color Line*. But in answering Theodore Roosevelt's vigorous criticism of his division of society into the "Few" and the "Many" and of his thesis that the Negro problem was really part of a larger struggle for democracy, Baker insisted that the political revolution in the South offered proof that *"class action is a condition now existent."*

Although Baker contended that the Vardamans and Jeff Davises represented "a genuine movement for a more democratic government in the South," his interpretation was scarcely an endorsement of southern conditions. He criticized the old aristocratic leadership in the region as being selfish and undemocratic, but he also realized that the new "men of the people" like Vardaman would exploit the passions and prejudices of the white masses. Yet he was hopeful. He found democracy at work in the overthrow of the old leadership and believed that it would not stop at the color line: "once its ferment begins to work in a nation it does not stop until it reaches and animates the uttermost man." In this sense Baker's work was anything but pro-southern. In fact, a note of impending political change runs strongly through the book. And despite his darker fears, he thought the South was ready for change and that the ferment of democracy would soon bring the Negro into more active participation in American society.

If Baker subscribed to many of the conservative ideas about race so commonplace in his day, he was nevertheless able to transcend many of the racist attitudes of his contemporaries. His genuine concern over the distressing conditions of American Negroes, his sympathy for the downtrodden, his ardor for justice, and his basic optimism

[3] For a suggestive essay on Baker's search for a philosophy, see David Chalmers, "Ray Stannard Baker's Search for Reform," *Journal of the History of Ideas,* XIX (June, 1958), pp. 422-34.

were inseparable from the argument of *Following the Color Line*. His broad humanity embraced the Negro and he considered racial conflict a spiritual as well as a social and economic problem. His very inconsistencies revealed as much. Thus it was impossible for him to reconcile his emphasis on the growing separation of the two races, into which he tried to read hopeful signs, with his belief in democracy and brotherhood. It was this confusion, this dilemma, that gave his chapter on the mulatto in America, the man caught in between, rare sensitiveness and pathos. The prophetic quality of *Following the Color Line* cannot compare with such a volume as W. E. B. Du Bois' *The Souls of Black Folk* (1903) but its very ambivalence makes it one of the most revealing documents of the progressive era. Baker had no ready solution for the American Dilemma; he could only suggest "a gradual substitution of understanding and sympathy for blind repulsion and hatred." But he was convinced that "the white man as well as the black is being tried by fire." And throughout his book he demonstrated a conviction that "the man farthest down" could be helped only if all Americans expressed a democratic spirit.

In the decade following the publication of *Following the Color Line* Baker retained his interest in the problem of the Negro in the United States, writing and speaking on the subject and stressing his conviction that the problem was basically one of democracy. For a time his optimism about an ultimate solution mounted. Thus in 1913 he predicted the early breakup of the Solid South, the entrance of many Negroes and poor whites into politics, and a rejuvenated southern political life in which basic issues could be attacked and solved. But events soon pricked the bubble of his optimism. In the fall of 1914 he conceded that in its patronage and segregation policies the Wilson administration had "surrendered a stronghold of democracy in the treatment of the Negro & given new territory to the occupation of the idea of caste in America." In 1916 he expressed alarm over the growing economic competition between the races in the South, the increasing migration of Negroes to northern cities, the growing resort to Jim Crow measures in South and North, and the mounting bitterness of Negroes because of the discriminatory treatment they suffered.

In investigating such great national problems as the role of organized labor and the most effective way for democracy to deal with powerful business aggregations, Ray Stannard Baker had shown remarkable capacity to enlarge his understanding and to grow in sympathetic appreciation of the human beings involved. This was also true of his experience in following the color line. Puzzled by the hostile response of the more aggressive Negro leaders to what he had written, he re-examined some of the opinions he had expressed in his book. With the passage of time he moved closer to Du Bois' philosophy of active agitation for Negro equality and in 1915 even accepted an honorary vice-presidency of the N.A.A.C.P. By that time he had begun to wonder "if social equality is not, after all, the crux of the whole problem?" He continued to have faith in the promise of progress through education, economic improvement, and humanitarianism. But as the signs of danger grew during the next few years he became appalled at "the contemptuous indifference of a large part of white America to what is going on in the depths of the volcano just below."

Following the Color Line was a pioneer work in the study of race relations in the United States. Baker's careful reporting and revealing insight make it a singularly useful account for the period it treats. Gunnar Myrdal and his associates used it as a major source in the preparation of *An American Dilemma* (1944), quoting from it more than two dozen times. In many respects it is superior to most southern travel accounts of the era, including Albert Bushnell Hart's *The Southern South* (1910), William Archer's *Through Afro-America* (1910), and Maurice S. Evans' *Black and White in the Southern States* (1915). Rupert B. Vance has described it as "the best account of race relations in the South during the period—one that reads like field notes for the future historian." [4] In its description of conditions and attitudes in the South the book often goes beyond race relations, and although not the work of a social scientist, it contributed to the conviction that the South invited disciplined sociological investigation.

Baker's volume is also significant as the most substantial contribution by any muckraker and progressive to the litera-

[4] Thomas D. Clark (ed.), *Travels in the New South: A Bibliography,* 2 vols. (Norman, 1962), II, 18.

ture on the American Negro. It is not, strictly speaking, a muckraking book, but it does recapture some of the muckraking spirit. More important, it reflects in a superb way the assumptions and aspirations of the progressive mind which Baker typified so well. The journalist understood that the problem he was discussing was ineluctably involved in the deeper currents of American democracy and he attempted to treat it from that perspective. He had hoped, like a good muckraker, that publicity and education would stimulate the American people to take action and gradually to set their democracy in order. But like many progressives Baker would go only so far toward greater equality. The tragedy is that even the limited reconstruction he envisaged in 1908 was largely neglected and the progressive movement failed to come to grips with the problem.

Baker was one of the first modern Americans to discuss the race issue comprehensively and in a spirit of fairness. His work contributed in some measure to the forces that eventually brought the question of the Negro's status in America to its rightful place as a compelling national issue. But *Following the Color Line's* greatest value is as a reliable and revealing source for those interested in the course of race relations in recent American history.

Nashville, Tennessee
December 1, 1963

A NOTE ABOUT THE TORCHBOOK EDITION

The original edition of *Following the Color Line* was published by Doubleday, Page & Company in 1908. In editing this new edition I have added notes of identification and explanation for certain individuals and events referred to by Ray Stannard Baker. But except for the correction of a few typographical errors and one or two minor mistakes in Baker's use of dates and statistics, this edition is a faithful reproduction of the original. Although the conventional American spelling of "color" has been used for the jacket and title page, Baker's "colour" has been retained for the text of the book itself.

I am deeply grateful to the Baker family for the help they have given me in preparing this Torchbook edition of *Following the Color Line*.

D. W. G.

PREFACE

My purpose in writing this book has been to make a clear statement of the exact present conditions and relationships of the Negro in American life. I am not vain enough to imagine that I have seen all the truth, nor that I have always placed the proper emphasis upon the facts that I here present. Every investigator necessarily has his personal equation or point of view. The best he can do is to set down the truth as he sees it, without bating a jot or adding a tittle, and this I have done.

I have endeavoured to see every problem, not as a Northerner, nor as a Southerner, but as an American. And I have looked at the Negro, not merely as a menial, as he is commonly regarded in the South, nor as a curiosity, as he is often seen in the North, but as a plain human being, animated with his own hopes, depressed by his own fears, meeting his own problems with failure or success.

I have accepted no statement of fact, however generally made, until I was fully persuaded from my own personal investigation that what I heard was really a fact and not a rumour.

Wherever I have ventured upon conclusions, I claim for them neither infallibility nor originality. They are offered frankly as my own latest and clearest thoughts upon the various subjects discussed. If any man can give me better evidence for the error of my conclusions than I have for the truth of them I am prepared to go with him, and gladly, as far as he can prove his way. And I have offered my conclusions, not in a spirit of controversy, nor in behalf of any party or section of the country, but in the hope that, by inspiring a broader outlook, they may lead, finally, to other conclusions more nearly approximating the truth than mine.

While these chapters were being published in the *American Magazine* (one chapter, that on lynching, in *McClure's Magazine*) I received many hundreds of letters from all parts of the country. I acknowledge them gratefully. Many of them contained friendly criticisms, suggestions, and corrections, which I have profited by in the revision of the chapters for book publication. Especially have the letters from the South, describing local conditions and expressing local points of view, been valuable to me. I wish here, also, to thank the many men and women, South and North, white and coloured, who have given me personal assistance in my inquiries.

CONTENTS

ILLUSTRATIONS

PART ONE

THE NEGRO IN THE SOUTH

CHAPTER I

A RACE RIOT, AND AFTER

UPON the ocean of antagonism between the white and Negro races in this country, there arises occasionally a wave, stormy in its appearance, but soon subsiding into quietude. Such a wave was the Atlanta riot. Its ominous size, greater by far than the ordinary race disturbances which express themselves in lynchings, alarmed the entire country and awakened in the South a new sense of the dangers which threatened it. A description of that spectacular though superficial disturbance, the disaster incident to its fury, and the remarkable efforts at reconstruction will lead the way naturally — as human nature is best interpreted in moments of passion — to a clearer understanding, in future chapters, of the deep and complex race feeling which exists in this country.

On the twenty-second day of September, 1906, Atlanta had become a veritable social tinder-box. For months the relation of the races had been growing more strained. The entire South had been sharply annoyed by a shortage of labour accompanied by high wages and, paradoxically, by an increasing number of idle Negroes. In Atlanta the lower class — the "worthless Negro" — had been increasing in numbers: it showed itself too evidently among the swarming saloons, dives, and "clubs" which a complaisant city administration allowed to exist in the very heart of the city. Crime had increased to an alarming extent; an insufficient and ineffective police force seemed unable to cope with it. With a population of 115,000 Atlanta had over 17,000 arrests in 1905; in 1906 the number increased to 21,602. Atlanta had many more arrests than New Orleans with nearly three times the population and twice as many Negroes; and almost four times as many as Milwaukee, Wisconsin, a city nearly three times as large. Race feeling had been sharpened through

3

a long and bitter political campaign, Negro disfranchisement being one of the chief issues under discussion. An inflammatory play called "The Clansman," though forbidden by public sentiment in many Southern cities, had been given in Atlanta and other places with the effect of increasing the prejudice of both races. Certain newspapers in Atlanta, taking advantage of popular feeling, kept the race issue constantly agitated, emphasising Negro crimes with startling headlines. One newspaper even recommended the formation of organisations of citizens in imitation of the Ku Klux movement of reconstruction days. In the clamour of this growing agitation, the voice of the right-minded white people and industrious, self-respecting Negroes was almost unheard. A few ministers of both races saw the impending storm and sounded a warning — to no effect; and within the week before the riot the citizens, the city administration and the courts all woke up together. There were calls for mass-meetings, the police began to investigate the conditions of the low saloons and dives, the country constabulary was increased in numbers, the grand jury was called to meet in special session on Monday the 24th.

Prosperity and Lawlessness

But the awakening of moral sentiment in the city, unfortunately, came too late. Crime, made more lurid by agitation, had so kindled the fires of hatred that they could not be extinguished by ordinary methods. The best people of Atlanta were like the citizens of prosperous Northern cities, too busy with money-making to pay attention to public affairs. For Atlanta is growing rapidly. Its bank clearings jumped from ninety millions in 1900 to two hundred and twenty-two millions in 1906, its streets are well paved and well lighted, its streetcar service is good, its sky-scrapers are comparable with the best in the North. In other words, it was progressive — few cities I know of more so — but it had forgotten its public duties.

Within a few months before the riot there had been a number of crimes of worthless Negroes against white women. Leading Negroes, while not one of them with whom I talked wished

1. In the Democratic primary of August 22, 1906, Hoke Smith, an Atlanta lawyer and Secretary of the Interior during the second Cleveland administration, won an overwhelming victory in the contest for the gubernatorial nomination.

to protect any Negro who was really guilty, asserted that the number of these crimes had been greatly exaggerated and that in special instances the details had been over-emphasised because the criminal was black; that they had been used to further inflame race hatred. I had a personal investigation made of every crime against a white woman committed in the few months before and after the riot. Three, charged to white men, attracted comparatively little attention in the newspapers, although one, the offence of a white man named Turnadge, was shocking in its details. Of twelve such charges against Negroes in the six months preceding the riot two were cases of rape, horrible in their details, three were aggravated attempts at rape, three may have been attempts, three were pure cases of fright on the part of the white woman, and in one the white woman, first asserting that a Negro had assaulted her, finally confessed attempted suicide.

The facts of two of these cases I will narrate — and without excuse for the horror of the details. If we are to understand the true conditions in the South, these things *must* he told.

Story of One Negro's Crime

One of the cases was that of Mrs. Knowles Etheleen Kimmel, twenty-five years old, wife of a farmer living near Atlanta. A mile beyond the end of the street-car line stands a small green bungalow-like house in a lonely spot near the edge of the pine woods. The Kimmels who lived there were not Southerners by birth but of Pennsylvania Dutch stock. They had been in the South four or five years, renting their lonesome farm, raising cotton and corn and hopefully getting a little ahead. On the day before the riot a strange rough-looking Negro called at the back door of the Kimmel home. He wore a soldier's cast-off khaki uniform. He asked a foolish question and went away. Mrs. Kimmel was worried and told her husband. He, too, was worried — the fear of this crime is everywhere present in the South — and when he went away in the afternoon he asked his nearest neighbour to look out for the strange Negro. When he came back a few hours later, he found fifty white men in his yard. He knew what had happened without being told: his wife was under medical atten-

---

He had campaigned for over a year on a platform urging Negro disfranchisement and stringent railroad regulation.
2. Atlanta *Georgian*, Atlanta *Journal*, and Atlanta *News*.

dance in the house.   She had been able to give a clear description of the Negro: bloodhounds were brought, but the pursuing white men had so obliterated the criminal's tracks that he could not be traced.   Through information given by a Negro a suspect was arrested and nearly lynched before he could be brought to Mrs. Kimmel for identification; when she saw him she said: "He is not the man."   The real criminal was never apprehended.

One day, weeks afterward, I found the husband working alone in his field; his wife, to whom the surroundings had become unbearable, had gone away to visit friends.   He told me the story hesitatingly.   His prospects, he said, were ruined: his neighbours had been sympathetic but he could not continue to live there with the feeling that they all knew.   He was preparing to give up his home and lose himself where people did not know his story.   I asked him if he favoured lynching, and his answer surprised me.

"I've thought about that," he said.   "You see, I'm a Christian man, or I try to be.   My wife is a Christian woman.   We've talked about it.   What good would it do?   We should make criminals of ourselves, should n't we?   No, let the law take its course.   When I came here, I tried to help the Negroes as much as I could.   But many of them won't work even when the wages are high: they won't come when they agree to and when they get a few dollars ahead they go down to the saloons in Atlanta.   Everyone is troubled about getting labour and everyone is afraid of prowling idle Negroes.   Now, the thing has come to me, and it's just about ruined my life."

When I came away the poor lonesome fellow followed me half-way up the hill, asking: "Now, what would you do?"

One more case.   One of the prominent florists in Atlanta is W. C. Lawrence.   He is an Englishman, whose home is in the outskirts of the city.   On the morning of August 20th his daughter Mabel, fourteen years old, and his sister Ethel, twenty-five years old, a trained nurse who had recently come from England, went out into the nearby woods to pick ferns. Being in broad daylight and within sight of houses, they had no fear.   Returning along an old Confederate breastworks, they were met by a brutal-looking Negro with a club in one hand and a stone in the other.   He first knocked the little girl down, then her aunt. When the child "came to" she found herself partially bound with a rope. "Honey," said the Negro, "I want you to come with me." With remarkable presence of mind the child said: "I can't, my leg is broken," and she let it swing limp from the knee. Deceived, the Negro went back to bind the aunt. Mabel, instantly untying the rope, jumped up and ran for help. When he saw the child escaping the Negro ran off.

"When I got there," said Mr. Lawrence, "my sister was lying against the bank, face down. The back of her head had been beaten bloody. The bridge of her nose was cut open, one eye had been gouged out of its socket. My daughter had three bad cuts on her head—thank God, nothing worse to either. But my sister, who was just beginning her life, will be totally blind in one eye, probably in both. Her life is ruined."

About a month later, through the information of a Negro, the criminal was caught, identified by the Misses Lawrence, and sent to the penitentiary for forty years (two cases), the limit of punishment for attempted criminal assault.

In both of these cases arrests were made on the information of Negroes.

Terror of Both White and Coloured People

The effect of a few such crimes as these may be more easily imagined than described. They produced a feeling of alarm which no one who has not lived in such a community can in any wise appreciate. I was astonished in travelling in the South to discover how widely prevalent this dread has become. Many white women in Atlanta dare not leave their homes alone after dark; many white men carry arms to protect themselves and their families. And even these precautions do not always prevent attacks.

But this is not the whole story. Everywhere I went in Atlanta I heard of the fear of the white people, but not much was said of the terror which the Negroes also felt. And yet every Negro I met voiced in some way that fear. It is difficult here in the North for us to understand what such a condition means: a whole community namelessly afraid!

The better-class Negroes have two sources of fear: one of the criminals of their own race — such attacks are rarely given much space in the newspapers — and the other the fear of the white people. My very first impression of what this fear of the Negroes might be came, curiously enough, not from Negroes but from a fine white woman on whom I called shortly after going South. She told this story:

"I had a really terrible experience one evening a few days ago. I was walking along —— Street when I saw a rather good-looking young Negro come out of a hallway to the side-walk. He was in a great hurry, and, in turning suddenly, as a person sometimes will do, he accidentally brushed my shoulder with his arm. He had not seen me before. When he turned and found it was a white woman he had touched, such a look of abject terror and fear came into his face as I hope never again to see on a human countenance. He knew what it meant if I was frightened, called for help, and accused him of insulting or attacking me. He stood still a moment, then turned and ran down the street, dodging into the first alley he came to. It shows, does n't it, how little it might take to bring punishment upon an innocent man!"

The next view I got was through the eyes of one of the able Negroes of the South, Bishop Gaines of the African Methodist Episcopal Church.[3] He is now an old man, but of imposing presence. Of wide attainments, he has travelled in Europe, he owns much property, and rents houses to white tenants. He told me of services he had held some time before in south Georgia. Approaching the church one day through the trees, he suddenly encountered a white woman carrying water from a spring. She dropped her pail instantly, screamed, and ran up the path toward her house.

"If I had been some Negroes," said Bishop Gaines, "I should have turned and fled in terror; the alarm would have been given, and it is not unlikely that I should have had a posse of white men with bloodhounds on my trail. If I had been caught what would my life have been worth? The woman would have identified me — and what could I have said? But I did not run. I stepped out in the path, held up one hand and said:

" 'Don't worry, madam, I am Bishop Gaines, and I am

3. Bishop Wesley John Gaines of Atlanta.

holding services here in this church.' So she stopped running and I apologised for having startled her."

The Negro knows he has little chance to explain, if by accident or ignorance he insults a white woman or offends a white man. An educated Negro, one of the ablest of his race, telling me of how a friend of his who by merest chance had provoked a number of half-drunken white men, had been set upon and frightfully beaten, remarked: "It might have been me!"

Now, I am telling these things just as they look to the Negro; it is quite as important, as a problem in human nature, to know how the Negro feels and what he says, as it is to know how the white man feels.

How the Newspapers Fomented the Riot

On the afternoon of the riot the newspapers in flaming headlines chronicled four assaults by Negroes on white women. I had a personal investigation made of each of those cases. Two of them may have been attempts at assaults, but two palpably were nothing more than fright on the part of both the white woman and the Negro. As an instance, in one case an elderly woman, Mrs. Martha Holcombe, going to close her blinds in the evening, saw a Negro on the sidewalk. In a terrible fright she screamed. The news was telephoned to the police station, but before the officials could respond, Mrs. Holcombe telephoned them not to come out. And yet this was one of the "assaults" chronicled in letters five inches high in a newspaper extra.

And finally on this hot Saturday half-holiday, when the country people had come in by hundreds, when everyone was out of doors, when the streets were crowded, when the saloons had been filled since early morning with white men and Negroes, both drinking — certain newspapers in Atlanta began to print extras with big headings announcing new assaults on white women by Negroes. The Atlanta *News* published five such extras, and newsboys cried them through the city:

"Third assault."

"Fourth assault.'

The whole city, already deeply agitated, was thrown into a

veritable state of panic. The news in the extras was taken as truthful; for the city was not in a mood then for cool investigation. Calls began to come in from every direction for police protection. A loafing Negro in a backyard, who in ordinary times would not have been noticed, became an object of real terror. The police force, too small at best, was thus distracted and separated.

In Atlanta the proportion of men who go armed continually is very large; the pawnshops of Decatur and Peters Streets, with windows like arsenals, furnish the low class of Negroes and whites with cheap revolvers and knives. Every possible element was here, then, for a murderous outbreak. The good citizens, white and black, were far away in their homes; the bad men had been drinking in the dives permitted to exist by the respectable people of Atlanta; and here they were gathered, by night, in the heart of the city.

The Mob Gathers

And, finally, a trivial incident fired the tinder. Fear and vengeance generated it: it was marked at first by a sort of rough, half-drunken horseplay, but when once blood was shed, the brute, which is none too well controlled in the best city, came out and gorged itself. Once permit the shackles of law and order to be cast off, and men, white or black, Christian or pagan, revert to primordial savagery. There is no such thing as an orderly mob.

Crime had been committed by Negroes, but this mob made no attempt to find the criminals: it expressed its blind, unreasoning, uncontrolled race hatred by attacking every man, woman, or boy it saw who had a black face. A lame boot-black, an inoffensive, industrious Negro boy, at that moment actually at work shining a man's shoes, was dragged out and cuffed, kicked and beaten to death in the street. Another young Negro was chased and stabbed to death with jack-knives in the most unspeakably horrible manner. The mob entered barber shops where respectable Negro men were at work shaving white customers, pulled them away from their chairs and beat them. Cars were stopped and inoffensive Negroes were thrown through the windows or dragged out and

JAMES H. WALLACE

"The asphalt workers are nearly all coloured. In New York . . . the chosen representative who sits with the Central Federated Union of the city is James H. Wallace, a coloured man."

R. R. WRIGHT

Organiser of the Negro State Fair in Georgia. Of full-blooded African descent, his grandmother, who reared him, being an African Negro of the Mandingo tribe.

H. O. TANNER

One of whose pictures hangs in the Luxembourg; winner N. W. Harris prize for the best American painting at Chicago.

REV. H. H. PROCTOR

Pastor of the First Congregational Church (coloured), to which belong many of the best coloured families of Atlanta.

DR. W. F. PENN

This prosperous Negro physician's home in Atlanta was visited by the mob.

Photograph by Sexton & Maxwell

GEORGE W. CABLE

Chairman of the coloured probation officers of the Juvenile Court, Indianapolis.

AN OLD BLACK "MAMMY" WITH WHITE CHILD

beaten. They did not stop with killing and maiming; they broke into hardware stores and armed themselves, they demolished not only Negro barber shops and restaurants, but they robbed stores kept by white men.

Of course the Mayor came out, and the police force and the fire department, and finally the Governor ordered out the militia — to apply that pound of cure which should have been an ounce of prevention.

It is highly significant of Southern conditions — which the North does not understand — that the first instinct of thousands of Negroes in Atlanta, when the riot broke out, was not to run away from the white people but to run to them. The white man who takes the most radical position in opposition to the Negro race will often be found loaning money to individual Negroes, feeding them and their families from his kitchen, or defending "his Negroes" in court or elsewhere. All of the more prominent white citizens of Atlanta, during the riot, protected and fed many coloured families who ran to them in their terror. Even Hoke Smith, Governor-elect of Georgia, who is more distrusted by the Negroes as a race probably than any other white man in Georgia, protected many Negroes in his house during the disturbance. In many cases white friends armed Negroes and told them to protect themselves. One widow I know of who had a single black servant, placed a shot-gun in his hands and told him to fire on any mob that tried to get him. She trusted him absolutely. Southern people possess a real liking, wholly unknown in the North, for individual Negroes whom they know.

So much for Saturday night. Sunday was quiescent but nervous — the atmosphere full of the electricity of apprehension. Monday night, after a day of alarm and of prowling crowds of men, which might at any moment develop into mobs, the riot broke forth again — in a suburb of Atlanta called Brownsville.

Story of the Mob's Work in a Southern Negro Town

When I went out to Brownsville, knowing of its bloody part in the riot, I expected to find a typical Negro slum. I looked for squalour, ignorance, vice. And I was surprised to find a large settlement of Negroes practically every one of whom owned his own home, some of the houses being as attractive without and as well furnished within as the ordinary homes of middle-class white people. Near at hand, surrounded by beautiful grounds, were two Negro colleges — Clark University and Gammon Theological Seminary. The post-office was kept by a Negro. There were several stores owned by Negroes. The school-house, though supplied with teachers by the county, was built wholly with money personally contributed by the Negroes of the neighbourhood, in order that there might be adequate educational facilities for their children. They had three churches and not a saloon. The residents were all of the industrious, property-owning sort, bearing the best reputation among white people who knew them.

Think, then, of the situation in Brownsville during the riot in Atlanta. All sorts of exaggerated rumours came from the city. *The Negroes of Atlanta were being slaughtered wholesale.* A condition of panic fear developed. Many of the people of the little town sought refuge in Gammon Theological Seminary, where, packed together, they sat up all one night praying. President Bowen did not have his clothes off for days, expecting the mob every moment.[4] He telephoned for police protection on Sunday, but none was provided. Terror also existed among the families which remained in Brownsville; most of the men were armed, and they had decided, should the mob appear, to make a stand in defence of their homes.

At last, on Monday evening, just at dark, a squad of the county police, led by Officer Poole, marched into the settlement at Brownsville. Here, although there had been not the slightest sign of disturbance, they began arresting Negroes for being armed. Several armed white citizens, who were not officers, joined them.

Finally, looking up a little street they saw dimly in the next block a group of Negro men. Part of the officers were left with the prisoners and part went up the street. As they approached the group of Negroes, the officers began firing: the Negroes responded. Officer Heard was shot dead; another officer was wounded, and several Negroes were killed or injured.

The police went back to town with their prisoners. On

4. John Wesley Edward Bowen, theologian and author.

the way two of the Negroes in their charge were shot. A white man's wife, who saw the outrage, being with child, dropped dead of fright.

The Negroes (all of this is now a matter of court record) declared that they were expecting the mob; that the police— not mounted as usual, not armed as usual, and accompanied by citizens — looked to them in the darkness like a mob. In their fright the firing began.

The wildest reports, of course, were circulated. One sent broadcast was that five hundred students of Clark University, all armed, had decoyed the police in order to shoot them down. As a matter of fact, the university did not open its fall session until October 3d, over a week later—and on this night there were just two students on the grounds. The next morning the police and the troops appeared and arrested a very large proportion of the male inhabitants of the town. Police officers, accompanied by white citizens, entered one Negro home, where lay a man named Lewis, badly wounded the night before. He was in bed; they opened his shirt, placed their revolvers at his breast, and in cold blood shot him through the body several times in the presence of his relatives. They left him for dead, but he has since recovered.

President Bowen, of Gammon Thelogical Seminary, one of the able Negroes in Atlanta, who had nothing whatever to do with the riot, was beaten over the head by one of the police with his rifle-butt. The Negroes were all disarmed, and about sixty of them were finally taken to Atlanta and locked up charged with the murder of Officer Heard.

In the Brownsville riot four Negroes were killed. One was a decent, industrious, though loud-talking, citizen named Fambro, who kept a small grocery store and owned two houses besides, which he rented. He had a comfortable home, a wife and one child. Another was an inoffensive Negro named Wilder, seventy years old, a pensioner as a soldier of the Civil War, who was well spoken of by all who knew him. He was found — not shot, but murdered by a knife-cut in the abdomen — lying in a woodshed back of Fambro's store. McGruder, a brick mason, who earned $4 a day at his trade, and who had laid aside enough to earn his own home, was killed while under arrest by the police; and Robinson, an industrious Negro carpenter, was shot to death on his way to work Tuesday morning after the riot.

Results of the Riot

And after the riot in Brownsville, what? Here was a self-respecting community of hard-working Negroes, disturbing no one, getting an honest living. How did the riot affect them? Well, it demoralised them, set them back for years. Not only were four men killed and several wounded, but sixty of their citizens were in jail. Nearly every family had to go to the lawyers, who would not take their cases without money in hand. Hence the little homes had to be sold or mortgaged, or money borrowed in some other way to defend those arrested, doctors' bills were to be paid, the undertaker must be settled with. A riot is not over when the shooting stops! And when the cases finally came up in court and all the evidence was brought out every Negro went free; but two of the county policemen who had taken part in the shooting, were punished. George Muse, one of the foremost merchants of Atlanta, who was foreman of the jury which tried the Brownsville Negroes, said:

"We think the Negroes were gathered just as white people were in other parts of the town, for the purpose of defending their homes. We were shocked by the conduct which the evidence showed some of the county police had been guilty of."

After the riot was over many Negro families, terrified and feeling themselves unprotected, sold out for what they could get — I heard a good many pitiful stories of such sudden and costly sacrifices — and left the country, some going to California, some to Northern cities. The best and most enterprising are those who go: the worst remain. Not only did the Negroes leave Brownsville, but they left the city itself in considerable numbers. Labour was thus still scarcer and wages higher in Atlanta because of the riot.

Report of a White Committee on the Riot

It is significant that not one of the Negroes killed and wounded in the riot was of the criminal class. Every one was industrious, respectable and law-abiding. A white committee, composed of W. G. Cooper, Secretary of the Chamber of Commerce, and George Muse, a prominent merchant, backed by the sober citizenship of the town, made an honest investigation and issued a brave and truthful report. Here are a few of its conclusions:

1. Among the victims of the mob there was not a single vagrant.
2. They were earning wages in useful work up to the time of the riot.
3. They were supporting themselves and their families or dependent relatives.
4. Most of the dead left small children and widows, mothers or sisters with practically no means and very small earning capacity.
5. The wounded lost from one to eight weeks' time, at 50 cents to $4 a day each.
6. About seventy persons were wounded, and among these there was an immense amount of suffering. In some cases it was prolonged and excruciating pain.
7. Many of the wounded are disfigured, and several are permanently disabled.
8. Most of them were in humble circumstances, but they were honest, industrious and law-abiding citizens and useful members of society.
9. These statements are true of both white and coloured.
10. Of the wounded, ten are white and sixty are coloured. Of the dead, two are white and ten are coloured; two female, and ten male. This includes three killed at Brownsville.
11. Wild rumours of a larger number killed have no foundation that we can discover. As the city was paying the funeral expenses of victims and relief was given their families, they had every motive to make known their loss. In one case relatives of a man killed in a broil made fruitless efforts to secure relief.
12. Two persons reported as victims of the riot had no connection with it. One, a Negro man, was killed in a broil over a crap game; and another, a Negro woman, was killed by her paramour. Both homicides occurred at some distance from the scene of the riot.

The men who made this brave report did not mince matters. They called murder, murder; and robbery, robbery. Read this:

13. As twelve persons were killed and seventy were murderously assaulted, and as, by all accounts, a number took part in each assault, it is clear that several hundred murderers or would-be murderers are at large in this community.

At first, after the riot, there was an inclination in some quarters to say:

"Well, at any rate, the riot cleared the atmosphere. The Negroes have had their lesson. There won't be any more trouble soon."

But read the sober conclusions in the Committee's report. The riot did not prevent further crime.

14. Although less than three months have passed since the riot, events have already demonstrated that the slaughter of the innocent does not deter the criminal class from committing more crimes. Rapes and robbery have been committed in the city during that time.

15. The slaughter of the innocent does drive away good citizens. From one small neighbourhood twenty-five families have gone. A great many of them were buying homes on the instalment plan.

16. The crimes of the mob include robbery as well as murder. In a number of cases the property of innocent and unoffending people was taken. Furniture was destroyed, small shops were looted, windows were smashed, trunks were burst open, money was taken from the small hoard, and articles of value were appropriated. In the commission of these crimes the victims, both men and women, were treated with unspeakable brutality.

17. As a result of four days of lawlessness there are in this glad Christmas-time widows of both races mourning their husbands, and husbands of both races mourning for their wives; there are orphan children of both races who cry out in vain for faces they will see no more; there are grown men of both races disabled for life, and all this sorrow has come to people who are absolutely innocent of any wrong-doing.

In trying to find out exactly the point of view and the feeling of the Negroes — which is most important in any honest consideration of conditions — I was handed the following letter, written by a young coloured man, a former resident in Atlanta now a student in the North. He is writing frankly to a friend. It is valuable as showing a *real* point of view — the bitterness, the hopelessness, the distrust.

". . . It is possible that you have formed at least a good idea of how we feel as the result of the horrible eruption in Georgia. I have not spoken to a Caucasian on the subject since then. But, listen: How would you feel, if with our history, there came a time when, after speeches and papers and teachings you acquired property and were educated, and were a fairly good man, it were impossible for you to walk the street (for whose maintenance you were taxed) with your sister without being in mortal fear of death if you resented any insult offered to her? How would you feel if you saw a governor, a mayor, a sheriff, whom you could not oppose at the polls, encourage by deed or word or both, a mob of 'best' and worst citizens to slaughter your people in the streets and in their own homes and in their places of business? Do you think that you could resist the same wrath that caused God to slay the Philistines and the Russians to throw bombs? I can resist it, but with each new outrage I am less able to resist it. And yet if I gave way to my feelings I should become just like other men . . . of the mob! But I do not . . . not quite, and I must hurry through the only life I shall live on earth, tortured by these experiences and these horrible impulses, with no hope of ever getting away from them. They are ever present, like the just God, the devil, and my conscience.

"If there were no such thing as Christianity we should be hopeless."

Besides this effect on the Negroes the riot for a week or more practically paralysed the city of Atlanta. Factories were closed, railroad cars were left unloaded in the yards, the street-car system was crippled, and there was no cab-service (cab-drivers being Negroes), hundreds of servants deserted their places, the bank clearings slumped by hundreds of thousands of dollars, the state fair, then just opening, was a failure. It was, indeed, weeks before confidence was fully restored and the city returned to its normal condition.

Who Made Up the Mob?

One more point I wish to make before taking up the extraordinary reconstructive work which followed the riot. I have not spoken of the men who made up the mob. We know the dangerous Negro class — after all a very small proportion of the entire Negro population. There is a corresponding low class of whites quite as illiterate as the Negroes.

The poor white hates the Negro, and the Negro dislikes the poor white. It is in these lower strata of society, where the races rub together in unclean streets, that the fire is generated. Decatur and Peters streets, with their swarming saloons and dives, furnish the point of contact. I talked with many people who saw the mobs at different times, and the universal testimony was that it was made up largely of boys and young men, and of the low criminal and semi-criminal class. The ignorant Negro and the uneducated white; there lies the trouble!

This idea that 115,000 people of Atlanta — respectable, law-abiding, good citizens, white and black — should be disgraced before the world by a few hundred criminals was what aroused the strong, honest citizenship of Atlanta to vigorous action.

The riot brought out all that was worst in human nature; the reconstruction brought out all that was best and finest.

Almost the first act of the authorities was to close every saloon in the city, afterward revoking all the licences — and for two weeks no liquor was sold in the city. The police, at first accused of not having done their best in dealing with the mob, arrested a good many white rioters, and Judge Broyles, to show that the authorities had no sympathy with such disturbers of the peace, sent every man brought before him, twenty-four in all, to the chain gang for the largest possible sentence, without the alternative of a fine. The grand jury met and boldly denounced the mob; its report said in part:

"That the sensationalism of the afternoon papers in the presentation of the criminal news to the public prior to the riots of Saturday night, especially in the case of the Atlanta *News,* deserves our severest condemnation."

But the most important and far-reaching effect of the riot was in arousing the strong men of the city. It struck at the pride of those men of the South, it struck at their sense of law and order, it struck at their business interests. On Sunday following the first riot a number of prominent men gathered at the Piedmont Hotel, and had a brief discussion; but it was not until Tuesday afternoon, when the worst of the news from Brownsville had come in, that they gathered in the courthouse with the serious intent of stopping the riot at all costs. Most of the prominent men of Atlanta were present. Sam D. Jones, president of the Chamber of Commerce, presided. One of the first speeches was made by Charles T. Hopkins, who had been the leading spirit in the meetings on Sunday and Monday. He expressed with eloquence the humiliation which Atlanta felt.

"Saturday evening at eight o'clock," he said, "the credit of Atlanta was good for any number of millions of dollars in New York or Boston or any financial centre; to-day we could n't borrow fifty cents. The reputation we have been building up so arduously for years has been swept away in two short hours. Not by men who have made and make Atlanta, not by men who represent the character and strength of our city, but by hoodlums, understrappers and white criminals. Innocent Negro men have been struck down for no crime whatever, while peacefully enjoying the life and liberty guaranteed to every American citizen. The Negro race is a child race. We are a strong race, their guardians. We have boasted of our superiority and we have now sunk to this level — we have shed the blood of our helpless wards. Christianity and humanity demand that we treat the Negro fairly. He is here, and here to stay. He only knows how to do those things we teach him to do; it is our Christian duty to protect him. I for one, and I believe I voice the best sentiment of this city, am willing to lay down my life rather than to have the scenes of the last few days repeated."

The Plea of a Negro Physician

In the midst of the meeting a coloured man arose rather doubtfully. He was, however, promptly recognized as Dr. W. F. Penn, one of the foremost coloured physicians of Atlanta, a graduate of Yale College — a man of much influence among his people. He said that he had come to ask the protection of the white men of Atlanta. He said that on the day before a mob had come to his home; that ten white men, some of whose families he knew and had treated professionally, had been sent into his house to look for concealed arms; that his little girl had run to them, one after another, and begged them not to shoot her father; that his life and the lives of his family had afterward been threatened, so that he had had to leave his home; that he had been saved from a gathering mob by a white man in an automobile.

"What shall we do?" he asked the meeting — and those who heard his speech said that the silence was profound. "We have been disarmed: how shall we protect our lives and property? If living a sober, industrious, upright life, accumulating property and educating his children as best he knows how, is not the standard by which a coloured man can live and be protected in the South, what is to become of him? If the kind of life I have lived isn't the kind you want, shall I leave and go North?

"When we aspire to be decent and industrious we are told

that we are bad examples to other coloured men. Tell us what your standards are for coloured men. What are the requirements under which we may live and be protected? What shall we do?"

When he had finished, Colonel A. J. McBride, a real estate owner and a Confederate veteran, arose and said with much feeling that he knew Dr. Penn and that he was a good man, and that Atlanta meant to protect such men.

"If necessary," said Colonel McBride, "I will go out and sit on his porch with a rifle."

Such was the spirit of this remarkable meeting. Mr. Hopkins proposed that the white people of the city express their deep regret for the riot and show their sympathy for the Negroes who had suffered at the hands of the mob by raising a fund of money for their assistance. Then and there $4,423 was subscribed, to which the city afterward added $1,000.

But this was not all. These men, once thoroughly aroused, began looking to the future, to find some new way of preventing the recurrence of such disturbances.

A committee of ten, appointed to work with the public officials in restoring order and confidence, consisted of some of the foremost citizens of Atlanta:

Charles T. Hopkins, Sam D. Jones, President of the Chamber of Commerce; L. Z. Rosser, president of the Board of Education; J. W. English, president of the Fourth National Bank; Forrest Adair, a leading real estate owner; Captain W. D. Ellis, a prominent lawyer; A. B. Steele, a wealthy lumber merchant; M. L. Collier, a railroad man; John E. Murphy, capitalist; and H. Y. McCord, president of a wholesale grocery house.

One of the first and most unexpected things that this committee did was to send for several of the leading Negro citizens of Atlanta: the Rev. H. H. Proctor, B. J. Davis, editor of the *Independent*, a Negro journal, the Rev. E. P. Johnson, the Rev. E. R. Carter, the Rev. J. A. Rush, and Bishop Holsey.[5]

Committees of the Two Races Meet

This was the first important occasion in the South upon which an attempt was made to get the two races together for any serious consideration of their differences.

5. Bishop Lucius Henry Holsey of the Colored Methodist Episcopal Church.

They held a meeting. The white men asked the Negroes, "What shall we do to relieve the irritation?" The Negroes said that they thought that coloured men were treated with unnecessary roughness on the street-cars and by the police. The white members of the committee admitted that this was so and promised to take the matter up immediately with the street-car company and the police department, which was done. The discussion was harmonious. After the meeting Mr. Hopkins said:

"I believe those Negroes understood the situation better than we did. I was astonished at their intelligence and diplomacy. They never referred to the riot: they were looking to the future. I did n't know that there were such Negroes in Atlanta."

Out of this beginning grew the Atlanta Civic League. Knowing that race prejudice was strong, Mr. Hopkins sent out 2,000 cards, inviting the most prominent men in the city to become members. To his surprise 1,500 immediately accepted, only two refused, and those anonymously; 500 men not formally invited were also taken as members. The league thus had the great body of the best citizens of Atlanta behind it. At the same time Mr. Proctor and his committee of Negroes had organised a Coloured Co-operative Civic League, which secured a membership of 1,500 of the best coloured men in the city. A small committee of Negroes met a small committee of the white league.

Fear was expressed that there would be another riotous outbreak during the Christmas holidays, and the league proceeded with vigour to prevent it. New policemen were put on, and the committee worked with Judge Broyles and Judge Roan in issuing statements warning the people against lawlessness. They secured an agreement among the newspapers not to publish sensational news; the sheriff agreed, if necessary, to swear in some of the best men in town as extra deputies; they asked that saloons be closed at four o'clock on Christmas Eve; and through the Negro committee, they brought influence to bear to keep all coloured people off the streets. When two county police got drunk at Brownsville and threatened Mrs. Fambro, the wife of one of the Negroes killed in the riot, a member of the committee, Mr. Seeley,[6]

6. Fred Loring Seely, later prominent in the campaigns for state-wide prohibition and abolition of the convict leasing system in Georgia.

publisher of the *Georgian,* informed the sheriff and sent his automobile to Brownsville, where the policemen were arrested and afterward discharged from the force. As a result, it was the quietest Christmas Atlanta had had in years.

But the most important of all the work done, because of the spectacular interest it aroused, was the defence of a Negro charged with an assault upon a white woman. It is an extraordinary and dramatic story.

Does a Riot Prevent Further Crime?

Although many people said that the riot would prevent any more Negro crime, several attacks on white women occurred within a few weeks afterward. On November 13th Mrs. J. D. Camp, living in the suburbs of Atlanta, was attacked in broad daylight in her home and brutally assaulted by a Negro, who afterward robbed the house and escaped. Though the crime was treated with great moderation by the newspapers, public feeling was intense. A Negro was arrested, charged with the crime. Mr. Hopkins and his associates believed that the best way to secure justice and prevent lynchings was to have a prompt trial. Accordingly, they held a conference with Judge Roan, as a result of which three lawyers in the city, Mr. Hopkins, L. Z. Rosser, and J. E. McClelland, were appointed to defend the accused Negro, serving without pay. A trial-jury, composed of twelve citizens, among the most prominent in Atlanta, was called — one of the ablest juries ever drawn in Georgia. There was a determination to have immediate and complete justice.

The Negro arrested, one Joe Glenn, had been completely identified by Mrs. Camp as her assailant. Although having no doubt of his guilt, the attorneys went at the case thoroughly. The first thing they did was to call in two members of the Negro committee, Mr. Davis and Mr. Carter. These men went to the jail and talked with Glenn, and afterward they all visited the scene of the crime. They found that Glenn, who was a man fifty years old with grandchildren, bore an excellent reputation. He rented a small farm about two miles from Mrs. Camp's home and had some property; he was sober and industrious. After making a thorough examination and getting all the evidence they could, they came back to Atlanta, persuaded, in spite of the fact that the Negro had been positively identified by Mrs. Camp — which in these cases is usually considered conclusive — that Glenn was not guilty. It was a most dramatic trial; at first, when Mrs. Camp was placed on the stand she failed to identify Glenn; afterward, reversing herself she broke forth into a passionate denunciation of him. But after the evidence was all in, the jury retired, and reported two minutes later with a verdict "Not guilty." Remarkably enough, just before the trial was over the police informed the court that another Negro, named Will Johnson, answering Mrs. Camp's description, had been arrested, charged with the crime. He was subsequently identified by Mrs. Camp.

Without this energetic defence, an innocent, industrious Negro would certainly have been hanged — or if the mob had been ahead of the police, as it usually is, he would have been lynched.

But what of Glenn afterward?

When the jury left the box Mr. Hopkins turned to Glenn and said:

"Well, Joe, what do you think of the case?"

He replied: "Boss I 'spec's they will hang me, for that lady said I was the man, but they won't hang me, will they, 'fore I sees my wife and chilluns again?"

He was kept in the tower that night and the following day for protection against a possible lynching. Plans were made by his attorneys to send him secretly out of the city to the home of a farmer in Alabama, whom they could trust with the story. Glenn's wife was brought to visit the jail and Glenn was told of the plans for his safety, and instructed to change his name and keep quiet until the feeling of the community could be ascertained.

A ticket was purchased by his attorneys, with a new suit of clothes, hat, and shoes. He was taken out of jail about midnight under a strong guard, and safely placed on the train. From that day to this he has never been heard of. He did not go to Alabama. The poor creature, with the instinct of a hunted animal, did not dare after all to trust the white men who had befriended him. He is a fugitive, away from his family, not daring, though innocent, to return to his home.

Other Reconstruction Movements

Another strong movement also sprung into existence. Its inspiration was religious. Ministers wrote a series of letters to the Atlanta *Constitution*. Clark Howell, its editor, responded with an editorial entitled "Shall We Blaze the Trail?" W. J. Northen, Ex-Governor of Georgia, and one of the most highly respected men in the state, took up the work, asking himself, as he says:

"What am I to do, who have to pray every night?"

He answered that question by calling a meeting at the Coloured Y. M. C. A. building, where some twenty white men met an equal number of Negroes, mostly preachers, and held a prayer meeting.

The South still looks to its ministers for leadership — and they really lead. The sermons of men like the Rev. John E. White, the Rev. C. B. Wilmer, the Rev. W. W. Landrum, who have spoken with power and ability against lawlessness and injustice to the Negro, have had a large influence in the reconstruction movement.

Ex-Governor Northen travelled through the state of Georgia, made a notable series of speeches, urged the establishment of law and order organisations, and met support wherever he went. He talked against mob-law and lynching in plain language. Here are some of the things he said:

"We shall never settle this until we give absolute justice to the Negro. We are not now doing justice to the Negro in Georgia.

"Get into contact with the best Negroes; there are plenty of good Negroes in Georgia. What we must do is to get the good white folks to leaven the bad white folks and the good Negroes to leaven the bad Negroes."

"There must be no aristocracy of crime: a white fiend is as much to be dreaded as a black brute."

These movements did not cover specifically, it will be observed, the enormously difficult problems of politics, and the political relationships of the races, nor the subject of Negro

education, nor the most exasperating of all the provocatives —
those problems which arise from human contact in street cars,
railroad trains, and in life generally.

That they had to meet the greatest difficulties in their work
is shown by such an editorial as the following, published
December 12th by the Atlanta *Evening News:*

> No law of God or man can hold back the vengeance of our white men upon
> such a criminal [the Negro who attacks a white woman]. If necessary, we
> will double and treble and quadruple the law of Moses, and hang off-hand the
> criminal, or failing to find that a remedy, we will hang two, three, or four of
> the Negroes nearest to the crime, until the crime is no longer done or feared
> in all this Southern land that we inhabit and love.

On January 31, 1907, the newspaper, which published this
editorial went into the hands of a receiver — its failure being
due largely to the strong public sentiment against its course
before and during the riot.

After the excitement of the riot and the evil results which
followed it began to disappear it was natural that the reconstruction movements should quiet down. Ex-Governor
Northen continued his work for many months and is indeed,
still continuing it: and there is no doubt that his campaigns
have had a wide influence. The feeling that the saloons and
dives of Atlanta were partly responsible for the riot was a
powerful factor in the anti-saloon campaign which took place
in 1907 and resulted in closing every saloon in the state of
Georgia on January 1, 1908. And the riot and the revulsion
which followed it will combine to make a recurrence of such
a disturbance next to impossible.

CHAPTER II

FOLLOWING THE COLOUR LINE IN THE SOUTH

BEFORE entering upon a discussion of the more serious aspects of the Negro question in the South, it may prove illuminating if I set down, briefly, some of the more superficial evidences of colour line distinctions in the South as they impress the investigator. The present chapter consists of a series of sketches from my note-books giving the earliest and freshest impressions of my studies in the South.

When I first went South I expected to find people talking about the Negro, but I was not at all prepared to find the subject occupying such an overshadowing place in Southern affairs. In the North we have nothing at all like it; no question which so touches every act of life, in which everyone, white or black, is so profoundly interested. In the North we are mildly concerned in many things; the South is overwhelmingly concerned in this one thing.

And this is not surprising, for the Negro in the South is both the labour problem and the servant question; he is preëminently the political issue, and his place, socially, is of daily and hourly discussion. A Negro minister I met told me a story of a boy who went as a sort of butler's assistant in the home of a prominent family in Atlanta. His people were naturally curious about what went on in the white man's house. One day they asked him:

"What do they talk about when they 're eating?"

The boy thought a moment; then he said:

"Mostly they discusses us culled folks."

What Negroes Talk About

The same consuming interest exists among the Negroes. A very large part of their conversation deals with the race

FAC–SIMILES OF CERTAIN ATLANTA NEWSPAPERS OF SEPTEMBER 22, 1906
Showing the sensational news headings

COMPANION PICTURES

Showing how the colour line was drawn by the saloons at Atlanta, Georgia.
Many of the saloons for Negroes were kept by foreigners, usually Jews

question. I had been at the Piedmont Hotel only a day or two when my Negro waiter began to take especially good care of me. He flecked off imaginary crumbs and gave me unnecessary spoons. Finally, when no one was at hand, he leaned over and said:

"I understand you're down here to study the Negro problem."

"Yes," I said, a good deal surprised. "How did you know it?"

"Well, sir," he replied, "we've got ways of knowing things."

He told me that the Negroes had been much disturbed ever since the riot and that he knew many of them who wanted to go North. "The South," he said, "is getting to be too dangerous for coloured people." His language and pronunciation were surprisingly good. I found that he was a college student, and that he expected to study for the ministry.

"Do you talk much about these things among yourselves?" I asked.

"We don't talk about much else," he said. "It's sort of life and death with us."

Another curious thing happened not long afterward. I was lunching with several fine Southern men, and they talked, as usual, with the greatest freedom in the full hearing of the Negro waiters. Somehow, I could not help watching to see if the Negroes took any notice of what was said. I wondered if they were sensitive. Finally, I put the question to one of my friends:

"Oh," he said, "we never mind them; they don't care."

One of the waiters instantly spoke up:

"No, don't mind me; I'm only a block of wood."

First Views of the Negroes

I set out from the hotel on the morning of my arrival to trace the colour line as it appears, outwardly, in the life of such a town.

Atlanta is a singularly attractive place, as bright and new as any Western city. Sherman left it in ashes at the close of the war; the old buildings and narrow streets were swept away

and a new city was built, which is now growing in a manner
not short of astonishing.   It has 115,000 to 125,000 inhabitants,
about a third of whom are Negroes, living in more or less
detached quarters in various parts of the city, and giving an
individuality to the life interesting enough to the unfamiliar
Northerner.   A great many of them are always on the streets
far better dressed and better-appearing than I had expected
to see — having in mind, perhaps, the tattered country speci-
mens of the penny postal cards.   Crowds of Negroes were
at work mending the pavement, for the Italian and Slav have
not yet appeared in Atlanta, nor indeed to any extent anywhere in the South.   I stopped to watch a group of them.   A
good deal of conversation was going on, here and there a Negro
would laugh with great good humour, and several times I
heard a snatch of a song: much jollier workers than our grim
foreigners, but evidently not working so hard.   A fire had
been built to heat some of the tools, and a black circle of
Negroes were gathered around it like flies around a drop of
molasses and they were all talking while they warmed their
shins — evidently having plenty of leisure.

As I continued down the street, I found that all the drivers
of waggons and cabs were Negroes; I saw Negro newsboys,
Negro porters, Negro barbers, and it being a bright day, many
of them were in the street — on the sunny side.

I commented that evening to some Southern people I met,
on the impression, almost of jollity, given by the Negro workers
I had seen.   One of the older ladies made what seemed to me
a very significant remark.

"They don't sing as they used to," she said.   "You should
have known the old darkeys of the plantation.   Every
year, it seems to me, they have been losing more and
more of their care-free good humour.   I sometimes feel
that I don't know them any more.   Since the riot they have
grown so glum and serious that I'm free to say I'm scared
of them!"

One of my early errands that morning led me into several
of the great new office buildings, which bear testimony to the
extraordinary progress of the city.   And here I found one
of the first evidences of the colour line for which I was
looking.   In both buildings, I found a separate elevator

for coloured people.   In one building, signs were placed reading:

FOR WHITES ONLY

In another I copied this sign:

THIS CAR FOR COLOURED PASSENGERS,
FREIGHT, EXPRESS AND PACKAGES

Curiously enough, as giving an interesting point of view, an intelligent Negro with whom I was talking a few days later asked me:

"Have you seen the elevator sign in the Century Building?"
I said I had.

"How would you like to be classed with 'freight, express and packages'?"

I found that no Negro ever went into an elevator devoted to white people, but that white people often rode in cars set apart for coloured people.   In some cases the car for Negroes is operated by a white man, and in other cases, all the elevators in a building are operated by coloured men.   This is one of the curious points of industrial contact in the South which somewhat surprise the Northern visitor.   In the North a white workman will often refuse to work with a Negro; in the South, while the social prejudice is strong, Negroes and whites work together side by side in many kinds of employment.

I had an illustration in point not long afterward.   Passing the post office, I saw several mail-carriers coming out, some white, some black, talking and laughing, with no evidence, at first, of the existence of any colour line.   Interested to see what the real condition was, I went in and made inquiries.   A most interesting and significant condition developed.   I found that the postmaster, who is a wise man, sent Negro carriers up Peachtree and other fashionable streets, occupied by wealthy white people, while white carriers were assigned to beats in the mill districts and other parts of town inhabited by the poorer classes of white people.

"You see," said my informant, "the Peachtree people

know how to treat Negroes. They really prefer a Negro carrier to a white one; it's natural for them to have a Negro doing such service. But if we sent Negro carriers down into the mill district they might get their heads knocked off."

Then he made a philosophical observation:

"If we had only the best class of white folks down here and the industrious Negroes, there would n't be any trouble."

The Jim Crow Car

One of the points in which I was especially interested was the "Jim Crow" regulations, that is, the system of separation of the races in street cars and railroad trains. Next to the question of Negro suffrage, I think the people of the North have heard more of the Jim Crow legislation than of anything else connected with the Negro problem. The street car is an excellent place for observing the points of human contact between the races, betraying as it does every shade of feeling upon the part of both. In almost no other relationship do the races come together, physically, on anything like a common footing. In their homes and in ordinary employment, they meet as master and servant; but in the street cars they touch as free citizens, each paying for the right to ride, the white not in a place of command, the Negro without an obligation of servitude. Street-car relationships are, therefore, symbolic of the new conditions. A few years ago the Negro came and went in the street cars in most cities and sat where he pleased, but gradually Jim Crow laws or local regulations were passed, forcing him into certain seats at the back of the car.

While I was in Atlanta, the newspapers reported two significant new developments in the policy of separation. In Savannah Jim Crow ordinances have gone into effect for the first time, causing violent protestations on the part of the Negroes and a refusal by many of them to use the cars at all. Montgomery, Ala., about the same time, went one step further and demanded, not separate seats in the same car, but entirely separate cars for whites and blacks. There could be no better visible evidence of the increasing separation of the races, and of the determination of the white man to make the Negro "keep his place," than the evolution of the Jim Crow regulations.

I was curious to see how the system worked out in Atlanta. Over the door of each car, I found this sign:

> WHITE PEOPLE WILL SEAT FROM FRONT OF CAR TOWARD THE BACK AND COLORED PEOPLE FROM REAR TOWARD FRONT

Sure enough, I found the white people in front and the Negroes behind. As the sign indicates, there is no definite line of division between the white seats and the black seats, as in many other Southern cities. This very absence of a clear demarcation is significant of many relationships in the South. The colour line is drawn, but neither race knows just where it is. Indeed, it can hardly be definitely drawn in many relationships, because it is constantly changing. This uncertainty is a fertile source of friction and bitterness. The very first time I was on a car in Atlanta, I saw the conductor — all conductors are white — ask a Negro woman to get up and take a seat farther back in order to make a place for a white man. I have also seen white men requested to leave the Negro section of the car.

At one time, when I was on a car the conductor shouted: "Heh, you nigger, get back there," which the Negro, who had taken a seat too far forward, proceeded hastily to do.

No other one point of race contact is so much and so bitterly discussed among the Negroes as the Jim Crow car. I don't know how many Negroes replied to my question: "What is the chief cause of friction down here?" with a complaint of their treatment on street cars and in railroad trains.

Why the Negro Objects to the Jim Crow Car

Fundamentally, of course they object to any separation which gives them inferior accommodations. This point of view — and I am trying to set down every point of view, both coloured and white, exactly as I find it, is expressed in many ways.

"We pay first-class fare," said one of the leading Negroes in Atlanta, "exactly as the white man does, but we don't get first-class service. I say it is n't fair."

In answer to this complaint, the white man says: "The

Negro is inferior, he must be made to keep his place. Give him a chance and he assumes social equality, and that will lead to an effort at intermarriage and amalgamation of the races. The Anglo-Saxon will never stand for that."

One of the first complaints made by the Negroes after the riot, was of rough and unfair treatment on the street cars.

The committee admitted that the Negroes were not always well treated on the cars, and promised to improve conditions. Charles T. Hopkins, a leader in the Civic League and one of the prominent lawyers of the city, told me that he believed the Negroes should be given their definite seats in every car; he said that he personally made it a practice to stand up rather than to take any one of the four back seats, which he considered as belonging to the Negroes. Two other leading men, on a different occasion, told me the same thing.

One result of the friction over the Jim Crow regulations is that many Negroes ride on the cars as little as possible. One prominent Negro I met said he never entered a car, and that he had many friends who pursued the same policy; he said that Negro street car excursions, familiar a few years ago, had entirely ceased. It is significant of the feeling that one of the features of the Atlanta riot was an attack on the street cars in which all Negroes were driven out of their seats. One Negro woman was pushed through an open window, and, after falling to the pavement, she was dragged by the leg across the sidewalk and thrown through a shop window. In another case when the mob stopped a car the motorman, instead of protecting his passengers, went inside and beat down a Negro with his brass control-lever.

Story of an Encounter on a Street Car

I heard innumerable stories from both white people and Negroes of encounters in the street cars. Dr. W. F. Penn, one of the foremost Negro physicians of the city, himself partly white, a graduate of Yale College, told me of one occasion in which he entered a car and found there Mrs. Crogman, wife of the coloured president of Clark University.[1] Mrs. Crogman is a mulatto so light of complexion as to be practically undistinguishable from white people. Dr. Penn, who knew her

[1]. William Henry Crogman had been associated with Clark University for more than thirty years.

well, sat down beside her and began talking. A white man who occupied a seat in front with his wife turned and said:

"Here, you nigger, get out of that seat. What do you mean by sitting down with a white woman?"

Dr. Penn replied somewhat angrily:

"It's come to a pretty pass when a coloured man cannot sit with a woman of his own race in his own part of the car."

The white man turned to his wife and said:

"Here, take these bundles. I'm going to thrash that nigger."

In half a minute the car was in an uproar, the two men struggling. Fortunately the conductor and motorman were quickly at hand, and Dr. Penn slipped off the car.

Conditions on the railroad trains, while not resulting so often in personal encounters, are also the cause of constant irritation. When I came South, I took particular pains to observe the arrangement on the trains. In some cases Negroes are given entire cars at the front of the train, at other times they occupy the rear end of a combination coach and baggage car, which is used in the North as a smoking compartment. The complaint here is that, while the Negro is required to pay first-class fare, he is provided with second-class accommodations. Well-to-do Negroes who can afford to travel, also complain that they are not permitted to engage sleeping-car berths. Booker T. Washington usually take a compartment where he is entirely cut off from the white passengers. Some other Negroes do the same thing, although they are often refused even this expensive privilege. Railroad officials with whom I talked, and it is important to hear what they say, said that it was not only a question of public opinion — which was absolutely opposed to any intermingling of the races in the cars — but that Negro travel in most places was small compared with white travel, that the ordinary Negro was unclean and careless, and that it was impractical to furnish them the same accommodations, even though it did come hard on a few educated Negroes. They said that when there was a delegation of Negroes, enough to fill an entire sleeping car, they could always get accommodations. All of which gives a glimpse of the enormous difficulties accompanying the separation of the races in the South.

Another interesting point significant of tendencies came

early to my attention.　They had recently finished at Atlanta
one of the finest railroad stations in this country.　The ordinary
depot in the South has two waiting-rooms of about the same
size, one for whites and one for Negroes.　But when this new
station was built the whole front was given up to white people,
and the Negroes were assigned a side entrance, and a small
waiting-room.　Prominent coloured men regarded it as a new
evidence of the crowding out of the Negro, the further attempt
to give him unequal accommodations, to handicap him in his
struggle for survival.　A delegation was sent to the railroad
people to protest, but to no purpose.　Result: further bitterness.　There are in the station two lunch-rooms, one for whites,
one for Negroes.

A leading coloured man said to me:

"No Negro goes to the lunch-room in tne station who can
help it.　We don't like the way we have been treated."

A Negro Boycott

Of course this was an unusually intelligent coloured man,
and he spoke for his own sort; how far the same feeling of a
race consciousness strong enough to carry out such a boycott
as this — and it is like the boycott of a labour union — actuates
the masses of ignorant Negroes is a question upon which I
hope to get more light as I proceed.　I have already heard
more than one coloured leader complain that Negroes do not
stand together.　And a white planter, whom I met in the
hotel, said a significant thing along this very line:

"If once the Negroes got together and saved their money,
they'd soon own the country, but they can't do it, and they
never will."

After I had begun to trace the colour line I found evidences
of it everywhere —literally in every department of life.　In
the theatres, Negroes never sit downstairs, but the galleries
are black with them.　Of course, white hotels and restaurants
are entirely barred to Negroes, with the result that coloured
people have their own eating and sleeping places, many of
them inexpressibly dilapidated and unclean.　"Sleepers
wanted" is a familiar sign in Atlanta, giving notice of places
where for a few cents a Negro can find a bed or a mattress

on the floor, often in a room where there are many other sleepers, sometimes both men and women in the same room crowded together in a manner both unsanitary and immoral. No good public accommodations exist for the educated or well-to-do Negro in Atlanta, although other cities are developing good Negro hotels.   Indeed one cannot long remain in the South without being impressed with extreme difficulties which beset the exceptional coloured man.

In slavery time many Negroes attended white churches and Negro children were often taught by white women.   Now, a Negro is never (or very rarely) seen in a white man's church. Once since I have been in the South, I saw a very old Negro woman, some much-loved mammy, perhaps — sitting down in front near the pulpit, but that is the only exception to the rule that has come to my attention.   Negroes are not wanted in white churches.   Consequently the coloured people have some sixty churches of their own in Atlanta.   Of course, the schools are separate, and have been ever since the Civil War.

In one of the parks of Atlanta I saw this sign:

NO NEGROES ALLOWED IN THIS PARK

Colour Line in the Public Library

A story significant of the growing separation of the races is told about the public library at Atlanta, which no Negro is permitted to enter.   Carnegie gave the money for building it, and when the question came up as to the support of it by the city, the inevitable colour question arose.   Leading Negroes asserted that their people should be allowed admittance, that they needed such an educational advantage even more than white people, and that they were to be taxed their share — even though it was small — for buying the books and maintaining the building.   They did not win their point of course, but Mr. Carnegie proposed a solution of the difficulty by offering more money to build a Negro branch library, provided the city would give the land and provide for its support.   The city said to the Negroes:

"You contribute the land and we will support the library."

Influential Negroes at once arranged for buying and contributing a site for the library. Then the question of control arose. The Negroes thought that inasmuch as they gave the land and the building was to be used entirely for coloured people, they should have one or two members on the board of control. This the city officials, who had charge of the matter, would not hear of; result, the Negroes would not give the land, and the branch library has never been built.

Right in this connection: while I was in Atlanta, the Art School, which in the past has often used Negro models, decided to draw the colour line there, too, and no longer employ them.

Formerly Negroes and white men went to the same saloons, and drank at the same bars, as they do now, I am told, in some parts of the South. In a few instances, in Atlanta, there were Negro saloon-keepers, and many Negro bartenders. The first step toward separation was to divide the bar, the upper end for white men, the lower for Negroes. After the riot, by a new ordinance no saloon was permitted to serve both white and coloured men.

Consequently, going along Decatur Street, one sees the saloons designated by conspicuous signs:*

"WHITES ONLY"	"COLOURED ONLY"

And when the Negro suffers the ordinary consequences of a prolonged visit to Decatur Street, and finds himself in the city prison, he is separated there, too, from the whites. And afterward in court, if he comes to trial, two Bibles are provided; he may take his oath on one; the other is for the white man. When he dies he is buried in a separate cemetery.

One curious and enlightening example of the infinite ramifications of the colour line was given me by Mr. Logan,[2] secretary of the Atlanta Associated Charities, which is supported by voluntary contributions. One day, after the riot, a subscriber called Mr. Logan on the telephone and said: "Do you help Negroes in your society?"

"Why, yes, occasionally," said Mr. Logan.

"What do you do that for?"

*Since these notes were made, in 1907, the prohibition movement has abolished all the saloons in Georgia.

2. Joseph C. Logan, one of the early social workers in the South.

"A Negro gets hungry and cold like anybody else," answered Mr. Logan.

"Well, you can strike my name from your subscription list. I won't give any of my money to a society that helps Negroes."

Psychology of the South

Now, this sounds rather brutal, but behind it lies the peculiar psychology of the South. This very man who refused to contribute to the associated charities, may have fed several Negroes from his kitchen and had a number of Negro pensioners who came to him regularly for help. It was simply amazing to me, considering the bitterness of racial feeling, to see how lavish many white families are in giving food, clothing, and money to individual Negroes whom they know. A Negro cook often supports her whole family, including a lazy husband, on what she gets daily from the white man's kitchen. In some old families the "basket habit" of the Negroes is taken for granted; in the newer ones, it is, significantly, beginning to be called stealing, showing that the old order is passing and that the Negro is being held more and more strictly to account, not as a dependent vassal, but as a moral being, who must rest upon his own responsibility.

And often a Negro of the old sort will literally bulldoze his hereditary white protector into the loan of quarters and half dollars, which both know will never be paid back.

Mr. Brittain, superintendent of schools in Fulton County, gave me an incident in point. A big Negro with whom he was wholly unacquainted came to his office one day, and demanded — he did not ask, but demanded — a job.

"What's your name?" asked the superintendent.

"Marion Luther Brittain," was the reply.

"That sounds familiar," said Mr. Brittain — it being, indeed, his own name.

"Yas, sah. Ah 'm the son of yo' ol' mammy."

In short, Marion Luther had grown up on the old plantation; it was the spirit of the hereditary vassal demanding the protection and support of the hereditary baron, and he got it, of course.

The Negro who makes his appeal on the basis of this old

relationship finds no more indulgent or generous friend than the Southern white man, indulgent to the point of excusing thievery and other petty offences, but the moment he assumes or demands any other relationship or stands up as an independent citizen, the white men — at least some white men — turn upon him with the fiercest hostility. The incident of the associated charities may now be understood. It was not necessarily cruelty to a cold or hungry Negro that inspired the demand of the irate subscriber, but the feeling that the associated charities helped Negroes and whites on the same basis, as men; that, therefore, it encouraged "social equality," and that, therefore, it was to be stopped.

Most of the examples so far given are along the line of social contact, where, of course, the repulsion is intense. Negroes and whites can go to different schools, churches, and saloons, and sit in different street cars, and still live pretty comfortably. But the longer I remain in the South, the more clearly I come to understand how wide and deep, in other, less easily discernible ways, the chasm between the races is becoming.

The New Racial Consciousness Among Negroes

One of the natural and inevitable results of the effort of the white man to set the Negro off, as a race, by himself, is to awaken in him a new consciousness — a sort of racial consciousness. It drives the Negroes together for defence and offence. Many able Negroes, some largely of white blood, cut off from all opportunity of success in the greater life of the white man, become of necessity leaders of their own people. And one of their chief efforts consists in urging Negroes to work together and to stand together. In this they are only developing the instinct of defence against the white man which has always been latent in the race. This instinct exhibits itself in the way in which the mass of Negroes sometimes refuse to turn over a criminal of their colour to white justice; it is like the instinctive clannishness of the Highland Scotch or the peasant Irish. I don't know how many Southern people have told me in different ways of how extremely difficult it is to get at the real feeling of a Negro, to make him tell what goes on in his clubs and churches or in his innumerable societies.

A Southern woman told me of a cook who had been in her service for nineteen years. The whole family really loved the old servant: her mistress made her a confidant, in the way of the old South, in the most intimate private and family matters, the daughters told her their love affairs; they all petted her and even submitted to many small tyrannies upon her part.

"But do you know," said my hostess, "Susie never tells us a thing about her life or her friends, and we could n't, if we tried, make her tell what goes on in the society she belongs to."

The Negro has long been defensively secretive. Slavery made him that. In the past, the instinct was passive and defensive; but with growing education and intelligent leadership it is rapidly becoming conscious, self-directive and offensive. And right there, it seems to me, lies the great cause of the increased strain in the South.

Let me illustrate. In the People's Tabernacle in Atlanta, where thousands of Negroes meet every Sunday, I saw this sign in huge letters:

> FOR PHOTOGRAPHS, GO TO AUBURN PHOTO
> GALLERY OPERATED BY COLOURED MEN

The old-fashioned Negro preferred to go to the white man for everything; he did n't trust his own people; the new Negro, with growing race consciousness, and feeling that the white man is against him, urges his friends to patronise Negro doctors and dentists, and to trade with Negro storekeepers. The extent to which this movement has gone was one of the most surprising things that I, as an unfamiliar Northerner, found in Atlanta. In other words, the struggle of the races is becoming more and more rapidly economic.

Story of a Negro Shoe-store

One day, walking in Broad Street, I passed a Negro shoe-store. I did not know that there was such a thing in the country. I went in to make inquiries. It was neat, well kept, and evidently prosperous. I found that it was owned by a stock company, organised and controlled wholly by Negroes; the manager was a brisk young mulatto named Harper, a graduate of Atlanta University. I found him dictating to a Negro girl stenographer. There were two reasons, he said, why the store had been opened; one was because the promoters thought it a good business opportunity, and the other was because many Negroes of the better class felt that they did not get fair treatment at white stores. At some places — not all, he said — when a Negro woman went to buy a pair of shoes, the clerk would hand them to her without offering to help her try them on; and a Negro was always kept waiting until all the white people in the store had been served. Since the new business was opened, he said, it had attracted much of the Negro trade; all the leaders advising their people to patronise him. I was much interested to find out how this young man looked upon the race question. His first answer struck me forcibly, for it was the universal and typical answer of the business man the world over whether white, yellow, or black:

"All I want," he said, "is to be protected and let alone, so that I can build up this business."

"What do you mean by protection?" I asked.

"Well, justice between the races. That does n't mean social equality. We have a society of our own, and that is all we want. If we can have justice in the courts, and fair protection, we can learn to compete with the white stores and get along all right."

Such an enterprise as this indicates the new, economic separation between the races.

"Here is business," says the Negro, "which I am going to do."

Considering the fact that only a few years ago, the Negro did no business at all, and had no professional men, it is really surprising to a Northerner to see what progress he has made. One of the first lines he took up was — not unnaturally — the undertaking business. Some of the most prosperous Negroes in every Southern city are undertakers, doing work exclusively, of course, for coloured people. Other early enterprises, growing naturally out of a history of personal service, were barbering and tailoring. Atlanta has many small Negro tailor and clothes-cleaning shops.

Wealthiest Negro in Atlanta

The wealthiest Negro in Atlanta, A. F. Herndon, operates the largest barber shop in the city; he is the president of a Negro insurance company (of which there are four in the city) and he owns and rents some fifty dwelling houses. He is said to be worth $80,000, all made, of course, since slavery.

Another occupation developing naturally from the industrial training of slavery was the business of the building contractor. Several such Negroes, notably Alexander Hamilton, do a considerable business in Atlanta, and have made money. They are employed by white men, and they hire for their jobs both white and Negro workmen.

Small groceries and other stores are of later appearance; I saw at least a score of them in various parts of Atlanta. For the most part they are very small, many are exceedingly dirty and ill-kept; usually much poorer than corresponding places kept by foreigners, indiscriminately called "Dagoes" down here, who are in reality mostly Russian Jews and Greeks. But there are a few Negro grocery stores in Atlanta which are highly creditable. Other business enterprises include restaurants (for Negroes), printing establishments, two newspapers, and several drug-stores. In other words, the Negro is rapidly building up his own business enterprises, tending to make himself independent as a race.

The appearance of Negro drug-stores was the natural result of the increasing practice of Negro doctors and dentists. Time was when all Negroes preferred to go to white practitioners, but since educated coloured doctors became common, they have taken a very large part — practically all, I am told — of the practice in Atlanta. Several of them have had degrees from Northern universities, two from Yale; and one of them, at least, has some little practice among white people. The doctors are leaders among their people. Naturally they give prescriptions to be filled by druggists of their own race; hence the growth of the drug business among Negroes everywhere in the South. The first store to be estab-

lished in Atlanta occupies an old wooden building in Auburn
Avenue. It is operated by Moses Amos, a mulatto, and
enjoys, I understand, a high degree of prosperity. I visited
it. A post-office occupies one corner of the room; and it is
a familiar gathering place for coloured men. Moses Amos
told me his story, and I found it so interesting, and so significant of the way in which Negro business men have come up,
that I am setting it down briefly here.

Rise of a Negro Druggist

"I never shall forget," he said, "my first day in the drug
business. It was in 1876. I remember I was with a crowd
of boys in Peachtree Street, where Dr. Huss, a Southern white
man, kept a drug-store. The old doctor was sitting out in
front smoking his pipe. He called one little Negro after
another, and finally chose me. He said:

" 'I want you to live with me, work in the store, and look
after my horse.'

"He sent me to his house and told me to tell his wife to
give me some breakfast, and I certainly delivered the first
message correctly. His wife, who was a noble lady, not only
fed me, but made me take a bath in a sure enough porcelain
tub, the first I had ever seen. When I went back to the store,
I was so regenerated that the doctor had to adjust his spec-
tacles before he knew me. He said to me:

" 'You can wash bottles, put up castor oil, salts and turpentine, sell anything you *know* and put the money in the drawer.'

"He showed me how to work the keys of the cash drawer.
'I am going to trust you,' he said. 'Don't steal from me; if
you want anything ask for it, and you can have it. And don't
lie; I hate a liar. A boy who will lie will steal, too.'

"I remained with Dr. Huss thirteen years. He sent me
to school and paid my tuition out of his own pocket; he trusted
me fully, often leaving me in charge of his business for weeks
at a time. When he died I formed a partnership with Dr.
Butler, Dr. Slater, and others, and bought the store. Our
business grew and prospered, so that within a few years we
had a stock worth $3,000, and cash of $800. That made us
ambitious. We bought land, built a new store, and went

into debt to do it.   We did n't know much about business —
that 's the Negro's chief trouble — and we lost trade by
changing our location, so that in spite of all we could do, we
failed and lost everything, though we finally paid our creditors
every cent.   After many trials we started again in 1896 in
our present store; to-day we are doing a good business; we
can get all the credit we want from wholesale houses, we employ six clerks, and pay good interest on the capital invested."

Greatest Difficulties Met by Negro Business Men

I asked him what was the greatest difficulty he had to meet.
He said it was the credit system; the fact that many Negroes
have not learned financial responsibility.   Once, he said, he
nearly stopped business on this account.

"I remember," he said, "the last time we got into trouble.
We needed $400 to pay our bills.   I picked out some of our
best customers and gave them a heart-to-heart talk and told
them what trouble we were in.   They all promised to pay; but
on the day set for payment, out of $1,680 which they owed
us we collected just $8.25.   After that experience we came
down to a cash basis.   We trust no one, and since then we
have been doing well."

He said he thought the best opportunity for Negro development was in the South where he had his whole race behind
him.   He said he had once been tempted to go North looking
for an opening.

"How did you make out?" I asked.

"Well, I 'll tell you," he said, "when I got there I wanted
a shave; I walked the streets two hours visiting barber shops,
and they all turned me away with some excuse.   I finally
had to buy a razor and shave myself!   That was just a sample.
I came home disgusted and decided to fight it out down here
where I understood conditions."

Of course only a comparatively few Negroes are able to get
ahead in business.   They must depend almost exclusively on
the trade of their own race, and they must meet the highly
organised competition of white men.   But it is certainly
significant that even a few are able to make progress along
these unfamiliar lines.   Many Southern men I met had little

or no idea of the remarkable extent of this advancement among the better class of Negroes. Here is a strange thing. I don't know how many Southern men have prefaced their talks with me with words something like this:

"You can't expect to know the Negro after a short visit. You must live down here like we do. Now, I know the Negroes like a book. I was brought up with them. I know what they'll do and what they won't do. I have had Negroes in my house all my life."

But curiously enough I found that these men rarely knew anything about the better class of Negroes — those who were in business, or in independent occupations, those who owned their own homes. They *did* come into contact with the servant Negro, the field hand, the common labourer, who make up, of course, the great mass of the race. On the other hand, the best class of Negroes did not know the higher class of white people, and based their suspicion and hatred upon the acts of the poorer sort of whites with whom they naturally came into contact. The best elements of the two races are as far apart as though they lived in different continents; and that is one of the chief causes of the growing danger of the Southern situation. It is a striking fact that one of the first—almost instinctive—efforts at reconstruction after the Atlanta riot was to bring the best elements of both races together, so that they might, by becoming acquainted and gaining confidence in each other, allay suspicion and bring influence to bear upon the lawless elements of both white people and coloured.

Many Southerners look back wistfully to the faithful, simple, ignorant, obedient, cheerful, old plantation Negro and deplore his disappearance. They want the New South, but the old Negro. That Negro is disappearing forever along with the old feudalism and the old-time exclusively agricultural life.

A new Negro is not less inevitable than a new white man and a new South. And the new Negro, as my clever friend says, does n't laugh as much as the old one. It is grim business he is in, this being free, this new, fierce struggle in the open competitive field for the daily loaf. Many go down to vagrancy and crime in that struggle; a few will rise. The more rapid the progress (with the trained white man setting the pace), the more frightful the mortality.

CHAPTER III

THE SOUTHERN CITY NEGRO

AFTER my arrival in Atlanta, and when I had begun to understand some of the more superficial ramifications of the colour line (as I related in the last chapter,) I asked several Southern men whose acquaintance I had made where I could best see the poorer or criminal class of Negroes. So much has been said of the danger arising from this element of Southern population and it plays such a part in every discussion of the race question that I was anxious to learn all I could about it.

"Go down any morning to Judge Broyles's court," they said to me, "and you 'll see the lowest of the low."

So I went down — the first of many visits I made to police and justice courts. I chose a Monday morning that I might see to the best advantage the accumulation of the arrests of Saturday and Sunday.

The police station stands in Decatur Street, in the midst of the very worst section of the city, surrounded by low saloons, dives, and pawn-shops. The court occupies a great room upstairs, and it was crowded that morning to its capacity. Besides the police, lawyers, court officers, and white witnesses, at least one hundred and fifty spectators filled the seats behind the rail, nearly all of them Negroes. The ordinary Negro loves nothing better than to sit and watch the proceedings of a court. Judge Broyles kindly invited me to a seat on the platform at his side where I could look into the faces of the prisoners and hear all that was said.

In a Southern Police Court

It was a profoundly interesting and significant spectacle. In the first place the very number of cases was staggering. The docket that morning carried over one hundred names — men,

45

women, and children, white and black; the court worked hard, but it was nearly two o'clock in the afternoon before the room was cleared. Atlanta, as I showed in a former chapter, has the largest number of arrests, considering the population, of any important city in the United States. I found that 13,511 of the total of 21,702 persons arrested in 1906 were Negroes, or 62 per cent., whereas the coloured population of the city is only 40 per cent. of the total.*

A very large proportion of the arrests that Monday morning were Negroes, with a surprising proportion of women and of mere children. In 1906 3,194 Negro women were arrested in Atlanta. It was altogether a pitiful and disheartening exhibition, a spectacle of sodden ignorance, reckless vice, dissipation. Most of the cases, ravelled out, led back to the saloon.

"Where's your home?" the judge would ask, and in a number of cases the answer was:

"Ah come here fum de country."

Over and over again it was the story of the country Negro, or the Negro who had been working on the railroad, in the cotton fields or in the sawmills, who had entered upon the more complex life of the city. Most of the country districts of the South prohibit the sale of liquor; and Negroes, especially, have comparatively little temptation of this nature, nor are they subjected to the many other glittering pitfalls of city life. But of late years the opportunities of the city have attracted the black people, just as they have the whites, in large numbers. Atlanta had many saloons and other places of vice; and the results are to be seen in Judge Broyles's court any morning. And not only Negroes, but the "poor whites" who have come in from the mountains and the small farms to work in the mills: they, too, suffer fully as much as the Negroes.

Negro Cocaine Victims

Not a few of the cases both black and white showed evidences of cocaine or morphine poisoning — the blear eyes, the unsteady nerves.

* Since the closing of the saloons on January 1, 1908, the number of arrests has largely decreased, but the observations here made still apply to a large number of Southern cities.

"What's the trouble here?" asked the judge.

"Coke," said the officer.

"Ten-seventy-five," said the judge, naming the amount of the fine.

They buy the "coke" in the form of a powder and snuff it up the nose; a certain patent catarrh medicine which is nearly all cocaine is sometimes used; ten cents will purchase enough to make a man wholly irresponsible for his acts, and capable of any crime. The cocaine habit, which seems to be spreading, for there are always druggists who will break the law, has been a curse to the Negro and has resulted, directly, as the police told me, in much crime. I was told of two cases in particular, of offences against women, in which the Negro was a victim of the drug habit.

So society, in pursuit of wealth, South and North, preys upon the ignorant and weak — and then wonders why crime is prevalent!

One has only to visit police courts in the South to see in how many curious ways the contact of the races generates fire.

"What's the trouble here?" inquires the judge.

The white complainant — a boy — says:

"This nigger insulted me!" and he tells the epithet the Negro applied.

"Did you call him that?"

"No sah, I never called him no such name."

"Three-seventy-five — you must n't insult white people."

And here is the report of the case of a six-year-old Negro boy from the *Georgian*:

Because Robert Lee Buster, a six-year-old Negro boy, insulted Maggie McDermott, a little girl, who lives at 507 Simpson Street, Wednesday afternoon, he was given a whipping in the police station Thursday morning that will make him remember to be good.

The case was heard in the juvenile court before Judge Broyles. It was shown that the little Negro had made an insulting remark to the little girl.

Story of a Negro Arrest

The very suspicion and fear that exist give rise to many difficulties. One illuminating case came up that morning. A strapping Negro man was brought before the judge. He showed no marks of dissipation and was respectably dressed.

Confronting him were two plain-clothes policemen, one with his neck wrapped up, one with a bandage around his arm. Both said they had been stabbed by the Negro with a jack-knife. The Negro said he was a hotel porter and he had the white manager of the hotel in court to testify to his good character, sobriety, and industry. It seems that he was going home from work at nine o'clock in the evening, and it was dark. He said he was afraid and had been afraid since the riot. At the same time the two policemen were looking for a burglar. They saw the Negro porter and ordered him to stop. Not being in uniform the Negro said he thought the officers were "jes' plain white men" who were going to attack him. When he started to run the officers tried to arrest him, and he drew his jack-knife and began to fight. And here he was in court! The judge said:

"You must n't attack officers," and bound him over to trial in the higher court.

A White Man and a Negro Woman

Another case shows one of the strange relationships which grow out of Southern conditions. An old white man, much agitated and very pale, was brought before the judge. With him came a much younger, comely appearing woman. Both were well dressed and looked respectable — so much so, indeed, that there was a stir of interest and curiosity among the spectators. Why had they been arrested? As they stood in front of the judge's desk, the old man hung his head, but the woman looked up with such an expression, tearless and tragic, as I hope I shall not have to see again.

"What 's the charge?" asked the judge.

"Adultery," said the officer.

The woman winced, the old man did not look up.

The judge glanced from one to the other in surprise.

"Why don 't you get married?" he asked.

"The woman," said the officer, "is a nigger."

She was as white as I am, probably an octoroon; I could not have distinguished her from a white person, and she deceived even the experienced eye of the judge.

"Is that so?" asked the judge.

The man continued to hang his head, the woman looked up; neither said a word. It then came out that they had lived together as man and wife for many years and that they had children nearly grown. One of the girls — and a very bright, ambitious girl — as I learned later, was a student in Atlanta University, a Negro college, where she was supported by her father, who made good wages as a telegraph operator. Some neighbour had complained and the man and woman were arrested.

"Is this all true?" asked the judge.

Neither said a word.

"You can't marry under the Georgia law," said the judge; "I'll have to bind you over for trial in the county court."

They were led back to the prisoners' rooms. A few minutes later the bailiff came out quickly and said to the judge:

"The old man has fallen in a faint."

Not long afterward they half led, half carried him out across the court room.

One thing impressed me especially, not only in this court but in all others I have visited: a Negro brought in for drunkenness, for example, was punished much more severely than a white man arrested for the same offence. The injustice which the weak everywhere suffer — North and South — is in the South visited upon the Negro. The white man sometimes escaped with a reprimand, he was sometimes fined three dollars and costs, but the Negro, especially if he had no white man to intercede for him, was usually punished with a ten or fifteen dollar fine, which often meant that he must go to the chain-gang. One of the chief causes of complaint by the Negroes of Atlanta has been of the rough treatment of the police and of unjust arrests. After the riot, when the Civic League, composed of the foremost white citizens of Atlanta, was organised, one of the first subjects that came up was that of justice to the Negro. Mr. Hopkins, the leader of the League, said to me: "We complain that the Negroes will not help to bring the criminals of their race to justice. One reason for that is that the Negro has too little confidence in our courts. We must give him that, above all things."

In accordance with this plan, the Civic League, heartily supported by Judge Broyles, employed a young lawyer, Mr.

Underwood, to appear regularly in court and look after the
interests of Negroes.

Convicts Making a Profit for Georgia

One reason for the very large number of arrests — in Georgia
particularly — lies in the fact that the state and the counties
make a profit out of their prison system. No attempt is ever
made to reform a criminal, either white or coloured. Convicts
are hired out to private contractors or worked on the public
roads. Last year the net profit to Georgia from its chain-
gangs, to which the prison commission refers with pride,
reached the great sum of $354,853.55.

Of course a very large proportion of the prisoners are
Negroes. The demand for convicts by rich sawmill operators,
owners of brick-yards, large farmers, and others is far in
advance of the supply. The natural tendency is to convict
as many men as possible — it furnishes steady, cheap labour to
the contractors and a profit to the state. Undoubtedly this
explains in some degree the very large number of criminals,
especially Negroes, in Georgia. One of the leading political
forces in Atlanta is a very prominent banker who is a dominant
member of the city police board. He is also the owner of
extensive brick-yards near Atlanta, where many convicts
are employed. Some of the large fortunes in Atlanta
have come chiefly from the labour of chain-gangs of convicts
leased from the state.[2]

Fate of the Black Boy

As I have already suggested, one of the things that impressed
me strongly in visiting Judge Broyles's court—and others like
it — was the astonishing number of children, especially
Negroes, arrested. Some of them were very young and often
exceedingly bright-looking. From the records I find that in
1906 1 boy six years old, 7 of seven years, 33 of eight years, 69
of nine years, 107 of ten years, 142 of eleven years, and 219
of twelve years were arrested and brought into court — in other
words, 578 boys and girls, mostly Negroes, under twelve
years of age!

1. E. Marvin Underwood.
2. The convict leasing system, which was widely used by southern states in
the late nineteenth century, was abolished by Georgia in 1908. But, unfortu-

"I should think," I said to a police officer, "you would have trouble in taking care of all these children in your reformatories.

"Reformatories!" he said, "there are n't any."

"What do you do with them?"

"Well, if they 're bad we put 'em in the stockade or the chain-gang, otherwise they 're turned loose."

I found, however, that a new state juvenile reformatory was just being opened at Milledgeville — which may accommodate a few Negro boys. An attempt is also being made in Atlanta to get hold of some of the children through a new probation system. I talked with the excellent officer, Mr. Gloer, who works in conjunction with Judge Broyles. He reaches a good many white boys, but very few Negroes. Of 1,011 boys and girls under sixteen, arrested in 1905, 819 were black, but of those given the advantage of the probation system, 50 were white and only 7 coloured. In other words, out of 819 arrests of Negro children only 7 enjoyed the benefit of the probation system.

Mr. Gloer has endeavoured to secure a coloured assistant who would help look after the swarming Negro children who are becoming criminals. The city refused to appropriate money for that purpose, but some of the leading coloured citizens agreed to contribute one dollar a month each, and a Negro woman was employed to help with the coloured children brought into court. Excellent work was done, but owing to the feeling after the riot the Negro assistant discontinued her work.

Care of Negro Orphans

With many hundreds of Negro orphans, waifs, and foundlings, the state or city does very little to help them. If it were not for the fact that the Negroes, something like the Jews, are wonderfully helpful to one another, adopting orphan children with the greatest willingness, there would be much suffering. Several orphanages in the state are conducted by the coloured people themselves, either through their churches or by private subscription. In Atlanta the Carrie Steele orphanage, which is managed by Negroes, has received an appropriation yearly from the city, and has taken children sent by the city charities

nately, the county chain gang system which replaced the Lease was little better than the old arrangement.

department. After the riot the appropriation was suddenly cut off without explanation, but through the activities of the new Civic League, it was, I understand, restored.

Without proper reformatories or asylums, with small advantage of the probation system, hundreds of Negro children are on the streets of Atlanta every day — shooting craps, stealing, learning to drink. A few, shut up in the stockade, or in chain-gangs, without any attempt to reform them or teach them, take lessons in crime from older offenders and come out worse than they went in. They spread abroad the lawlessness they learn and finally commit some frightful crime and get back into the chain-gang for life — where they make a profit for the state!

Every child, white or coloured, is getting an education somewhere. If that education is not in schools, or at home, or, in cases of incorrigibility, in proper reformatories, then it is on the streets or in chain-gangs.

Why Negro Childern Are Not in School

My curiosity, aroused by the very large number of young prisoners, led me next to inquire why these children were not in school. I visited a number of schools and I talked with L. M. Landrum, the assistant superintendent. Compulsory education is not enforced anywhere in the South, so that children may run the streets unless their parents insist upon sending them to school.[3] I found more than this, however, that Atlanta did not begin to have enough school facilities for the children who wanted to go. Like many rapidly growing cities, both South and North, it has been difficult to keep up with the demand. Just as in the North the tenement classes are often neglected, so in the South the lowest class — which is the Negro — is neglected. Several new schools have been built for white children, but there has been no new school for coloured children in fifteen or twenty years (though one Negro private school has been taken over within the last few years by the city). So crowded are the coloured schools that they have two sessions a day, one squad of children coming in the forenoon, another in the afternoon. The coloured teachers, therefore, do double work, for which they receive about two-thirds as much salary as the white teachers.

3. Before 1900 only Kentucky among the southern states required compulsory school attendance. North Carolina in 1907 and several other southern states during the next few years enacted modest compulsory education statutes.

Though many Southern cities have instituted industrial training in the public schools, Atlanta so far has done nothing. The president of the board of education in his last published report (1903) calls attention to this fact, and says also:

> While on the subject of Negro schools, permit me to call your attention to their overcrowded condition.　In every Negro school many teachers teach two sets of pupils, each set for one-half of a school day.
> The last bond election was carried by a majority of only thirty-three votes. To my personal knowledge more than thirty-three Negroes voted for the bonds on the solemn assurance that by the passage of the bonds the Negro children would receive more school accommodations.

The eagerness of the coloured people for a chance to send their children to school is something astonishing and pathetic. They will submit to all sorts of inconveniences in order that their children may get an education.　One day I visited the mill neighbourhood of Atlanta to see how the poorer classes of white people lived.　I found one very comfortable home occupied by a family of mill employees.　They hired a Negro woman to cook for them, and while they sent their children to the mill to work, the cook sent her children to school!

How Negroes Educate Themselves

Here is a curious and significant thing I found in Atlanta. Because there is not enough room for Negro children in public schools, the coloured people maintain many private schools. The largest of these, called Morris Brown College, has nearly 1,000 pupils.　Some of them are boarders from the country, but the greater proportion are day pupils from seven years old up who come in from the neighbourhood.　This "college," in reality a grammar school, is managed and largely supported by tuition and contributions from Negroes, though some subscriptions are obtained in the North.　Besides this "college" there are many small private schools conducted by Negro women and supported wholly by the tuition paid — the Negroes thus voluntarily taxing themselves heavily for their educational opportunities.　One afternoon in Atlanta I passed a small, rather dilapidated home.　Just as I reached the gate I heard a great cackling of voices and much laughter.　Coloured children began to pour out of the house.　"What's this?" I said, and I turned in to see. I found a Negro woman, the teacher, standing in the doorway. She had just dismissed her pupils for recess. She was holding school in two little rooms where some fifty children must have been crowded to suffocation. Everything was very primitive and inconvenient — but it was a school! She collected, she told me, a dollar a month tuition for each child. Mollie McCue's school, perhaps the best known private school for Negroes in the city, has 250 pupils.

Many children also find educational opportunities in the Negro colleges of the city — Clark University, Atlanta University and Spellman Seminary, which are supported partly by the Negroes themselves but mostly by Northern philanthropy.

Mr. Landrum gave me a copy of the last statistical report of the school board (1903), from which these facts appear:

	School Population	No. of Schools	Teachers	With Seats	Without Seats
White	14,465	20	200	10,052	4,413
Coloured	8,118	5	49	2,445	5,673

Even with a double daily session for coloured pupils nearly half of the Negro children in Atlanta, even in 1903, were barred from the public schools from lack of facilities, and the number has increased largely in the last four years. Some of these are accommodated in the private schools and colleges which I have mentioned, but there still remain hundreds, even thousands, who are getting no schooling of any kind, but who are nevertheless being educated — on the streets, and for criminal lives.

White Instruction for Black Children

I made a good many inquiries to find out what was being done outside of the public schools by the white people toward training the Negro either morally, industrially or intellectually — and I was astonished to find that it was next to nothing. The Negro is, of course, not welcome at the white churches or Sunday schools, and the sentiment is so strong against teaching the Negro that it is a brave Southern man or woman, indeed, who dares attempt anything of the sort. I did find, however, that the Central Presbyterian Church of Atlanta conducted a Negro Sunday School. Of this Dr. Theron H. Rice, the pastor, said:

"The Sunday School conducted in Atlanta by my church is the outcome of the effort of some of the most earnest and thoughtful of our people to give careful religious training to the Negroes of this generation and thus to conserve the influence begun with the fathers and mothers and the grandfathers and grandmothers of these coloured children when they were taught personally by their devoted Christian masters and mistresses. The work is small in point of the number reached, but it has been productive of sturdy character and law-abiding citizenship."

A white man or woman, and especially a Northern white man or woman, in Atlanta who teaches Negroes is rigorously ostracised by white society. I visited one of the Negro colleges where there are a number of white teachers from the North. We had quite a talk. When I came to leave one of the teachers said to me:

"You don't know how good it seems to talk with some one from the outside world. We work here year in and year out without a white visitor, except those who have some necessary business with the institution."

Explaining the attitude toward these Northern teachers (and we must understand just how the Southern people feel in this matter), a prominent clergyman said that a lady who made a social call upon a teacher in that institution would not feel secure against having to meet Negroes socially and that when the call was returned a similar embarrassing situation might be created.

Apologising for Helping Negroes

Just in this connection: I found a very remarkable and significant letter published in the Orangeburg, S. C., *News*, signed by a well-to-do white citizen who thus apologises for a kind act to a Negro school:

I had left my place of business here on a business trip a few miles below, on returning I came by the above-mentioned school (the Prince Institute, coloured), and was held up by the teacher and begged to make a few remarks to the children. Very reluctantly I did so, not thinking that publicity would be given to it or that I was doing anything that would offend anyone. I wish to say here and now that I am heartily sorry for what I did, and I hope after this humble confession and expression of regret that all whom I have offended will forgive me.

The sentiment indicated by this letter, while widely prevalent, is by no means universal. I have seen Southern white men address Negro schools and Negro gatherings many times since I have been down here. Some of the foremost men in the South have accepted Booker T. Washington's invitations to speak at Tuskegee. And concerning the very letter that I reproduce above, the *Charlotte Observer*, a strong Southern newspaper, which copied it, said:

A man would better be dead than to thus abase himself. This man did right to address the pupils of a coloured school, but has spoiled all by apologising for it. Few people have conceived that race prejudice went so far, even in South Carolina, as is here indicated. Logically it is to be assumed that this jelly-fish was about to be put under the ban, and to secure exemption from this, published this abject card. To it was appended a certificate from certain citizens, saying they 'are as anxious to see the coloured race elevated as any people, but by all means let it be done inside the colour line.' . . . The narrowness and malignity betrayed in this Orangeburg incident is exceedingly unworthy, and those guilty of it should be ashamed of themselves.

The Rev. H. S. Bradley, for a long time one of the leading clergymen of Atlanta, now of St. Louis, said in a sermon published in the Atlanta *Constitution:*

. . . We have not been wholly lacking in our effort to help. There are a few schools and churches supported by Southern whites for the Negroes. Here and there a man like George Williams Walker, of the aristocracy of South Carolina, and a woman like Miss Belle H. Bennett, of the blue blood of Kentucky, goes as teacher to the Negro youth, and seeks in a Christly spirit of fraternity to bring them to a higher plane of civil and moral manhood, but the number like them can almost be counted on fingers of both hands.

Our Southern churches have spent probably a hundred times as much money since the Civil War in an effort to evangelise the people of China, Japan, India, South America, Africa, Mexico, and Cuba, as they have spent to give the Gospel to the Negroes at our doors. It is often true that opportunity is overlooked because it lies at our feet.

Concerning the Vagrant Negro

Before I get away from observations of the low-class Negro, I must speak of the subject of vagrancy. Many white men have told me with impatience of the great number of idle or partly idle Negroes — idle while every industry and most of the farming districts of Georgia are crying for more labour. And from my observation in Atlanta, I should say that there were good many idle or partly idle Negroes — even after the riot,

which served, I understand, to drive many of them away. Five
days before the riot of last September, a committee of the city
council visited some forty saloons one afternoon, and by actual
count found 2,455 Negroes (and 152 white men) drinking
at the bars or lounging around the doorways. In some of
these saloons — conducted by white men and permitted to exist
by the city authorities — pictures of nude white women were
displayed as an added attraction. Has this anything to do
with Negro crimes against white women? After the riot these
conditions in Atlanta were much improved and in January,
1908, all the saloons were closed.

Increased Negro idleness is the result, in large measure, of
the marvellous and rapid changes in Southern conditions. The
South has been and is to-day dependent on a single labour supply
— the Negro. Now Negroes, though recruited by a high birth
rate, have not been increasing in any degree as rapidly as the
demand for labour incident to the development of every sort of
industry, railroads, lumbering, mines, to say nothing of the
increased farm area and the added requirements of growing
cities. With this enormous increased demand for labour the
Negro supply has, relatively, been decreasing. Many have
gone North and West, many have bought farms of their own,
thousands, by education, have became professional men,
teachers, preachers, and even merchants and bankers — always
draining away the best and most industrious men of the race
and reducing by so much the available supply of common labour.
In short, those Negroes who were capable have been going the
same way as the unskilled Irishman and German in the North
— upward through the door of education — but, unlike the
North, there have been no other labourers coming in to take
their places.

What has been the result? Naturally a fierce contest
between agriculture and industry for the limited and dwindling
supply of the only labour they had.

Negro Monopoly on Labour

So they bid against one another — it was as though the Negro
had a monopoly on labour — and within the last few years day
wages for Negro workers have jumped from fifty or sixty cents

to $1.25 and$1.50, often more — a pure matter of competition. A similar advance has affected all sorts of servant labour — cooks, waiters, maids, porters.

High wages, scarcity of labour, and the consequent loss of opportunity for taking advantage of the prevailing prosperity would, in any community, South or North, whether the labour was white or black, produce a spirit of impatience and annoyance on the part of the employing class. I found it evident enough last summer in Kansas where the farmers were unable to get workers to save their crops; and the servant problem is not more provoking, certainly, in the South than in the North and West. Indeed, it is the labour problem more than any other one cause, that has held the South back and is holding it back to-day.

But the South has an added cause of annoyance. Higher wages, instead of producing more and better labour, as they would naturally be expected to do, have actually served to reduce the supply. This may, at first, seem paradoxical: but it is easily explainable and it lies deep down beneath many of the perplexities which surround the race problem.

Most Negroes, as I have said, were (and still are, of course) farm-dwellers, and farm-dwellers in the hitherto wasteful Southern way. Their living is easy to get and very simple. In that warm climate they need few clothes; a shack for a home. Their living standards are low; they have not learned to save; there has not been time since slavery for them to attain the sense of responsibility which would encourage them to get ahead. And moreover they have been and are to-day largely under the discipline of white land owners.

What was the effect, then, of a rapid advance in wages? The poorer class of Negroes, naturally indolent and happy-go-lucky, found that they could make as much money in two or three days as they had formerly earned in a whole week. It was enough to live on as well as they had ever lived: why, then, work more than two days a week? It was the logic of a child, but it was the logic used. Everywhere I went in the South I heard the same story: high wages coupled with the difficulty of getting anything like continuous work from this class of coloured men.

On the other hand the better and more industrious Negroes, who would work continuously — and there are unnumbered thousands of them, as faithful as any workers — occasionally saved their surplus, bought little farms or businesses of their own and began to live on a better scale. One of the first things they did after getting their footing was to take their wives and daughters out of the white man's kitchen, and to send their children from the cotton fields (where the white man needed them) to the school-house where the tendency (exactly as with white children) was to educate them away from farm employment. With the development of ambition and a higher standard of living, the Negro follows the steps of the rising Irishman or Italian: he has a better home, he wants his wife to take care of it, and he insists upon the education of his children.

In this way higher wages have tended to cut down the already limited supply of labour, producing annoyance, placing greater obstacles in the way of that material development of which the Southerner is so justly proud. And this, not at all unnaturally, has given rise on the one hand to complaints against the lazy Negro who will work only two days in the week that he may loaf the other five; and on the other hand it has found expression in blind and bitter hostility to the education which enables the better sort of Negro to rise above the unskilled employment and the domestic service of which the South is so keenly in need. It is human nature to blame men, not conditions. Here is unlimited work to do: here is the Negro who has been for centuries and is to-day depended upon to do it; it is not done. The natural result is to throw the blame wholly upon the Negro, and not upon the deep economic conditions and tendencies which have actually caused the scarcity of labour.

Immigrants to Take the Negroes' Places

But within the last year or two thinking men in the South have begun to see this particular root of the difficulty and a great new movement looking to the encouragement of immigration from foreign countries has been started. In November, 1906, the first shipload of immigrants ever brought from Europe directly to a South Carolina port were landed at Charleston with great ceremony and rejoicing.[4] If a steady stream of

4. By 1900 every state in the South had established some kind of immigration bureau and the region's interest in attracting foreign settlers steadily mounted during the next few years. But these efforts were largely unrewarded, for the great mass of foreign immigrants during this period bypassed the South.

immigrants can be secured and if they can be employed on satisfactory terms with the Negro it will go far toward relieving race tension in the South.

Of course idleness leads to crime, and one of the present efforts in the South is toward a more rigid enforcement of laws against vagrancy. In this the white people have the sympathy of the leading Negroes. I was struck with one passage in the discussion at the last Workers' Conference at Tuskegee. William E. Holmes, president of a coloured college at Macon, Georgia, was speaking. Some one interrupted him:

"I would like to ask if you think the Negro is any more disposed to become a loafer or vagrant than any other people under the same conditions?"

"Well," said Mr. Holmes, taking a deep breath, "we cannot afford to do what other races do. We have n't a single, solitary man or woman among us we can afford to support as an idler. It may be that other races have made so much progress that they can afford to support loafers. But we are not yet in that condition. Some of us have the impression that the world owes us a living. That is a misfortune. I must confess that I have become convinced that at the present time we furnish a larger number of loafers than any other race of people on this continent."

These frank remarks did not meet with the entire approval of the members of the conference, but the discussion seemed to indicate that there was a great deal more of truth in them than the leaders and teachers of the Negro are disposed to admit.

The Worthless Negro

I tried to see as much as I could of this "worthless Negro," who is about the lowest stratum of humanity, it seems to me, of any in our American life. He is usually densely ignorant, often a wanderer, working to-day with a railroad gang, to-morrow on some city works, the next day picking cotton. He has lost his white friends — his "white folks," as he calls them — and he has not attained the training or self-direction to stand alone. He works only when he is hungry, and he is as much a criminal as he dares to be. Many such Negroes are supported by their wives or by women with whom they live — for morality and the home virtues among this class are unknown. A woman who works as a cook in a white family will often take enough from the kitchen to feed a worthless vagabond of a man and keep him in idleness — or worse. A Negro song exactly expresses this state of beatitude:

> "I doan has to work so ha'd
> I 's got a gal in a white man's ya'd;
> Ebery night 'bout half pas' eight
> I goes 'round to the white man's gate:
> She brings me butter and she brings me la'd —
> I doan has to work so ha'd!"

This worthless Negro, without training or education, grown up from the neglected children I have already spoken of, evident in his idleness around saloons and depots — this Negro provokes the just wrath of the people, and gives a bad name to the entire Negro race. In numbers he is, of course, small, compared with the 8,000,000 Negroes in the South, who perform the enormous bulk of hard manual labour upon which rests Southern prosperity.

How the Working Negro Lives

Above this low stratum of criminal or semi-criminal Negroes is a middle class, comprising the great body of the race — the workers. They are crowded into straggling settlements like Darktown and Jackson Row, a few owning their homes, but the majority renting precariously, earning good wages, harmless for the most part, but often falling into petty crime. Poverty here, however, lacks the tragic note that it strikes in the crowded sections of Northern cities. The temperament of the Negro is irrepressibly cheerful, he overflows from his small home and sings and laughs in his streets; no matter how ragged or forlorn he may be good humour sits upon his countenance, and his squalour is not unpicturesque. A banjo, a mullet supper from time to time, an exciting revival, give him real joys. Most of the families of this middle class, some of whom are deserted wives with children, have their "white folks" for whom they do washing, cooking, gardening, or other service, and all have church connections, so that they have a real place in the social fabric and a certain code of self-respect.

I tried to see all I could of this phase of life. I visited many of the poorer Negro homes and I was often received in squalid rooms with a dignity of politeness which would have done credit to a society woman. For the Negro, naturally, is a sort of Frenchman. And if I can sum up the many visits I made in a single conclusion I should say, I think, that I was chiefly impressed by the tragic punishment meted out to ignorance and weakness by our complex society. I would find a home of one or two rooms meanly furnished, but having in one corner a glittering cottage organ, or on the mantel shelf a glorified gilt clock; crayon portraits, inexpressibly crude and ugly, but framed gorgeously, are not uncommon — the first uncertain, primitive (not unpitiful) reachings out after some of the graces of a broader life. Many of these things are bought from agents and the prices paid are extortionate. Often a Negro family will pay monthly for a year or so on some showy clock or chromo or music-box or decorated mirror — paying the value of it a dozen times over, only to have it seized when through sickness, or lack of foresight, they fail to meet a single note. Installment houses prey upon them, pawnbrokers suck their blood, and they are infinitely the victims of patent medicines. It is rare, indeed, that I entered a Negro cabin, even the poorest, without seeing one or more bottles of some abominable cure-all. The amount yearly expended by Negroes for patent medicines, which are glaringly advertised in all Southern newspapers, must be enormous — millions of dollars. I had an interesting side light on conditions one day while walking in one of the most fashionable residence districts of Atlanta. I saw a magnificent gray-stone residence standing somewhat back from the street. I said to my companion, who was a resident of the city:

"That's a fine home."

"Yes; stop a minute," he said, "I want to tell you about that. The anti-kink man lives there."

"Anti-kink?" I asked in surprise.

"Yes; the man who occupies that house is one of the wealthiest men here. He made his money by selling to Negroes a preparation to smooth the kinks out of their wool. They're simply crazy on that subject."

"Does it work?"

"You have n't seen any straight-haired Negroes, have you?"
he asked.

Ignorance carries a big burden and climbs a rocky road!

Old Mammies and Nurses

The mass of coloured people still maintain, as I have said,
a more or less intimate connection with white families —
frequently a very beautiful and sympathetic relationship like
that of the old mammies or nurses. To one who has heard so
much of racial hatred as I have since I have been down here, a
little incident that I observed the other day comes with a charm
hardly describable. I saw a carriage stop in front of a home.
The expected daughter had arrived — a very pretty girl indeed.
She stepped out eagerly. Her father was halfway down to the
gate; but ahead of him was a very old Negro woman in the
cleanest of clean starched dresses.

"Honey," she said eagerly.

"Mammy!" exclaimed the girl, and the two rushed into each
other's arms, clasping and kissing — the white girl and the old
black woman.

I thought to myself: "There's no Negro problem there:
that 's just plain human love!"

"Master" Superseded by "Boss"

Often I have heard Negroes refer to "my white folks" and
similarly the white man still speaks of "my Negroes." The
old term of slavery, the use of the word "master," has wholly
disappeared, and in its place has arisen, not without significance,
the round term "Boss," or sometimes "Cap," or "Cap'n."
To this the white man responds with the first name of the Negro,
"Jim" or "Susie" — or if the Negro is old or especially
respected: "Uncle Jim" or "Aunt Susan."

To an unfamiliar Northerner one of the very interesting and
somewhat amusing phases of conditions down here is the panic
fear displayed over the use of the word "Mr." or "Mrs." No
Negro is ever called Mr. or Mrs. by a white man; that would
indicate social equality. A Southern white man told me with
humour of his difficulties:

"Now I admire Booker Washington. I regard him as a great man, and yet I could n't call him Mr. Washington. We were all in a quandary until a doctor's degree was given him. That saved our lives! We all call him 'Dr.' Washington now."

Sure enough! I don't think I have heard him called Mr. Washington since I came down here. It is always "Dr." or just "Booker." They are ready to call a Negro "Professor" or "Bishop" or "The Reverend" — but not "Mr."

In the same way a Negro may call Miss Mary Smith by the familiar "Miss Mary," but if he called her Miss Smith she would be deeply incensed. The formal "Miss Smith" would imply social equality.

I digress: but I have wanted to impress these relationships. There are all gradations of Negroes between the wholly dependent old family servant and the new, educated Negro professional or business man, and, correspondingly, every degree of treatment from indulgence to intense hostility.

I must tell, in spite of lack of room, one beautiful story I heard at Atlanta, which so well illustrates the old relationship. There is in the family of Dr. J. S. Todd, a well-known citizen of Atlanta, an old, old servant called, affectionately, Uncle Billy. He has been so long in the family that in reality he is served as much as he serves. During the riot last September he was terrified: he did not dare to go home at night. So Miss Louise, the doctor's daughter, took Uncle Billy home through the dark streets. When she was returning one of her friends met her and was much alarmed that she should venture out in a time of so much danger.

"What are you doing out here this time of night?" he asked.

"Why," she replied, as if it were the most natural answer in the world, "I had to take Uncle Billy safely home."

Over against this story I want to reproduce a report from a Kentucky newspaper which will show quite the other extreme:

*Tennessee Farmer Has Negro Bishop and His Wife
Ejected from a Sleeping Car*

Irvine McGraw, a Tennessee farmer, brought Kentucky's Jim Crow law into prominent notice yesterday on an Illinois Central Pullman car. When McGraw entered the car he saw the coloured divine, Rev. Dr. C. H. Phillips, bishop of the coloured Methodist Episcopal Churches in Tennessee, North Carolina, Texas and a portion of Arizona and New Mexico, and his wife pre-

INTERIOR OF A NEGRO WORKINGMAN'S HOME, ATLANTA, GEORGIA

INTERIOR OF A NEGRO HOME OF THE POOREST SORT IN INDIANAPOLIS

WHERE WHITE MILL HANDS LIVE IN ATLANTA, GEORGIA

WHERE SOME OF THE POORER NEGROES LIVE IN ATLANTA, GEORGIA

COMPANION PICTURES
to show that there is comparatively little difference in the material comfort of
the two classes

paring to retire for the night. He demanded that the conductor order them out of the car, but the conductor refused.

After he entered Kentucky he hunted for an officer at every station and finally at Hopkinsville Policeman Bryant Baker agreed to undertake the task of ejecting the Negroes from the car. The train was held nine minutes while they dressed and repaired to the coloured compartment.

I have now described two of the three great classes of Negroes: First, the worthless and idle Negro, often a criminal, comparatively small in numbers but perniciously evident. Second, the great middle class of Negroes who do the manual work of the South. Above these, a third class, few in numbers, but most influential in their race, are the progressive, property-owning Negroes, who have wholly severed their old intimate ties with the white people — and who have been getting further and further away from them.

A White Man's Problem

It keeps coming to me that this is more a white man's problem than it is a Negro problem. The white man as well as the black is being tried by fire. The white man is in full control of the South, politically, socially, industrially: the Negro, as ex-Governor Northen points out, is his helpless ward. What will he do with him? Speaking of the education of the Negro, and in direct reference to the conditions in Atlanta which I have already described, many men have said to me:

"Think of the large sums that the South has spent and is spending on the education of the Negro. The Negro does not begin to pay for his education in taxes."

Neither do the swarming Slavs, Italians, and Poles in our Northern cities. They pay little in taxes and yet enormous sums are expended in their improvement. For their benefit? Of course, but chiefly for ours. It is better to educate men in school than to let them so educate themselves as to become a menace to society. The present *kind* of education in the South may possibly be wrong; but for the protection of society it is as necessary to train every Negro as it is every white man.

When I saw the crowds of young Negroes being made criminal — through lack of proper training — I could not help thinking how pitilessly ignorance finally revenges itself upon that society which neglects or exploits it.

CHAPTER IV

IN THE BLACK BELT: THE NEGRO FARMER

THE cotton picking season was drawing to its close when I left for the black belt of Georgia. So many friends in Atlanta had said:

"The city Negro is n't the real Negro. You must go out on the cotton plantations in the country; there you'll see the genuine black African in all his primitive glory."

It is quite true that the typical Negro is a farmer. The great mass of the race in the South dwells in the country. According to the last census, out of 8,000,000 Negroes in the Southern states 6,558,173, or 82 per cent., lived on the farms or in rural villages. The crowded city life which I have already described represents not the common condition of the masses of the Negro race but the newer development which accompanies the growth of industrial and urban life. In the city the races are forced more violently together, socially and economically, than in the country, producing acute crises, but it is in the old agricultural regions where the Negro is in such masses, where ideas change slowly, and old institutions persist, that the problem really presents the greatest difficulties.

There is no better time of year to see the South than November; for then it wears the smile of abundance. The country I went through — rolling red hills, or black bottoms, pine-clad in places, with pleasant farm openings dotted with cabins, often dilapidated but picturesque, and the busy little towns — wore somehow an air of brisk comfort. The fields were lively with Negro cotton pickers; I saw bursting loads of the new lint drawn by mules or oxen, trailing along the country roads; all the gins were puffing busily; at each station platform cotton bales by scores or hundreds stood ready for shipment and the towns were cheerful with farmers white and black, who now had money to spend. The heat of the summer had gone, the air bore the tang of a brisk autumn coolness. It was a good time of the year — and everybody seemed to feel it. Many Negroes got on or off at every station with laughter and shouted good-byes.

What Is the Black Belt?

And so, just at evening, after a really interesting journey, I reached Hawkinsville, a thriving town of some 3,000 people just south of the centre of Georgia. Pulaski County, of which Hawkinsville is the seat, with an ambitious new court-house, is a typical county of the black belt. A census map which is here reproduced well shows the region of largest proportionate

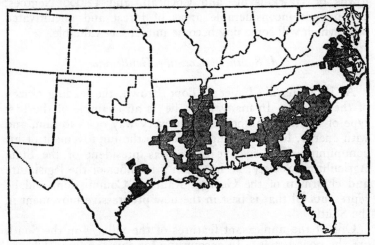

THE BLACK BELT
In the region shaded more than half of the inhabitants are negroes

Negro population, extending from South Carolina through central Georgia and Alabama to Mississippi. More than half the inhabitants of all this broad belt, including also the Atlantic coastal counties and the lower Mississippi Valley (as shaded on the map), are Negroes — chiefly farm Negroes. There the race question, though perhaps not so immediately difficult as in cities like Atlanta, is with both white and coloured people the imminent problem of daily existence. Several times while

in the black belt I was amused at the ardent response of people
to whom I mentioned the fact that I had already seen something
of conditions in Kentucky, Maryland, and Virginia:

"Why, they have n't any Negro problem. They 're *North*."

In Maryland, Kentucky, and Texas the problem is a sharp
irritant — as it is, for that matter, in Ohio, in Indianapolis,
and on the west side of New York City — but it is not
the life and death question that it is in the black belt or in
the Yazoo delta.

All the country of Central Georgia has been long settled.
Pulaski County was laid out in 1808; and yet the population
to-day may be considered sparse. The entire county has only
8,000 white people, a large proportion of whom live in the
towns of Hawkinsville and Cochran, and 12,000 Negroes,
leaving not inconsiderable areas of forest and uncultivated
land which will some day become immensely valuable.

A Southern Country Gentleman

At Hawkinsville I met J. Pope Brown, the leading citizen
of the county. In many ways he is an example of the best
type of the new Southerner. In every way open to him, and
with energy, he is devoting himself to the improvement of his
community. For five years he was president of the State
Agricultural Society; he has been a member of the legislature
and chairman of the Georgia Railroad Commission, and he
represents all that is best in the new progressive movement in
the South.

One of the unpleasant features of the villages in the South
are the poor hotels. In accounting for this condition I heard
a story illustrating the attitude of the old South toward public
accommodations. A number of years ago, before the death
of Robert Toombs, who, as a member of Jefferson Davis's
cabinet was called the "backbone of the confederacy," the
spirit of progress reached the town where Toombs lived. The
thing most needed was a new hotel. The business men got
together and subscribed money with enthusiasm, counting
upon Toombs, who was their richest man, for the largest
subscription. But when they finally went to him, he said:

"What do we want of a hotel? When a gentleman comes

to town I will entertain him myself; those who are not gentlemen we don't want!"

That was the old spirit of aristocratic individualism; the town did not get its hotel.

One of the public enterprises of Mr. Brown at Hawkinsville is a good hotel; and what is rarer still, North and South, he has made his hotel building really worthy architecturally.

Mr. Brown took me out to his plantation — a drive of some eight miles. In common with most of the larger plantation owners, as I found not only in Georgia, but in other Southern states which I afterward visited, Mr. Brown makes his home in the city. After a while I came to feel a reasonable confidence in assuming that almost any prominent merchant, banker, lawyer, or politician whom I met in the towns owned a plantation in the country. From a great many stories of the fortunes of families that I heard I concluded that the movement of white owners from the land to nearby towns was increasing every year. High prices for cotton and consequent prosperity seem to have accelerated rather than retarded the movement. White planters can now afford to live in town where they can have the comforts and conveniences, where the servant question is not impossibly difficult, and where there are good schools for the children. Another potent reason for the movement is the growing fear of the whites, and especially the women and children, at living alone on great farms where white neighbours are distant. Statistics show that less crime is committed in the black belt than in other parts of the South. I found that the fear was not absent even among these people.

I have a letter from a white man, P. S. George, of Greenwood, Mississippi, which expresses the country white point of view with singular earnestness:

> I live in a country of large plantations; if there are 40,000 people in that country, at least 30,000 are Negroes, and we never have any friction between the races. I have been here as a man for twenty years and I never heard of but one case of attempted assault by a Negro on a white woman. That Negro was taken out and hanged. I said that we never had any trouble with Negroes, but it's because we never take our eyes off the gun. You may wager that I never leave my wife and daughter at home without a man in the house after ten o'clock at night—because I am afraid.

As a result of these various influences a traveller in the black belt sees many plantation houses, even those built in recent years, standing vacant and forlorn or else occupied by white overseers, who are in many parts of the South almost as difficult to keep as the Negro tenants.

Thousands of small white farmers, both owners and renters, of course, remain, but when the leading planters leave the country, these men, too, grow discontented and get away at the first opportunity. Going to town, they find ready employment for the whole family in the cotton mill or in other industries where they make more money and live with a degree of comfort that they never before imagined possible.

Story of the Mill People

Many cotton mills, indeed, employ agents whose business it is to go out through the country urging the white farmers to come to town and painting glowing pictures of the possibilities of life there. I have visited a number of mill neighbourhoods and talked with the operatives. I found the older men sometimes homesick for free life of the farm. One lanky old fellow said rather pathetically:

"When it comes to cotton picking time and I know that they are grinding cane and hunting possums, I jest naturally get lonesome for the country."

But nothing would persuade the women and children to go back to the old hard life. Hawkinsville has a small cotton mill and just such a community of white workers around it. Owing to the scarcity of labour, wages in the mills have been going up rapidly all over the South, during the last two or three years, furnishing a still more potent attraction for country people.

All these various tendencies are uniting to produce some very remarkable conditions in the South. A natural segregation of the races is apparently taking place. I saw it everywhere I went in the black belt. The white people were gravitating toward the towns or into white neighbourhoods and leaving the land, even though still owned by white men, more and more to the exclusive occupation of Negroes. Many black counties are growing blacker while not a few white counties are growing whiter.

Take, for example, Pulaski County, through which I drove

that November morning with Mr. Brown. In 1870 the coloured and white population were almost exactly equal — about 6,000 for each. In 1880 the Negroes had increased to 8,225 while the whites showed a loss. By 1890 the towns had begun to improve and the white population grew by about 700, but the Negroes increased nearly 2,000. And, finally, here are the figures for 1900: Negroes 11,029; Whites 7,460.

I have not wished to darken our observations with too many statistics, but this tendency is so remarkable that I wish to set down for comparison the figures of a "white county" in northern Georgia — Polk County — which is growing whiter every year.

	Negroes	Whites
1880	4,147	7,805
1890	4,654	10,289
1900	4,916	12,940

Driving out Negroes

One of the most active causes of this movement is downright fear — or race repulsion expressing itself in fear. White people dislike and fear to live in dense coloured neighbourhoods, while Negroes are often terrorised in white neighbourhoods — and not in the South only but in parts of Ohio, Indiana, Illinois, as I shall show when I come to treat of Northern race conditions. I have accumulated many instances showing how Negroes are expelled from white neighbourhoods. There is a significant report from Little Rock, Arkansas:

(Special to the Georgian.)

Little Rock, Ark., Jan. 1.—Practically every Negro in Evening Shade, Sharp County, in this state, has left town as the result of threats which have been made against the Negroes. For several years a small colony of Negroes has lived just on the outskirts of the town. A short time ago notices were posted warning the Negroes to leave the town at once. About the same time Joe Brooks, a Negro who lived with his family two miles north of town, was called to his door and fired upon by unknown persons. A load of shot struck the house close by his side and some of the shot entered his arm. Brooks and his family have left the country, and practically every member of the Negro colony has gone. They have abandoned their property or disposed of it for whatever they could get.

From the New Orleans *Times Democrat* of March 20, 1907, I cut the following dispatch showing one method pursued by the whites of Oklahoma:

BLACKS ORDERED OUT

Lawton, Okla., March 20.—"Negroes, beware the cappers. We, the Sixty Sons of Waurika, demand the Negroes to leave here at once. We mean Go! Leave in twenty-four hours, or after that your life is uncertain." These were the words on placards which the eighty Negroes of the town of Waurika, forty miles south of Lawton, saw posted conspicuously in a number of public places this morning.

Dispatches from here to-night stated that the whites are in earnest, and that the Negroes will be killed if they do not leave town.

Not a few students of Southern conditions like John Temple Graves among the whites and Bishop Turner[1] among the coloured people have argued that actual physical separation of the races (either by deportation of the Negroes to Africa or elsewhere, or by giving them certain reservation-like parts of the South to live in) is the only solution. But there is, in actuality, a natural segregation going forward in certain parts of the South, though in a very different way from that recommended by Mr. Graves and Bishop Turner; for even in the blackest counties the white people own most of the land, occupy the towns, and dominate everywhere politically, socially, and industrially.

Mr. Brown's plantation contains about 5,000 acres, of which some 3,500 acres are in cultivation, a beautiful rolling country, well watered, with here and there clumps of pines, and dotted with the small homes of the tenantry.

As we drove along the country road we met or passed many Negroes who bowed with the greatest deference. Some were walking, but many drove horses or mules and rode not infrequently in top buggies, looking most prosperous, as indeed, Mr. Brown informed me that they were. He knew them all, and sometimes stopped to ask them how they were getting along. The outward relationship between the races in the country seems to me to be smoother than it is in the city.

Cotton, as in all this country, is almost the exclusive crop. In spite of the constant preaching of agricultural reformers, like Mr. Brown himself, hardly enough corn is raised to supply

1. Henry M. Turner of Atlanta, a bishop in the African Methodist Episcopal Church.

the people with food, and I was surprised here and elsewhere at seeing so few cattle and hogs. Sheep are non-existent. In Hawkinsville, though the country round about raises excellent grass,I saw in front of a supply store bales of hay which had been shipped in 400 miles — from Tennessee. Enough sugar cane is raised, mostly in small patches, to supply syrup for domestic uses. At the time of my visit the Negroes were in the cane-fields with their long knives, getting in the crop. We saw several little one-horse grinding mills pressing the juice from the cane, while near at hand, sheltered by a shanty-like roof, was the great simmering syrup kettle, with an expert Negro at work stirring and skimming. And always there were Negroes round about, all the boys and girls with jolly smeared faces — and the older ones peeling and sucking the fresh cane.

It was a great time of year!

How does the landlord — and a lord he is in a very true sense — manage his great estate ? The same system is in use with slight variations everywhere in the cotton country and a description of Mr. Brown's methods, with references here and there to what I have seen or heard elsewhere, will give an excellent idea of the common procedure.

A *Country of Great Plantations*

The black belt is a country of great plantations, some owners having as high as 30,000 acres, interspersed with smaller farms owned by the poorer white families or Negroes. In one way the conditions are similar to those prevailing in Ireland; great landlords and a poor tenantry or peasantry, the tenants here being very largely black.

It requires about 100 families, or 600 people, to operate Mr. Brown's plantation. Of these, 90 per cent. are coloured and 10 per cent. white. I was much interested in what Mr. Brown said about his Negro tenants, which varies somewhat from the impression I had in the city of the younger Negro generation.

"I would much rather have young Negroes for tenants," he said, "because they work better and seem more disposed to take care of their farms. The old Negroes ordinarily will shirk — a habit of slavery."

Besides the residence of the overseer and the homes of the tenants there is on the plantation a supply store owned by Mr. Brown, a blacksmith shop and a Negro church, which is also used as a school-house. This is, I found all through the black belt, a common equipment.

Three different methods are pursued by the landlord in getting his land cultivated. First, the better class of tenants rent the land for cash, a "standing rent" of some $3 an acre, though in many places in Mississippi it ranges as high as $6 and $8 an acre. Second, a share-crop rental, in which the landlord and the tenant divide the cotton and corn produced. Third, the ordinary wage system; that is, the landlord hires workers at so much a month and puts in his own crop. All three of these methods are usually employed on the larger plantations. Mr. Brown rents 2,500 acres for cash, 400 on shares, and farms 600 himself with wage workers.

All the methods of land measurement are very different here from what they are in the North. The plantation is irregularly divided up into what are called one-mule or one-plough farms — just that amount of land which a family can cultivate with one mule — usually about thirty acres. Some ambitious tenants will take a two-mule or even a four-mule farm.

The Negro Tenant

Most of the tenants, especially the Negroes, are very poor, and wholly dependent upon the landlord. Many Negro families possess practically nothing of their own, save their ragged clothing, and a few dollars' worth of household furniture, cooking utensils and a gun. The landlord must therefore supply them not only with enough to live on while they are making their crop, but with the entire farming outfit. Let us say that a Negro comes in November to rent a one-mule farm from the landlord for the coming year.

"What have you got?" asks the landlord.

"Noting', boss," he is quite likely to say.

The "boss" furnishes him with a cabin to live in — which goes with the land rented — a mule, a plough, possibly a one-

A "POOR WHITE" FAMILY

"Among them is a spirit of pride and independence which, rightly directed, would uplift and make them prosperous, but which, misguided and blind, as it sometimes is, keeps them in poverty."

A MODEL NEGRO SCHOOL

Inspired by Tuskegee; different, indeed, from the ordinary country Negro school in the South

COMPANION PICTURES

Old and new cabins for Negro tenants on the Brown plantation

horse waggon and a few tools. He is often given a few dollars in cash near Christmas time which (ordinarily) he immediately spends — wastes. He is then allowed to draw upon the plantation supply store a regular amount of corn to feed his mule, and meat, bread, and tobacco, and some clothing for his family. The cost of the entire outfit and supplies for a year is in the neighbourhood of $300, upon which the tenant pays interest at from 10 to 30 per cent. from the time of signing the contract in November, although most of the supplies are not taken out until the next summer. Besides this interest the planter also makes a large profit on all the groceries and other necessaries furnished by his supply store. Having made his contract the Negro goes to work with his whole family and keeps at it until the next fall when the cotton is all picked and ginned. Then he comes in for his "settlement" — a great time of year. The settlements were going forward while I was in the black belt. The Negro is credited with the amount of cotton he brings in and he is charged with all the supplies he has had, and interest, together with the rent of his thirty acres of land. If the season has been good and he has been industrious, he will often have a nice profit in cash, but sometimes he not only does not come out even, but closes his year of work actually in deeper debt to the landlord.

Some Negroes, nowadays usually of the poorer sort, work for wages. They get from $12 to $15 a month (against $5 to $8 a few years ago) with a cabin to live in. They are allowed a garden patch, where they can, if they are industrious and their families help, raise enough vegetables to feed them comfortably, or part of a bale of cotton, which is their own. But it is sadly to be commented upon that few Negro tenants, or whites either, as far as I could see, do anything with their gardens save perhaps to raise a few collards, peanuts, and peppers — and possibly a few sweet potatoes. This is due in part to indolence and lack of ambition, and in part to the steady work required by the planter. The wife and children of an industrious wage-working Negro nearly always help in the fields, earning an additional income from chopping cotton in spring and picking the lint in the fall.

This is the system as it is in theory; but the interest for us lies not in the plan, but in the actual practice.

How does it all work out for good or for evil, for landlord and for tenant?

Tenantry in the South is a very different thing from what it is in the North. In the North, a man who rents a farm is nearly as free to do as he pleases as if he were the owner. But in the South, the present tenant system is much nearer the condition that prevailed in slavery times than it is to the present Northern tenant system. This grows naturally out of slavery; the white man had learned to operate big plantations with ignorant help; and the Negro on his part had no training for any other system. The white man was the natural master and the Negro the natural dependent and a mere Emancipation Proclamation did not at once change the *spirit* of the relationship.

To-day a white overseer resides on every large plantation and he or the owner himself looks after and disciplines the tenants. The tenant is in debt to him (in some cases reaching a veritable condition of debt slavery or peonage) and he *must* see that the crop is made. Hence he watches the work of every Negro (and indeed that of the white tenants as well), sees that the land is properly fertilised, and that the dikes (to prevent washing) are kept up, that the cotton is properly chopped (thinned) and regularly cultivated. Some of the greater land-owners employ assistant overseers or "riders" who are constantly travelling from farm to farm. On one plantation I saw four such riders start out one day, each with a rifle on his saddle. And on a South Carolina plantation I had a glimpse of one method of discipline. A planter was telling me of his difficulties — how a spirit of unruliness sometimes swept abroad through a plantation, inspired by some "bigoty nigger."

"Do you know what I do with such cases?" he said. "Come with me, I'll show you."

He took me back through his house to the broad porch and reaching up to a shelf over the door he took down a hickory waggon spoke, as long as my arm.

"When there's trouble," he said, "I just go down with that and lay one or two of 'em out. That ends the trouble. We've got to do it; they're like children and once in a while they simply have to be punished. It's far better for them to take it this way, from a white man who is their friend, than to be arrested and taken to court and sent to the chain-gang."

Troubles of the Landlord

Planters told me of all sorts of difficulties they had to meet with their tenants.   One of them, after he had spent a whole evening telling me of the troubles which confronted any man who tried to work Negroes, summed it all up with the remark:

"You 've just got to make up your mind that you are dealing with children, and handle them as firmly and kindly as you know how."

He told me how hard it was to get a Negro tenant even in the busy season to work a full week — and it was often only by withholding the weekly food allowance that it could be done. Saturday afternoon (or "evening," as they say in the South) the Negro goes to town or visits his friends.   Often he spends all day Sunday driving about the country and his mule comes back so worn out that it cannot be used on Monday.   There are often furious religious revivals which break into the work, to say nothing of "frolics" and fish suppers at which the Negroes often remain all night long.   Many of them are careless with their tools, wasteful of supplies, irresponsible in their promises.   One planter told me how he had built neat fences around the homes of his Negroes, and fixed up their houses to encourage them in thrift and give them more comfort, only to have the fences and even parts of the houses used for firewood.

Toward fall, if the season has been bad, and the crop of cotton is short, so short that a Negro knows that he will not be able to "pay out" and have anything left for himself, he will sometimes desert the plantation entirely, leaving the cotton un-picked and a large debt to the landlord.   If he attempts that, however, he must get entirely away, else the planter will chase him down and bring him back to his work.   Illiterate, without discipline or training, with little ambition and much indolence, a large proportion of Negro tenants are looked after and driven like children or slaves.   I say "a large proportion"—but there are thousands of industrious Negro landowners and tenants who are rapidly getting ahead — as I shall show in my next chapter.

In this connection it is a noteworthy fact that a considerable number of the white tenants require almost as much attention as the Negroes, though they are, of course, treated in an entirely different way. One planter in Alabama said to me: "Give me Negroes every time. I would n't have a low-down white tenant on my place. You can get work out of any Negro if you know how to handle him; but there are some white men who won't work and can't be driven, because they are white."

Race Troubles in the Country

In short, when slavery was abolished it gave place to a sort of feudal tenantry system which continues widely to-day. And it has worked with comparative satisfaction, at least to the landlords, until within the last few years, when the next step in the usual evolution of human society — industrial and urban development — began seriously to disturb the feudal equilibrium of the cotton country. It was a curious idea — human enough — that men should attempt to legislate slaves immediately into freedom. But nature takes her own methods of freeing slaves; they are slower than men's ways, but more certain.

The change now going on in the South from the feudal agricultural life to sharpened modern conditions has brought difficulties for the planter compared with which all others pale into insignificance. I mean the scarcity of labour. Industry is competing with agriculture for the limited supply of Negro workers. Negroes, responding to exactly the same natural laws that control the white farmers, have been moving cityward, entering other occupations, migrating west or north — where more money is to be made. Agricultural wages have therefore gone up and rents, relatively, have gone down, and had the South not been blessed for several years with wonderful returns from its monopoly crop, there might have been a more serious crisis.

Cry of the South: "More Labour"

If the South to-day could articulate its chief need, we should hear a single great shout:

"More labour!"

Out of this struggle for tenants, servants, and workers has grown the chief complications of the Negro problem —

and I am not forgetting race prejudice, or the crimes against women. Indeed, it has seemed to me that the chief difficulty in understanding the Negro problem lies in showing how much of the complication in the South is due to economic readjustments and how much to instinctive race repulsion or race prejudice.

A Tenant Stealer

In one town I visited — not Hawkinsville — I was standing talking with some gentlemen in the street when I saw a man drive by in a buggy.

"Do you see that man?" they asked me. I nodded.

"Well, he is the greatest tenant-stealer in this country."

I heard a good deal about these "tenant stealers." A whole neighbourhood will execrate one planter who, to keep his land cultivated, will lure away his neighbours' Negroes. Sometimes he will offer more wages, sometimes he will give the tenants better houses to live in, and sometimes he succeeds by that sheer force of a masterful personality which easily controls an ignorant tenantry.

I found, moreover, that there was not only a struggle between individual planters for Negro tenants, but between states and sections. Many of the old farms in South Carolina and Alabama have been used so long that they require a steady and heavy annual treatment of fertiliser, with the result that cotton growing costs more than it does in the rich alluvial lands of Mississippi, or the newer regions of Arkansas and Texas. The result is that the planters of the West, being able to pay more wages and give the tenants better terms, lure away the Negroes of the East. Georgia and other states have met this competitive disadvantage in the usual way in which such disadvantages, when first felt but not fully understood, are met, by counteracting legislation. Georgia has made the most stringent laws to keep her Negroes on the land. The Georgian code (Section 601) says:

Any person who shall solicit or procure emigrants, or shall attempt to do so, without first procuring a licence as required by law, shall be guilty of a misdemeanour.

Ex-Congressman William H. Fleming, one of the ablest statesmen of Georgia, said:

"Land and other forms of capital cannot spare the Negro and will not give him up until a substitute is found. His labour is worth millions upon millions. In Georgia we now make it a crime for anyone to solicit emigrants without taking out a licence, and then we make the licence as nearly prohibitive as possible. One of the most dangerous occupations for any one to follow in this state would be that of an emigrant agent — as some have found by experience."

In this connection I have an account published in April, 1907, in an Augusta newspaper of just such a case:

The heaviest fine given in the city court of Richmond County within the last two years was imposed upon E. F. Arnett yesterday morning. He was sentenced to pay a fine of one thousand dollars or serve six months in the county jail.

Arnett was convicted of violating the state emigration laws regarding the carrying of labour out of the state. He was alleged to have employed thirteen Negroes to work on the Georgia and Atlantic Railroad, which operates in this state and Alabama. The jury on the case returned a verdict of guilty when court convened yesterday, although it had been reported that a mistrial was probable.

"Peg Leg" Williams

A famous railroad emigration agent called "Peg Leg" Williams, who promoted Negro emigration from Georgia to Mississippi and Texas a few years ago, was repeatedly prosecuted and finally driven out of business. In a letter which he wrote some time ago to the Atlanta *Constitution* he said:

I know of several counties not a hundred miles from Atlanta where it's more than a man's life is worth to go in to get Negroes to move to some other state. There are farmers that would not hesitate to shoot their brother were he to come from Mississippi to get "his niggers," as he calls them, even though he had no contract with them. I know personally numbers of Negro men who have moved West and after accumulating a little, return to get a brother, sister, or an old father or mother, and they were compelled to return without them, their lives being imperilled; they had to leave and leave quick.

In view of such a feeling it may be imagined how futile is the talk of the deportation of the Negro race. What the Southern planter wants to-day is not fewer Negroes but more Negroes — Negroes who will "keep their place."

Laws to Make the Negro Work

Many other laws have been passed in the Southern states which are designed to keep the Negro on the land, and having

him there, to make him work.   The contract law, the abuses of
which lead to peonage and debt slavery, is an excellent example
— which I shall discuss more fully in the next chapter.   The
criminal laws, the chain-gang system, and the hiring of Negro
convicts to private individuals are all, in one way or another,
devices to keep the Negro at work on farms, in brick-yards
and in mines.   The vagrancy laws, not unlike those of the
North and excellent in their purpose, are here sometimes
executed with great severity.   In Alabama the last legislature
passed a law under which a Negro arrested for vagrancy must
prove that he is not a vagrant.   In short, the old rule of law
that a man is innocent until proved guilty is here reversed for
the Negro so that the burden of proving that he is not guilty
of vagrancy rests upon him, not upon the state.   The last
Alabama legislature also passed a stringent game law, one
argument in its favour being that by preventing the Negro
from pot-hunting it would force him to work more steadily
in the cotton fields.

Race Hatred Versus Economic Necessity

One of the most significant things I saw in the South — and
I saw it everywhere — was the way in which the white people
were torn between their feeling of race prejudice and their
downright economic needs.   Hating and fearing the Negro
as a race (though often loving individual Negroes), they yet
want him to work for them; they can't get along without him.
In one impulse a community will rise to mob Negroes or to
drive them out of the country because of Negro crime or Negro
vagrancy, or because the Negro is becoming educated, acquiring
property and "getting out of his place"; and in the next impulse
laws are passed or other remarkable measures taken to keep
him at work — because the South can't get along without
him.   From the Atlanta *Georgian* I cut recently a letter which
well illustrates the way in which racial hatred clashes with
economic necessity.

TROUBLES OF COUNTRY FOLK

But are n't there two sides to every question ?   Here we are out here in the
country, right in the midst of hundreds of Negroes, and do you know, sir, that
all this talk about lynching and ku-kluxing is frightening the farm hands to such

an extent we begin to fear that soon the farmers will sustain a great loss of labour, by their running away? Already it is beginning to have its effect. After night the Negroes are afraid to leave their farm to go anywhere on errands of business. Why, sir, two miles from this town, the Negroes are afraid to come here to trade at night. The country merchants are feeling the force of it very sorely, and if this foolishness is n't stopped their losses in fall trade will be very heavy.

Even some of the ladies of our community are complaining of this rashness. That it is demoralising the labour in the home department. So in conclusion, in behalf of my community and other country communities, I feel it my duty to raise a warning voice against all such new foolish ku-kluxism.

Mableton, Ga.　　　　　　　　　　　　　　　　T. J. Lowe.

While I was in Georgia a case came up which threw a flood of light upon the inner complexities of this problem. In the county of Habersham in North Georgia the population is largely of the type known as "poor white" — the famous mountain folk who were never slave-owners and many of whom fought in the Union army during the Civil War. Habersham is one of the "white counties" which is growing whiter. It has about 2,000 Negroes and 12,000 whites — many of the latter having come in from the North to grow peaches and raise sheep. One of the Negroes of Habersham County was Frank Grant, described by a white neighbour as "a Negro of good character, a property owner, setting an example of thrift and honesty that ought to have made his example a benefit to any community."

Grant had saved money from his labour and bought a home. He was such a good worker that people were willing sometimes to pay him twice the wages of the average labourer, white or black. On the night of December 16, 1906, the Negro's house was fired into by a party of white men who then went to the house of his tenant, Henry Scism, also a Negro, and shot promiscuously around Scism's house, and warned him to leave the country in one week, threatening him with severe penalties if he did not go. As a result Grant had to sell out his little home, won after such hard work, and he and his tenant Scism with their families both fled the county.

"In Grant," said his white neighbour, "the county lost a capable labourer — in its present situation, a most valuable asset — and a good citizen."

Here, then, we have race hatred versus economic necessity. The important citizens and employers of Habersham County came to Atlanta and presented a petition to Governor Terrell, January 18, 1907, as follows:

To His Excellency, J. M. Terrell,
  Governor of Georgia, Atlanta:
  Whereas, on the night of December 16, 1906, parties unknown came to the quiet home of one Frank Grant, coloured, a citizen of this county, and shot into his residence, and then went to the home of Henry Scism, coloured, a tenant of said Frank Grant, and shot promiscuously around his (the said Scism's) house, and demanded of him to leave the county under severe penalty.
  This has caused the tenant, Henry Scism, to leave, and Frank Grant to sell his little house at a sacrifice and leave. It comes to us that Frank Grant is a quiet, innocent, hard-working citizen. Therefore, we, the undersigned officers and citizens of Habersham County, Georgia, pray you to offer a liberal reward for the arrest and conviction of these unknown parties — say $100 for the first and $50 for each succeeding one.
  (Signed)   C. W. Grant,
          County School Commissioner.
                J. A. Erwin, Clerk, S. C.,
                M. Franklin, Ordinary
                J. D. Hill, T. C. H. C.

But, of course, nothing could be done that would keep the Negroes on the land under such conditions.

Why Negroes Are Driven Out

What does it all mean? Listen to the explanation given by a prominent white man of Habersham County — not to me — but to the Atlanta *Georgian*, where it was published:

" It is not a problem of Negro labour, because there is little of that kind there. The white labour will not work for the fruit growers at prices they can afford, even when it is a good fruit year. Often they decline to work at any price. They have many admirable qualities; among them is a spirit of pride and independence, which, rightly directed, would uplift and make them prosperous, but which misguided and blind, as it sometimes is, keeps them in poverty and puts the region in which they live at great disadvantage.

" Landowners and employers, native, and new, are indignant but helpless. They are in the power of the shiftless element of the whites, who say, 'I will work or not, as I please, and when I please, and at my own price; and I will not have Negroes taking my work away from me.' This is not a race question, pure and simple; it is an industrial question, a labour issue, not confined to one part of the country."

Here, it will be observed, the same complaint is made against the "poor white" as against the Negro — that he is shiftless and that he won't work even for high wages.

Generally speaking, the race hatred in the South comes chiefly from the poorer class of whites who either own land which they work themselves or are tenant farmers in competition with Negroes and from politicians who seek to win the votes of this class of white men. The larger landowners and employers of labour, while they do not love the Negro, want him to work and work steadily, and will do almost anything to keep him on the land — so long as he is a faithful, obedient, unambitious worker. When he becomes prosperous, or educated, or owns land, many white people no longer "have any use for him" and turn upon him with hostility, but the best type of the Southern white men is not only glad to see the Negro become a prosperous and independent farmer but will do much to help him.

Vivid Illustration of Race Feeling

I have had innumerable illustrations of the extremes to which race feeling reaches among a certain class of Southerners. In a letter to the Atlanta *Constitution*, November 5, 1906, a writer who signs himself Mark Johnson, says:

The only use we have for the Negro is as a labourer. It is only as such that we need him; it is only as such that we can use him. If the North wants to take him and educate him we will bid him godspeed and contribute to his education if schools are located on the other side of the line.

And here are extracts from a remarkable letter from a Southern white working man signing himself Forrest Pope and published in the Atlanta *Georgian*, October 22, 1906:

When the skilled negro appears and begins to elbow the white man in the struggle for existence, don't you know the white man rebels and won't have it so? If you don't it won't take you long to find it out; just go out and ask a few of them, those who tell you the whole truth, and see what you will find out about it.

What Is the Negro's Place?

All the genuine Southern people like the Negro as a servant, and so long as he remains the hewer of wood and carrier of water, and remains strictly in what we choose to call his place, everything is all right, but when ambition, prompted by real education, causes the Negro to grow restless and he bestir himself to get out of that servile condition, then there is, or at least there will be, trouble, sure enough trouble, that all the great editors, parsons and philosophers can no more check than they can now state the whole truth and nothing but the truth, about this all-absorbing, far-reaching miserable race question. There are those among Southern editors and other public men who have been shouting into the ears of the North for twenty-five years that education would solve the Negro question; there is not an honest, fearless, thinking man in the South but who knows that to be a bare-faced lie. Take a young Negro of little more than ordinary intelligence, even, get hold of him in time, train him thoroughly as to books, and finish him up with a good industrial education, send him out into the South with ever so good intentions both on the part of his benefactor and himself, send him to take my work away from me and I will kill him.

The writer says in another part of this remarkable letter, giving as it does a glimpse of the bare bones of the economic struggle for existence:

I am, I believe, a typical Southern white workingman of the skilled variety, and I'll tell the whole world, including Drs. Abbott and Eliot, that I don't want any educated property-owning Negro around me. The Negro would be desirable to me for what I could get out of him in the way of labour that I don't want to have to perform myself, and I have no other uses for him.

Who Will Do the Dirty Work?

One illustration more and I am through. I met at Montgomery, Alabama, a lawyer named Gustav Frederick Mertins. We were discussing the "problem," and Mr. Mertins finally made a striking remark, not at all expressing the view that I heard from some of the strongest citizens of Montgomery, but excellently voicing the position of many Southerners.

"It's a question," he said, "who will do the dirty work. In this country the white man won't: the Negro must. There's got to be a mudsill somewhere. If you educate the Negroes they won't stay where they belong; and you must consider them as a race, because if you let a few rise it makes the others discontented."

Mr. Mertins presented me with a copy of his novel called "The Storm Signal," in which he further develops the idea (p. 342):

The Negro is the mudsill of the social and industrial South to-day. Upon his labour in the field, in the forest, and in the mine, the whole structure rests. Slip the mudsill out and the system must be reorganised . . . . Educate him and he quits the field. Instruct him in the trades and sciences and he enters into active competition with the white man in what are called the higher planes of life. That competition brings on friction, and that friction in the end means the Negroe's undoing.

Is not this mudsill stirring to-day, and is not that the deep reason for many of the troubles in the South — and in the North as well, where the Negro has appeared in large numbers? The friction of competition has arrived, and despite the demand for justice by many of the best class of the Southern whites, the struggle is certainly of growing intensity.

And out of this economic struggle of whites and blacks grows an ethical struggle far more significant. It is the struggle of the white man with himself. How shall he, who is supreme in the South as in the North, treat the Negro? That is the *real* struggle!

CHAPTER V

RACE RELATIONSHIPS IN THE SOUTH

I

GENERALLY speaking, the sharpest race prejudice in the South is exhibited by the poorer class of white people, whether farmers, artisans, or unskilled workers, who come into active competition with the Negroes, or from politicians who are seeking the votes of this class of people. It is this element which has driven the Negroes out of more than one community in the South and it commonly forms the lynching mobs. A similar antagonism of the working classes exists in the North wherever the Negro has appeared in large numbers — as I shall show when I come to write of the treatment of the Northern Negro.

On the other hand, the larger landowners and employers of the South, and all professional and business men who hire servants, while they dislike and fear the Negro as a race (though often loving and protecting individual Negroes), want the black man to work for them. More than that, they *must have him:* for he has a practical monopoly on labour in the South. White men of the employing class will do almost anything to keep the Negro on the land and his wife in the kitchen — so long as they are obedient and unambitious workers.

"Good" and "Bad" Landlords

But I had not been very long in the black belt before I began to see that the large planters — the big employers of labour — often pursued very different methods in dealing with the Negro. In the feudal middle ages there were good and bad barons; so in the South to-day there are "good" and "bad" landlords (for lack of a better designation) and every gradation between them.

The good landlord, generally speaking, is the one who knows by inheritance how a feudal system should be operated. In other words, he is the old slave-owner or his descendant, who not only feels the ancient responsibility of slavery times, but believes that the good treatment of tenants, as a policy, will produce better results than harshness and force.

The bad landlord represents the degeneration of the feudal system: he is in farming to make all he can out of it this year and next, without reference to human life.

I have already told something of J. Pope Brown's plantation near Hawkinsville. On the November day, when we drove out through it, I was impressed with the fact that nearly all the houses used by the Negro tenants were new, and much superior to the old log cabins built either before or after the war, some of which I saw still standing, vacant and dilapidated, in various parts of the plantation. I asked the reason why he had built new houses:

"Well," he answered, "I find I can keep a better class of tenants, if the accommodations are good."

Liquor and "the Resulting Trouble"

Mr. Brown has other methods for keeping the tenantry on his plantation satisfied. Every year he gives a barbecue and "frolic" for his Negroes, with music and speaking and plenty to eat. A big watermelon patch is also a feature of the plantation, and during all the year the tenants are looked after, not only to see that the work is properly done, but in more intimate and sympathetic ways. On one trip through the plantation we stopped in front of a Negro cabin. Inside lay a Negro boy close to death from a bullet wound in the head. He had been at a Negro party a few nights before where there was liquor. Someone had overturned the lamp: shooting began, and the young fellow was taken out for dead. Such accidents or crimes are all too familiar in the plantation country. Although Pulaski County, Georgia, prohibits the sale or purchase of liquor (most of the South, indeed, is prohibition in its sentiment), the Negroes are able from time to time to get jugs of liquor — and, as one Southerner put it to me, "enjoy the resulting trouble."

The boy's father came out of the field and told us with real eloquence of sorrow of the patient's condition.

"Las' night," he said, "we done thought he was a-crossin' de ribbah."

Mr. Brown had already sent the doctor out from the city; he now made arrangements to transport the boy to a hospital in Macon where he could be properly treated.

Use of Cocaine Among Negroes

As I have said before, the white landlord who really tries to treat his Negroes well, often has a hard time of it. Many of those (not all) he deals with are densely ignorant, irresponsible, indolent — and often rendered more careless from knowing that the white man must have labour. Many of them will not keep up the fences, or take care of their tools, or pick the cotton even after it is ready, without steady attention. A prominent Mississippi planter gave me an illustration of one of the troubles he just then had to meet. An eighteen-year-old Negro left his plantation to work in a railroad camp. There he learned to use cocaine, and when he came back to the plantation he taught the habit to a dozen of the best Negroes there, to their complete ruin. The planter had the entire crowd arrested, searched for cocaine and kept in jail until the habit was broken. Then he prosecuted the white druggist who sold the cocaine.

Some Southern planters, to prevent the Negroes from leaving, have built churches for them, and in one instance I heard of a school-house as well.

Another point of the utmost importance — for it strikes at the selfish interest of the landlord — lies in the treatment of the Negro, who, by industry or ability, can "get ahead." A good landlord not only places no obstacles in the way of such tenants, but takes a real pride in their successes. Mr. Brown said:

"If a tenant sees that other Negroes on the same plantation have been able to save money and get land of their own, it tends to make them more industrious. It pays the planter to treat his tenants well."

Negro with $1,000 in the Bank

The result is that a number of Mr. Brown's tenants have bought and own good farms near the greater plantation. The plantation, indeed, becomes a sort of central sun around which revolves like planets the lesser life of the Negro landowner.

Mr. Brown told me with no little pride of the successes of several Negroes. We met one farmer driving to town in a top buggy with a Negro school-teacher. His name was Robert Polhill — a good type of the self-respecting, vigorous, industrious Negro. Afterward we visited his farm. He had an excellent house with four rooms. In front there were vines and decorative "chicken-corn"; a fence surrounded the place and it was really in good repair. Inside the house everything was scrupulously neat, from the clean rag rugs to the huge post beds with their gay coverlets. The wife evidently had some Indian blood in her veins; she could read and write, but Polhill himself was a full black Negro, intelligent, but illiterate. The children, and there were a lot of them, are growing up practically without opportunity for education because the school held in the Negro church is not only very poor, but it is in session only a short time every year. Near the house was a one-horse syrup-mill then in operation, grinding cane brought in by neighbouring farmers — white as well as black — the whites thus patronising the enterprise of their energetic Negro neighbour.

"I first noticed Polhill when he began work on the plantation," said Mr. Brown, "because he was the only Negro on the place whom I could depend upon to stop hog-cracks in the fences."

His history is the common history of the Negro farmer who "gets ahead." Starting as a wages' hand, he worked hard and steadily, saving enough finally to buy a mule — the Negro's first purchase; then he rented land, and by hard work and close calculating made money steadily. With his first $75 he started out to see the world, travelling by railroad to Florida, and finally back home again. The "moving about" instinct is strong in all Negroes — sometimes to their destruction. Then he bought 100 acres of land on credit and having good crops, paid for it in six or seven years. Now he has a comfortable home, he is out of debt, and has money in the bank, a painted house, a top buggy and a cabinet organ! These are the values of his property:

His farm is worth	$2,000
Two mules	300
Horse	150
Other equipment	550
Money in the bank	1,000
	$4,000

Negro Who Owns 1,000 Acres of Land

All of this shows what a Negro who is industrious, and who comes up on a plantation where the landlord is not oppressive, can do. And despite the fact that much is heard on the one hand of the lazy and worthless Negro, and on the other of the landlord who holds his Negroes in practical slavery — it is significant that many Negroes are able to get ahead. In Pulaski County there are Negroes who own as high as 1,000 acres of land. Ben Gordon is one of them, his brother Charles has 500 acres, John Nelson has 400 acres worth $20 an acre, the Miller family has 1,000 acres, January Lawson, another of Mr. Brown's former tenants, has 500 acres; Jack Daniel 200 acres, Tom Whelan 600 acres. A mulatto merchant in Hawkinsville, whose creditable store I visited, also owns his plantation in the country and rents it to Negro tenants on the same system employed by the white landowners. Indeed, a few Negroes in the South are coming to be not inconsiderable landlords, and have many tenants.

Hawkinsville also has a Negro blacksmith, Negro barbers and Negro builders — and like the white man, the Negro also develops his own financial sharks. One educated coloured man in Hawkinsville is a "note shaver"; he "stands for" other Negroes and signs their notes — at a frightful commission.

Statistics will give some idea of how the industrious Negro in a black belt county like Pulaski has been succeeding.

	Acres of Land Owned	Total Assessed Value of Property
1875	4,490	$43,230
1880	5,988	60,760
1885	6,901	59,022
1890	12,294	122,926
1895	14,145	144,158
1900	13,205	138,800

It is surprising to an unfamiliar visitor to find out that the Negroes in the South have acquired so much land. In Georgia alone in 1906 coloured people owned 1,400,000 acres and were assessed for over $28,000,000 worth of property, practically all of which, of course, has been acquired in the forty years since slavery.

Negro farmers in some instances have made a genuine reputation for ability. John Roberts, a Richmond County Negro, won first prize over many white exhibitors in the fall of 1906 at the Georgia-Carolina fair at Augusta for the best bale of cotton raised.

Little Coloured Boy's Famous Speech

I was at Macon while the first State fair ever held by Negroes in Georgia was in progress. In spite of the fact that racial relationships, owing to the recent riot at Atlanta, were acute, the fair was largely attended, and not only by Negroes, but by many white visitors. The brunt of the work of organisation fell upon R. R. Wright, president of the Georgia State Industrial College (coloured) of Savannah. President Wright is of full-blooded African descent, his grandmother, who reared him, being an African Negro of the Mandingo tribe. Just at the close of the war he was a boy in a freedman's school at Atlanta. One Sunday General O. O. Howard came to address the pupils. When he had finished, he expressed a desire to take a message back to the people of the North.

"What shall I tell them for you?" he asked.

A little black boy in front stood up quickly, and said:

"Tell 'em, massa, we is rising."

Upon this incident John Greenleaf Whittier wrote a famous poem: and at the Negro fair, crowning the charts which had been prepared to show the progress of the Negroes of Georgia, I saw this motto:

> "WE ARE RISING"

The little black boy grew up, was graduated at Atlanta University, studied at Harvard, travelled in Europe, served in the Spanish-American War, and is now seeking to help his race to get an industrial training in the college which he organised in 1891. The attendance at the fair in Macon was between 25,000 and 30,000, the Negroes raised $11,000 and spent $7,000, and planned for a greater fair the next year. In this enterprise they had the sympathy and approval of the best white people. A vivid glimpse of what

CANE SYRUP KETTLE. EXPERT NEGRO STIRRING AND SKIMMING

CHAIN–GANG WORKERS ON THE ROADS

A TYPE OF THE COUNTRY CHAIN-GANG NEGRO

the fair meant is given by the *Daily News* of Macon — a white newspaper:

> The fair shows what progress can be accomplished by the industrious and thrifty Negro, who casts aside the belief that he is a dependent, and sails right in to make a living and a home for himself. Some of the agricultural exhibits of black farmers have never been surpassed in Macon. On the whole, the exposition just simply astounded folks who did not know what the Negro is doing for himself.
>
> Another significant feature about the fair was the excellent behaviour of the great throngs of coloured people who poured into the city during its progress. There was not an arrest on the fair grounds and very few in the city.

The better class of Negro farmers, indeed, have shown not only a capacity for getting ahead individually, but for organising for self-advancement, and even for working with corresponding associations of white farmers. The great cotton and tobacco associations of the South, which aim to direct the marketing of the product of the farms, have found it not only wise, but necessary to enlist the coöperation of Negro farmers. At the annual rally of the dark-tobacco growers at Guthrie, Kentucky, last September, many Negro planters were in the line of parade with the whites. The farmers' conferences held at Hampton, Tuskegee, Calhoun, and at similar schools, illustrate in other ways the possibilities of advancement which grow out of landownership by the Negroes.

The Penalties of Being Free

So much for the sunny side of the picture: the broad-gauge landlord and the prosperous tenantry. Conditions in the black belt are in one respect much as they were in slavery times, or as they would be under any feudal system: if the master or lord is "good," the Negro prospers; if he is harsh, grasping, unkind, the Negro suffers bitterly. It gets back finally to the white man. In assuming supreme rights in the South — political, social, and industrial, the white man also assumes heavy duties and responsibilities; he cannot have the one without the other: and he takes to himself the pain and suffering which goes with power and responsibility.

Of course, scarcity of labour and high wages have given the really ambitious and industrious Negro his opportunity, and many thousands of them are becoming more and more independent of the favour or the ill-will of the whites. And therein lies a profound danger, not only to the Negro, but to the South. Gradually losing the support and advice of the best type of white man, the independent Negro finds himself in competition with the poorer type of white man, whose jealousy he must meet. He takes the penalties of being really free. Escaping the exactions of a feudal life, he finds he must meet the sharper difficulties of a free industrial system. And being without the political rights of his poor white competitor and wholly without social recognition, discredited by the bestial crimes of the lower class of his own race, he has, indeed, a hard struggle before him. In many neighbourhoods he is peculiarly at the mercy of this lower class white electorate, and the self-seeking politicians whose stock in trade consists in playing upon the passions of race-hatred.

II

I come now to the reverse of the picture. When the Negro tenant takes up land or hires out to the landlord, he ordinarily signs a contract, or if he cannot sign (about half the Negro tenants of the black belt are wholly illiterate) he makes his mark. He often has no way of knowing certainly what is in the contract, though the arrangement is usually clearly understood, and he must depend on the landlord to keep both the rent and the supply-store accounts. In other words, he is wholly at the planter's mercy — a temptation as dangerous for the landlord as the possibilities which it presents are for the tenant. It is so easy to make large profits by charging immense interest percentages or outrageous prices for supplies to tenants who are too ignorant or too weak to protect themselves, that the stories of the oppressive landlord in the South are scarcely surprising. It is easy, when the tenant brings in his cotton in the fall not only to underweigh it, but to credit it at the lowest prices of the week; and this dealing of the strong with the weak is not Southern, it is human. Such a system has encouraged dishonesty, and wastefulness; it has made many landlords cruel and greedy, it has increased the helplessness, hopelessness and shiftlessness of the Negro. In many cases it has meant downright degeneration, not only to the Negro, but to the white man. These are strong words, but no one can travel in the black belt without seeing enough to convince him of the terrible consequences growing out of these relationships.

The Story of a Negro Tenant

A case which came to my attention at Montgomery, Alabama, throws a vivid light on one method of dealing with the Negro tenant. Some nine miles from Montgomery lives a planter named T. L. McCullough. In December, 1903, he made a contract with a Negro named Jim Thomas to work for him. According to this contract, a copy of which I have, the land-lord agreed to furnish Jim the Negro with a ration of 14 lbs. of meat and one bushel of meal a month, and to pay him besides $96 for an entire year's labour.

On his part Jim agreed to "do good and faithful labour for the said T. L. McCullough." "Good and faithful labour" means from sunrise to sunset every day but Sunday, and excepting Saturday afternoon.

A payment of five dollars was made to bind the bargain — just before Christmas. Jim probably spent it the next day. It is customary to furnish a cabin for the worker to live in; no such place was furnished, and Jim had to walk three or four miles morning and evening to a house on another planta-tion. He worked faithfully until May 15th. Then he ran away, but when he heard that the landlord was after him, threatening punishment, he came back and agreed to work twenty days for the ten he had been away. Jim stayed some time, but he was not only given no cabin and paid no money, but his food ration was cut off! So he ran away again, claiming that he could not work unless he had a place to live. The landlord went after him and had him arrested, and although the Negro had worked nearly half a year, McCullough prosecuted him for fraud because he had got $5 in cash at the signing of the con-tract. In such a case the Alabama law gives the landlord every advantage; it says that when a person receives money under a contract and stops work, the presumption is that he intended to defraud the landowner and that therefore he is criminally punishable. The practical effect of the law is to permit imprisonment for debt, for it places a burden of proof on the Negro that he can hardly overturn. The law is defended on the ground that Negroes will get money any way they can, sign any sort of paper for it, and then run off — if there is not a stringent law to punish them.   But it may be imagined how this law could be used, and is used, in the hands of unscrupulous men to keep the Negro in a sort of debt-slavery.   When the case came up before Judge William H. Thomas of Montgomery, the constitutionality of the law was brought into question, and the Negro was finally discharged.

Often an unscrupulous landlord will deliberately give a Negro a little money before Christmas, knowing that he will promptly waste it in a "celebration," thus getting him into debt so that he dare not leave the plantation for fear of arrest and criminal prosecution.   If he attempts to leave he is arrested and taken before a friendly justice of the peace, and fined or threatened with imprisonment.   If he is not in debt, it sometimes happens that the landlord will have him arrested on the charge of stealing a bridle or a few potatoes (for it is easy to find something against almost any Negro), and he is brought into court.   In several cases I know of the escaping Negro has even been chased down with bloodhounds.   On appearing in court the Negro is naturally badly frightened. The white man is there and offers as a special favour to take him back and let him work out the fine — which sometimes requires six months, often a whole year.   In this way Negroes are kept in debt — so-called debt-slavery or peonage — year after year, they and their whole family.   One of the things that I could n't at first understand in some of the courts I visited was the presence of so many white men to stand sponsor for Negroes who had committed various offences.   Often this grows out of the feudal protective instinct which the landlord feels for the tenant or servant of whom he is fond; but often it is merely the desire of the white man to get another Negro worker.   In one case in particular, I saw a Negro brought into court charged with stealing cotton.

"Does anybody know this Negro?" asked the judge.

Two white men stepped up and both said they did.

The judge fined the Negro $20 and costs, and there was a real contest between the two white men as to who should pay it — and get the Negro.   They argued for some minutes, but finally the judge said to the prisoner:

"Who do you want to work for, George?"

The Negro chose his employer, and agreed to work four months to pay off his $20 fine and costs.

Sometimes a man who has a debt against a Negro will sell the claim — which is practically selling the Negro — to some farmer who wants more labour.

A case of this sort came up in the winter of 1907 in Rankin County, Mississippi — the facts of which are all in testimony. A Negro named Dan January was in debt to a white farmer named Levi Carter. Carter agreed to sell the Negro and his entire family to another white farmer named Patrick. January refused to be sold. According to the testimony Carter and some of his companions seized January, bound him hand and foot and beat him most brutally, taking turns in doing the whipping until they were exhausted and the victim unconscious.

January's children removed him to his home, but the white men returned the next day, produced a rope and threatened to hang him unless he consented to go to the purchaser of the debt. The case came into court but the white men were never punished. January was in Jackson, Miss., when I was there; he still showed the awful effects of his beating.

Keeping Negroes Poor

This system has many bad results. It encourages the Negro in crime. He knows that unless he does something pretty bad, he will not be prosecuted because the landlord does n't want to lose the work of a single hand; he knows that if he *is* prosecuted, the white man will, if possible, "pay him out." It disorganises justice and confuses the ignorant Negro mind as to what is a crime and what is not. A Negro will often do things that he would not do if he thought he were really to be punished. He comes to the belief that if the white man wants him arrested, he will be arrested, and if he protects him, he won't suffer, no matter what he does. Thousands of Negroes, ignorant, weak, indolent, to-day work under this system. There are even landlords and employers who will trade upon the Negro's worst instincts — his love for liquor, for example — in order to keep him at work. An instance of this sort came to my attention at Hawkinsville while I was there. The white people of the town were making a strong fight for prohibition; the women held meetings, and on the day of the election marched in the streets singing and speaking. But the largest employer of Negro labor in the county had registered several hundred of his Negroes and declared his intention of voting them against prohibition. He said bluntly: "If my niggers can't get whisky they wont stay with me; you've got to keep a nigger poor or he won't work."

This employer actually voted sixty of his Negroes against prohibition, but the excitement was so great that he dared vote no more — and prohibition carried.

A step further brings the Negro to the chain-gang. If there is no white man to pay him out, or if his crime is too serious to be paid out, he goes to the chain-gang — and in several states he is then hired out to private contractors. The private employer thus gets him sooner or later. Some of the largest farms in the South are operated by chain-gang labour. The demand for more convicts by white employers is exceedingly strong. In the Montgomery *Advertiser* for April 10, 1907, I find an account of the sentencing of fifty-four prisoners in the city court, fifty-two of whom were Negroes. The *Advertiser* says:

The demand for their labour is probably greater now than it ever has been before. Numerous labour agents of companies employing convict labour reached Montgomery yesterday, and were busily engaged in manœuvring to secure part or even all of the convicts for their respective companies. The competition for labour of all kinds, it seems, is keener than ever before known.

The natural tendency of this demand, and from the further fact that the convict system makes yearly a huge profit for the State, is to convict as many Negroes as possible, and to punish the offences charged as severely as possible. From the Atlanta *Constitution* of October 13, 1906, I have this clipping:

SIX MONTHS FOR POTATO THEFT

COLUMBUS, GA., October 12 (Special)
In the city court yesterday Charley Carter, a Negro, was sentenced to six months on the chain-gang or to pay a fine of $25 for stealing a potato valued at 5 cents.

Serious crimes are sometimes compromised. In a newspaper dispatch, October 6, 1906, from Eaton Ga.,[1] I find a

1. Probably Eatonton, Georgia.

report of the trial of six Negroes charged with assault with the intent to kill. All were found guilty, but upon a recommendation of mercy they were sentenced as having committed misdemeanours rather than felonies. They could therefore have their fines paid, and five were immediately released by farmers who wanted their labour. The report says that of thirty-one misdemeanours during the month it is expected that "none will reach the chain-gang," since there are "three farmers to every convict ready to pay the fine."

Still other methods are pursued by certain landlords to keep their tenants on the land. In one extreme case a Negro tenant, after years of work, decided to leave the planter. He had had a place offered him where he could make more money. There was nothing against him; he simply wanted to move. But the landlord informed him that no waggon would be permitted to cross his (the planter's) land to get his household belongings. The Negro, being ignorant, supposed he could thus be prevented from moving, and although the friend who was trying to help him assured him that the landlord could not prevent his moving, he dared not go. In another instance — also extreme — a planter refused to let his tenants raise hogs, because he wanted them to buy salt pork at his store. It is, indeed, through the plantation store (which corresponds to the company or "truck" store of Northern mining regions) that the unscrupulous planter reaps his most exorbitant profits. Negroes on some plantations, whether they work hard or not, come out at the end of the year with nothing. Part of this is due, of course, to their own improvidence; but part, in too many cases, is due to exploitation by the landlord.

142076

One Biscuit to Eat and no Place to Sleep

Booker T. Washington, in a letter to the Montgomery *Advertiser* on the Negro labour problem, tells this story:

I recall that some years ago a certain white farmer asked me to secure for him a young coloured man to work about the house and to work in the field. The young man was secured, a bargain was entered into to the effect that he was to be paid a certain sum monthly and his board and lodging furnished as well. At the end of the coloured boy's first day on the farm he returned. I asked the reason, and he said that after working all the afternoon he was handed a buttered biscuit for his supper, and no place was provided for him to sleep.

At night he was told he could find a place to sleep in the fodder loft. This white farmer, whom I know well, is not a cruel man and seeks generally to do the right thing; but in this case he simply overlooked the fact that it would have paid him in dollars and cents to give some thought and attention to the comfort of his helper.

This case is more or less typical. Had this boy been well cared for, he would have advertised the place that others would have sought work there.

Such methods mean, of course, the lowest possible efficiency of labour—ignorant, hopeless, shiftless. The harsh planter naturally opposes Negro education in the bitterest terms and prevents it wherever possible; for education means the doom of the system by which he thrives.

Negro with Nineteen Children

Life for the tenants is often not a pleasant thing to contemplate. I spent much time driving about on the great plantations and went into many of the cabins. Usually they were very poor, of logs or shacks, sometimes only one room, sometimes a room and a sort of lean-to. At one side there was a fireplace, often two beds opposite, with a few broken chairs or boxes, and a table. Sometimes the cabin was set up on posts and had a floor, sometimes it was on the ground and had no floor at all. The people are usually densely ignorant and superstitious; the preachers they follow are often the worst sort of characters, dishonest and immoral; the schools, if there are any, are practically worthless. The whole family works from sunrise to sunset in the fields. Even children of six and seven years old will drop seed or carry water. Dr. W. E. B. DuBois, himself a Negro, who has made many valuable and scholarly studies of Negro life, gives this vivid glimpse into a home where the Negro and his wife had nineteen children. He says:

This family of twenty-one is a poverty stricken, reckless, dirty set. The children are stupid and repulsive, and fight for their food at the table. They are poorly dressed, sickly and cross. The table dishes stand from one meal to another unwashed, and the house is in perpetual disorder. Now and then the father and mother engage in a hand-to-hand fight.

Never Heard the Name of Roosevelt

It would be impossible to over-emphasise the ignorance of many Negro farmers. It seems almost unbelievable, but after

some good-humoured talk with a group of old Negroes I tried
to find out how much they knew of the outside world. I
finally asked them if they knew Theodore Roosevelt. They
looked puzzled, and finally one old fellow scratched his head
and said:

"Whah you say dis yere man libes?"

"In Washington," I said; "you 've heard of the President
of the United States?"

"I reckon I dunno," he said.

And yet this old man gave me a first-class religious exhor-
tation; and one in the group had heard of Booker T.
Washington, whom he described as a "pow'ful big nigger."

Why Negroes Go to Cities

I made inquiries among the Negroes as to why they wanted
to leave the farms and go to cities. The answer I got from
all sorts of sources was first, the lack of schooling in the
country, and second, the lack of protection.

And I heard also many stories of ill-treatment of various
sorts, the distrust of the tenant of the landlord in keeping his
accounts — all of which, dimly recognised, tends to make
many Negroes escape the country, if they can. Indeed, it is
growing harder and harder on the great plantations, especially
where the management is by overseers, to keep a sufficient
labour supply. In some places the white landlords have begun
to break up their plantations, selling small farms to ambitious
Negroes — a significant sign, indeed, of the passing of the
feudal system. An instance of this is found near Thomaston,
Ga., where Dr. C. B. Thomas has long been selling land to
Negroes, and encouraging them to buy by offering easy terms.
Near Dayton, Messrs. Price and Allen have broken up their
"Lockhart Plantation" and are selling it out to Negroes. I
found similar instances in many places I visited. Com-
menting on this tendency, the Thomaston *Post* says:

This is, in part, a solution of the so-called Negro problem, for those of the
race who have property interests at stake cannot afford to antagonise their
white neighbours or transgress the laws. The ownership of land tends to
make them better citizens in every way, more thoughtful of the right of others,
and more ambitious for their own advancement.

At this place a number of neat and comfortable homes, a commodious high school, and a large lodge building, besides a number of churches, testify to the enterprise and thrift the best class of our coloured population. . . . The tendency towards cutting up the large plantations is beginning to show itself, and when all of them are so divided, there will be no agricultural labour problem, except, perhaps, in the gathering of an especially large crop.

III

I have endeavoured thus to give a picture of both sides of conditions in the black belt exactly as I saw them. I can now do no better in further illumination of the conditions I have described than by looking at them through the eyes and experiences of two exceptionally able white men of the South, both leaders in their respective walks of life, neither of them politicians and both, incidentally, planters.

At Jackson, Miss., I met Major R. W. Millsaps, a leading citizen of the state. He comes of a family with the best Southern traditions behind it; he was born in Mississippi, graduated before the war at Harvard College, and although his father, a slave owner, had opposed secession, the son fought four years in the Confederate army, rising to the rank of Major. He came out of the war, as he says, "with no earthly possessions but a jacket and a pair of pants, with a hole in them." But he was young and energetic; he began hauling cotton from Jackson to Natchez when cotton was worth almost its weight in gold. He received $10 a bale for doing it and made $4,000 in three months. He is now the president of one of the leading banks in Mississippi, interested in many important Southern enterprises, and the founder of Millsaps College at Jackson: a modest, useful, Christian gentleman.

An Experiment in Trusting Negroes

Near Greenville, Miss., Major Millsaps owns a plantation of 500 acres, occupied by 20 tenants, some 75 people in all. It is in one of the richest agricultural sections — the Mississippi bottoms — in the United States. Up to 1890 he had a white overseer and he was constantly in trouble of one kind or another with his tenants. When the price of cotton dropped, he decided to dispense with the overseer entirely and try a rather daring experiment. In short, he planned to trust the Negroes. He got them together and said:

"I am going to try you. I'm going to give you every possible opportunity; if you don't make out, I will go back to the overseer system."

In the sixteen years since then no white man has been on that plantation except as a visitor. The land was rented direct to the Negroes on terms that would give both landlord and tenant a reasonable profit.

"Did it work?" I asked.

"I have never lost one cent," said Major Millsaps, "no Negro has ever failed to pay up and you could n't drive them off the place. When other farmers complain of shortage of labour and tenants, I never have had any trouble."

Every Negro on the place owns his own mules and waggons and is out of debt. Nearly every family has bought or is buying a home in the little town of Leland, nearby, some of which are comfortably furnished. They are all prosperous and contented.

"How do you do it?" I asked.

"The secret," he said, "is to treat the Negro well and give him a chance. I have found that a Negro, like a white man, is most responsive to good treatment. Even a dog responds to kindness! The trouble is that most planters want to make too much money out of the Negro; they charge him too much rent; they make too large profits on the supplies they furnish. I know merchants who expect a return of 50 per cent. on supplies alone. The best Negroes I have known are those who are educated; Negroes need more education of the right kind — not less — and it will repay us well if we give it to them. It makes better, not worse, workers."

I asked him about the servant problem.

"We never have any trouble," he said. "I apply the same rule to servants as to the farmers. Treat them well, don't talk insultingly of their people before them, don't expect them to do too much work. I believe in treating a Negro with respect. That does n't mean to make equals of them. You people in the North don't make social equals of your white servants."

Jefferson Davis's Way with Negroes

Then he told a striking story of Jefferson Davis.

"I got a lesson in the treatment of Negroes when I was a

young man returning South from Harvard. I stopped in Washington and called on Jefferson Davis, then United States Senator from Mississippi. We walked down Pennsylvania Avenue. Many Negroes bowed to Mr. Davis and he returned the bow. He was a very polite man. I finally said to him that I thought he must have a good many friends among the Negroes. He replied:

"'I can't allow any Negro to outdo me in courtesy.'"

Plain Words from a White Man

A few days later on my way North I met at Clarksdale, Miss., Walter Clark, one of the well-known citizens of the state and President of the Mississippi Cotton Association. In the interests of his organisation he has been speaking in different parts of the state on court-days and at fairs. And the burden of his talks has been, not only organisation by the farmers, but a more intelligent and progressive treatment of Negro labour. Recognising the instability of the ordinary Negro, the crime he commits, the great difficulties which the best-intentioned Southern planters have to meet, Mr. Clark yet tells his Southern audiences some vigorous truths. He said in a recent speech:

"Every dollar I own those Negroes made for me. Our ancestors chased them down and brought them here. They are just what we make them. By our own greed and extravagance we have spoiled a good many of them. It has been popular here — now happily growing less so — to exploit the Negro by high store-prices and by encouraging him to get into debt. It has often made him hopeless. We have a low element of white people who are largely responsible for the Negro's condition. They sell him whiskey and cocaine; they corrupt Negro women. A white man who shoots craps with Negroes or who consorts with Negro women is worse than the meanest Negro that ever lived."

At Coffeeville, where Mr. Clark talked somewhat to this effect, an old man who sat in front suddenly jumped up and said: "That's the truth! Bully for you; bully for you!"

In his talk with me, Mr. Clark said other significant things:

"Our people have treated the Negroes as helpless children all their days. The Negro has not been encouraged to develop even the capacities he has. He must be made to use his own brains, not ours; put him on his responsibility and he will become more efficient. A Negro came to me not long ago complaining that the farmer for whom he worked would not give him an itemised account of his charges at the store. I met the planter and asked him about it. He said to me:

" 'The black nigger! What does he know about it? He can't read it.'

" 'But he is entitled to it, is n't he?' I asked him — and the Negro got it.

"The credit system has been the ruin of many Negroes. It keeps them in hopeless debt and it encourages the planter to exploit them. That 's the truth. My plan is to put the Negro on a strict cash basis; give him an idea of what money is by letting him use it. Three years ago I started it on my plantation. A Negro would come to me and say: 'Boss, I want a pair of shoes.' 'All right,' I 'd say. 'I 'll pay you spot cash every night and you can buy your own shoes.' In the same way I made up my mind that we must stop paying Negroes' fines when they got into trouble. I know planters who expect regularly every Monday to come into court and pay out about so many Negroes. It encourages the Negroes to do things they would not think of doing if they knew they would be regularly punished. I 've quit paying fines; my Negroes, if they get into trouble, have got to recognise their own responsibility for it and take what follows. That 's the only way to make men of them.

"What we need in the South is intelligent labour, more efficient labour. I believe in the education of the Negro. Industrial training is needed, not only for the Negro, but for the whites as well. The white people down here have simply got to take the Negro and make a man of him; in the long run it will make him more valuable to us."

PART TWO

THE NEGRO IN THE NORTH

CHAPTER VI

FOLLOWING THE COLOUR LINE IN THE NORTH

HAVING followed the colour line in the South, it is of extraordinary interest and significance to learn how the Negro fares in the North. Is he treated better or worse? Is Boston a more favourable location for him than Atlanta or New Orleans? A comparison of the "Southern attitude" and the "Northern attitude" throws a flood of light upon the Negro as a national problem in this country.

Most of the perplexing questions in the North pertain to the city, but in the South the great problems are still agricultural. In the South the masses of Negroes live on the land; they are a part of the cotton, sugar, lumber and turpentine industries; but in the North the Negro is essentially a problem of the great cities. He has taken his place in the babel of the tenements; already he occupies extensive neighbourhoods like the San Juan Hill district in New York and Bucktown in Indianapolis, and, by virtue of an increasing volume of immigration from the South, he is overflowing his boundaries in all directions, expanding more rapidly, perhaps, than any other single element of urban population. In every important Northern city, a distinct race-problem already exists, which must, in a few years, assume serious proportions.

Country districts and the smaller cities in the North for the most part have no Negro question. A few Negroes are found in almost all localities, but an examination of the statistics of rural counties and of the lesser cities shows that the Negro population is diminishing in some localities, increasing slightly in others. In distinctly agricultural districts in the North the census exhibits an actual falling off of Negro population of 10 per cent. between 1880 and 1900. Cass County in Michigan, which has a famous Negro agricultural colony — one of the few in the North — shows a distinct loss in population. From 1,837 inhabitants in 1880 it dropped to 1,568 in 1900.

A few Negro farmers have done well in the North (at Wilberforce, Ohio, I met two or three who had fine large farms and
were prosperous), but the rural population is so small as to be
negligible.

Negroes of Small Northern Towns

Most of the Negroes in the smaller towns and cities of the
North are of the stock which came by way of the underground
railroad just before the Civil War or during the period of
philanthropic enthusiasm which followed it. They have
come to fit naturally into the life of the communities where they
live, and no one thinks especially of their colour. There is,
indeed, no more a problem with the Negro than with the
Greek or Italian. In one community (Lansing, Mich.) with
which I have been long familiar, the Negroes are mostly
mulattoes and their numbers have remained practically
stationary for thirty years, while the white population has increased rapidly. At present there are only about 500 Negroes
in a city of 25,000 people.

As a whole the coloured people of Lansing are peaceful and
industrious, a natural part of the wage-working population.
Individuals have become highly prosperous and are much
respected. A few of the younger generation are idle and
worthless.

So far as comfortable conditions of life are concerned, where
there is little friction or discrimination and a good opportunity
for earning a respectable livelihood, I have found no places
anywhere which seemed so favourable to Negroes as these
smaller towns and cities in the North and West where the
coloured population is not increasing. But the moment there
is new immigration from the South the conditions cease to be
Utopian — as I shall show.

The great cities of the North present a wholly different
aspect; the increases of population there are not short of extraordinary. In 1880 Chicago had only 6,480 coloured people;
at present (1908) it has about 45,000, an increase of some
600 per cent. The census of 1900 gives the Negro population
of New York as 60,666. It is now (1908) probably not less
than 80,000. Between 1890 and 1900 the Negroes of Phila-

delphia increased by 59 per cent., while the Caucasians added only 22 per cent., and the growth since 1900 has been even more rapid, the coloured population now exceeding 80,000.

It is difficult to realise the significance of these masses of coloured population. The city of Washington to-day has a greater community of Negroes (some 100,000) than were ever before gathered together in one community in any part of the world, so far as we know. New York and Philadelphia both now probably have as many Negroes as any Southern city (except Washington, if that be called a Southern city). Nor must it be forgotten that about a ninth of the Negro population of the United States is in the North and West. Crowded communities of Negroes in Northern latitudes have never before existed anywhere. Northern city conditions therefore present unique and interesting problems.

I went first to Indianapolis because I had heard so much of the political power of the Negroes there; afterward I visited Cincinnati, Philadelphia, New York, Boston, Chicago and several smaller cities and country neighbourhoods. In every large city both white and coloured people told me that race feeling and discrimination were rapidly increasing: that new and more difficult problems were constantly arising.

Generally speaking, the more Negroes the sharper the expression of prejudice.

While the Negroes were an inconsequential part of the population, they passed unnoticed, but with increasing numbers (especially of the lower sort of Negroes and black Negroes), accompanied by competition for the work of the city and active political power, they are inevitably kindling the fires of race-feeling. Prejudice has been incited also by echoes of the constant agitation in the South, the hatred-breeding speeches of Tillman and Vardaman, the incendiary and cruel books and plays of Dixon,[1] and by the increased immigration of Southern white people with their strong Southern point of view.

Pathetic Expectations of the Negro

One finds something unspeakably pathetic in the spectacle of these untold thousands of Negroes who are coming North. To many of them, oppressed within the limitations set up by

1. The Rev. Thomas Dixon, Jr., of North Carolina, one-time Baptist minister and author of *The Leopard's Spots* (1902), *The Clansman* (1905), and *The*

the South, it is indeed the promised land. I shall never forget the wistful eagerness of a Negro I met in Mississippi. He told me he was planning to move to Indianapolis. I asked him why he wanted to leave the South.

"They 're Jim Crowin' us down here too much," he said; "there 's no chance for a coloured man who has any self-respect."

"But," I said, "do you know that you will be better off when you get to Indianapolis?"

"I hear they don't make no difference up there between white folks and coloured, and that a hard-working man can get two dollars a day. Is that all so?"

"Yes, that 's pretty nearly so," I said — but as I looked at the fairly comfortable home he lived in, among his own people, I felt somehow that he would not find the promised land all that he anticipated.

And after that I visited Indianapolis and other cities and saw hundreds of just such eager Negroes after they had reached the promised land. Two classes of coloured people come North: the worthless, ignorant, semi-criminal sort who find in the intermittent, high-paid day labour in the North, accompanied by the glittering excitements of city life, just the conditions they love best. Two or three years ago the Governor of Arkansas, Jeff Davis, pardoned a Negro criminal on condition that he would go to Boston and stay there! The other class is composed of self-respecting, hard-working people who are really seeking better conditions of life, a better chance for their children.

And what do Negroes find when they reach the promised land?

In the first place the poorer sort find in Indianapolis the alley home, in New York the deadly tenement. Landowners in Indianapolis have been building long rows of cheap one-story frame tenements in back streets and alleys. The apartments have two or three rooms each. When new they are brightly painted and papered and to many Negroes from the South, accustomed to the primitive cabin, they are beautiful indeed.

Even the older buildings are more pretentious if not really better than anything they have known in the rural South; and how the city life, nearly as free to the coloured man as to the white, stirs their pulses! No people, either black or white, are

---

Traitor (1907). In 1915 *The Clansman* was made into a motion picture, "The Birth of a Nation."

really free until they feel free. And to many Negroes the first few weeks in a Northern city give them the first glimpses they have ever had of what they consider to be liberty.

A striking illustration of this feeling came to my notice at Columbia, South Carolina. One of the most respected Negro men there — respected by both races — was a prosperous tailor who owned a building on the main street of the city. He was well to do, had a family, and his trade came from both races. I heard that he was planning to leave the South and I went to see him.

"Yes," he said, "I am going away. It's getting to be too dangerous for a coloured man down here."

It was just after the Atlanta riot.

"Where are you going?" I asked.

"I think I shall go to Washington," he said.

"Why Washington?"

"Well, you see, I want to be as near the flag as I can."

What the Negro Really Finds in the Promised Land

But they soon begin to learn things! It is true that the workingman can get high wages, and the domestic servant is paid an amount which astonishes her, but on the other hand — a fact that somehow never occurs to many of these people, or indeed to the foreigners who come flocking to our shores — the living cost is higher. For his gaudy tenements the landlord extorts exorbitant rentals. Ignorance is ever roundly and mercilessly taxed! I saw a double house built for white people just on the edge of a Negro neighbourhood and held at a rental of $18 a month, but not being able to secure white tenants the landlord rented to Negroes for $25 a month.

When he came North the Negro (even though he had lived in cities in the South, as many of the immigrants have) never dreamed that it would require such an amount of fuel to keep him through the long Northern winter, or that his bill for lights, water, and everything else would be so high. And in the South many Negro families of the poorer sort are greatly assisted by baskets of food brought from the white man's kitchen and the gift of cast-off clothes and shoes, to say nothing of tobacco, and even money — a lingering loose survival of the relationships of slavery.   But in the North the Negro finds himself in an intense industrial atmosphere where relationships are more strictly impersonal and businesslike.   What he gets he must pay for. Charity exists on a large scale, as I shall show later, but it is the sharp, inquiring, organised charity of the North.

In short, coming North to find a place where he will be treated more like a man and less like a serf, the Negro discovers that he must meet the competitive struggle to which men of the working class are subjected in the highly developed industrial system of the North.

Sufferings of the Northern Negro

In the South the great mass of Negroes have lived with their doors open, fireplaces have kept their homes ventilated, they could leave the matter of sanitation to fresh air and sunshine. And the Negro's very lack of training for such an environment as that of the North causes him untold suffering.   To save fuel, and because he loves to be warm and sociable, he and his family and friends crowd into one close room, which is kept at fever temperature, not by a healthful fireplace, but by a tight stove.   This, with the lack of proper sanitary conveniences, often becomes a hotbed of disease.   Even in mild weather I have been in Negro houses in the North where the air was almost unendurably warm and impure.

I know of nothing more tragic than the condition of the swarming newer Negro populations of Northern cities — the more tragic because the Negro is so cheerful and patient about it all.   I looked into the statistics closely in several of them, and in no instance does the birth-rate keep pace with the death-rate. Even allowing for the fact that birth statistics are not very accurately kept in most cities it is probable that if it were not for the immigration constantly rolling upward from the South the Negro population in Northern cities would show a falling off.   Consumption and the diseases of vice ravage their numbers.   One of the ablest Negro physicians I have met, Dr. S. A. Furniss, who has practised among his people in Indianapolis for many years, has made a careful study of conditions.   In a paper read before a medical association Dr. Furniss says:

"The reports of the Indianapolis Board of Health show that for no month in the last ten years has the birth-rate among Negroes equalled the death-rate."

Here are the statistics from 1901 to 1905:

	Deaths	Births
1901	332	279
1902	329	280
1903	448	283
1904	399	327
1905	443	384

"Race Suicide" Among Negroes

From inquiries that I have made everywhere in the North there would seem, indeed, to be a tendency to "race suicide" among Negroes as among the old American white stock. Especially is this true among the better class Negroes. The ignorant Negro in Southern agricultural districts is exceedingly prolific, but his Northern city brother has comparatively few children. I have saved the record from personal inquiry of perhaps two hundred Northern Negro families of the better class. Many have no children at all, many have one or two, and the largest family I found (in Boston) was seven children. I found one Negro family in the South with twenty-one children! Industrialism, of course, is not favourable to a large birth-rate. All Northern cities show a notable surplus, according to the statistics, of Negro women over Negro men. Many of these are house servants and, like the large class of roving single men who do day labour on the streets and railroads, they are without family ties and have no children.

Dr. Furniss finds that the deaths of Negroes from tuberculosis constitute over half the total deaths from that cause in the city of Indianapolis, whereas, in proportion to Negro population, they should constitute only one-eighth.

His observations upon these startling facts are of great interest:

"I believe the reason for these conditions is plain. First of all it is due to Negroes leaving the country and crowding into the larger cities, especially in the North, where they live in a climate totally different from that with which they have been familiar. They occupy unsanitary homes; they are frequently compelled to labour with insufficient food and clothing and without proper rest. Of necessity they follow the hardest and most exposed occupations in order to make a livelihood. I regret to say that intemperance and immorality play a part in making these figures what they are. They easily fall victim to the unusual vices of the city.

"Another reason for increased mortality is improper medical attention. Not only among the ignorant but among the intelligent we find too much trust put in patent medicines; the belief, latent it is true in many cases, but still existing among the ignorant, in the hoodoo militates against the close following of the doctor's orders.

"What shall we do about it?" asks Dr. Furniss. "We must urge those around us to more personal cleanliness, insist on a pure home life, and less dissipation and intemperance: to have fewer picnics and save more money for a rainy day. Tell the young people in the South not to come to Northern cities, but to go to the smaller towns of the West, where they can have a fair chance. Unless something is done to change existing conditions, to stop this movement to our Northern cities, to provide proper habitations and surroundings for those who are already here, it will be only a question of time until the problem of the American Negro will reach a solution not at all desirable from our point of view."

Of course a doctor always sees the pathological side of life and his view is likely to be pessimistic. I saw much of the tragedy of the slum Negroes in the cities of the North, and yet many Negroes have been able to survive, many have learned how to live in towns and are making a success of their lives — as I shall show more particularly in the next chapter. It must not be forgotten that Negro families in Boston and Philadelphia (mostly mulattoes, it is true) as well as in Charleston, Savannah, and New Orleans, have lived and thrived under city conditions for many generations. Not a few Negroes in Indianapolis whose homes I visited are housed better than the average of white families.

Sickness Among Northern Negroes

Not only is the death-rate high in the North, but the Negro is hampered by sickness to a much greater degree than white people. Hospital records in Philadelphia show an excess of Negro patients over whites, according to population, of 125 per cent. About 5,000 Negroes passed through the hospitals of Philadelphia last year, averaging a confinement of three weeks each. Mr. Warner, in *American Charities*, makes sickness the chief cause of poverty among coloured people in New York, Boston, New Haven, and Baltimore. The percentage of sickness was twice or more as high as that of Germans, Irish, or white Americans.

Such are the pains of readjustment which the Negroes are having to bear in the North.

A question arises whether they can ever become a large factor of the population in Northern latitudes. They are certainly not holding their own in the country or in the smaller cities, and in the large cities they are increasing at present, not by the birth-rate, but by constant immigration.

Hostile physical conditions of life in the North are not the only difficulties that the Negro has to meet. He thought he left prejudice behind in the South, but he finds it also showing its teeth here in the North. And, as in the South, a wide difference is apparent between the attitude of the best class of white men and the lower class.

How Northerners Regard the Negro

One of the first things that struck me when I began studying race conditions in the North was the position of the better class of white people with regard to the Negro. In the South every white man and woman has a vigorous and vital opinion on the race question. You have only to apply the match, the explosion is sure to follow. It is not so in the North. A few of the older people still preserve something of the war-time sentiment for the Negro; but the people one ordinarily meets don't know anything about the Negro, don't discuss him, and don't care about him. In Indianapolis, and indeed in other cities, the only white people I could find who were much interested in the Negroes were a few politicians, mostly of the lower sort, the charity workers and the police. But that, of course, is equally true of the Russian Jews or the Italians.

One of the first white men with whom I talked (at Indianapolis) said to me with some impatience:

"There are too many Negroes up here; they hurt the city."

Another told me of the increasing presence of Negroes in the parks, on the streets, and in the street cars. He said:

"I suppose sooner or later we shall have to adopt some of the restrictions of the South."

He said it without heat, but as a sort of tentative conclusion, he had n't fully made up his mind.

Race Prejudice in Boston

In Boston, of all places, I expected to find much of the old sentiment. It does exist among some of the older men and women, but I was surprised at the general attitude which I encountered. It was one of hesitation and withdrawal. Summed up, I think the feeling of the better class of people in Boston (and elsewhere in Northern cities) might be thus stated:

We have helped the Negro to liberty; we have helped to educate him; we have encouraged him to stand on his own feet. Now let's see what he can do for himself. After all, he must survive or perish by his own efforts.

In short, they have "cast the bantling on the rocks."

Though they still preserve the form of encouraging the Negro, the spirit seems to have fled. Not long ago the Negroes of Boston organised a concert at which Theodore Drury, a coloured musician of really notable accomplishments, was to appear. Aristocratic white people were appealed to and bought a considerable number of tickets; but on the evening of the concert the large block of seats purchased by white people was conspicuously vacant. Northern white people would seem to be more interested in the distant Southern Negro than in the Negro at their doors.

Before I take up the cruder and more violent expressions of prejudice on the part of the lower class of white men in the North I want to show the beginnings of cold-shouldering as it exists in varying degrees in Northern cities, and especially in Boston, the old centre of abolitionism.

Superficially, at least, the Negro in Boston still enjoys the widest freedom; but after one gets down to real conditions he finds much complaint and alarm on the part of Negroes over growing restrictions.

Boston exercises no discrimination on the street cars, on railroads, or in theatres or other places of public gathering. The schools are absolutely free. A coloured woman, Miss Maria Baldwin, is the principal of the Agassiz school, of Cambridge, attended by 600 white children. I heard her spoken of in the highest terms by the white people. Eight Negro teachers, chosen through the ordinary channels of competitive examination, teach in the public schools. There are Negro policemen, Negro firemen, Negro officeholders — fully as many of them as the proportion of Negro population in Boston would warrant. A Negro has served as commander of a white post of the Grand Army.

Prosperous Negroes in Boston

Several prosperous Negro business men have won a large white patronage. One of the chief merchant-tailoring stores of Boston, with a location on Washington Street which rents for $10,000 a year, is owned by J. H. Lewis. He has been in business many years. He employs both white and Negro workmen and clerks and he has some of the best white trade in Boston. Not long ago he went to North Carolina and bought the old plantation where his father was a slave, and he even talks of going there to spend his old age. Another Negro, Gilbert H. Harris, conducts the largest wig-making establishment in New England. I visited his place. He employs coloured girls and his trade is exclusively white. Another Negro has a school of pharmacy in which all the students are white; another, George Hamm, has a prosperous news and stationery store. A dentist, Dr. Grant, who has a reputation in his profession for a cement which he invented, was formerly in the faculty of the Harvard dentistry school and now enjoys a good practice among white people. The real estate dealer who has the most extensive business in Cambridge, T. H. Raymond, is a Negro. He employs white clerks and his business is chiefly with white people. Two or three Negro lawyers, Butler Wilson in particular, have many white clients. Dr. Courtney, a coloured physician from the Harvard Medical

School, was for a time house physician of the Boston Lying-in-Hospital, in which the patients were practically all white, and has now a practice which includes both white and coloured patients. Dr. Courtney has also served on the School Board of Boston, an important elective office. The Negro poet, William Stanley Braithwaite, whose father took a degree at Oxford (England), is a member of the Authors' Club of Boston. His poems have appeared in various magazines, he has written a volume of poems, a standard anthology of Elizabethan verse, and he is about to publish a critical study of the works of William Dean Howells. Several of these men meet white people socially more or less.

I give these examples to show the place occupied by the better and older class of Boston Negroes. Most of those I have mentioned are mulattoes, some very light. It shows what intelligent Negroes can do for themselves in a community where there has been little or no prejudice against them.

But with crowding new immigration, and incited by all the other causes I have mentioned, these conditions are rapidly changing.

A few years ago no hotel or restaurant in Boston refused Negro guests; now several hotels, restaurants, and especially confectionery stores, will not serve Negroes, even the best of them. The discrimination is not made openly, but a Negro who goes to such places is informed that there are no accommodations, or he is overlooked and otherwise slighted, so that he does not come again. A strong prejudice exists against renting flats and houses in many white neighbourhoods to coloured people. The Negro in Boston, as in other cities, is building up "quarters," which he occupies to the increasing exclusion of other classes of people. The great Negro centre is now in the South End, a locality once occupied by some of the most aristocratic families of Boston. And yet, as elsewhere, they struggle for the right to live where they please. A case in point is that of Mrs. Mattie A. McAdoo, an educated coloured woman, almost white, who has travelled abroad, and is a woman of refinement. She had a flat in an apartment house among white friends. One of the renters, a Southern woman, finding out that Mrs. McAdoo had coloured blood, objected. The landlord refused to cancel Mrs. McAdoo's lease and the white woman left, but the next year Mrs. McAdoo found that she could not re-rent her apartment. The landlord in this instance was the son of an abolitionist. He said to her:

"You know I have no prejudice against coloured people. I will rent you an apartment in the building where I myself live if you want it, but I can't let you into my other buildings, because the tenants object."

An attempt was even made a year or so ago by white women to force Miss Baldwin, the coloured school principal to whom I have referred, and who is almost one of the institutions of Boston, to leave Franklin House, where she was living. No one incident, perhaps, awakened Boston to the existence of race prejudice more sharply than this.

Churches Draw the Colour Line

One would think that the last harbour of prejudice would be the churches, and yet I found strange things in Boston. There are, and have been for a long time, numerous coloured churches in Boston, but many Negroes, especially those of the old families, have belonged to the white churches. In the last two years increased Negro attendance, especially at the Episcopal churches, has become a serious problem. A quarter of the congregation of the Church of the Ascension is coloured and the vicar has had to refuse any further coloured attendance at the Sunday School. St. Peter's and St. Philip's Churches in Cambridge have also been confronted with the colour problem.

A proposition is now afoot to establish a Negro mission which shall gradually grow into a separate coloured Episcopal Church, a movement which causes much bitterness among the coloured people. I shall not soon forget the expression of hopelessness in the face of a prominent white church leader as he exclaimed:

"What *shall* we do with these Negroes! I for one would like to have them stay. I believe it is in accordance with the doctrine of Christ, but the proportion is growing so large that white people are drifting away from us. Strangers avoid us. Our organisation is expensive to keep up and the Negroes are able to contribute very little in proportion to their numbers.

Think about it yourself: What shall we do? If we allow the Negroes to attend freely it means that eventually all the white people will leave and we shall have a Negro church whether we want it or not."

In no other city are there any considerable number of Negroes who attend white churches — except a few Catholic churches. At New Orleans, I have seen white and coloured people worshipping together at the cathedrals. White ministers sometimes have spasms of conscience that they are not doing all they should for the Negro.

Let me tell two significant incidents from Philadelphia. The worst Negro slum in that city is completely surrounded by business houses and the homes of wealthy white people. Within a few blocks of it stand several of the most aristocratic churches of Philadelphia. Miss Bartholomew conducts a neighbourhood settlement in the very centre of this social bog. Twice during the many years she has been there white ministers have ventured down from their churches. One of them said he had been troubled by the growing masses of ignorant coloured people.

"Can't I do something to help?"

Miss Bartholomew was greatly pleased and cheered.

"Of course you can," she said heartily. "We're trying to keep some of the Negro children off the streets. There is plenty of opportunity for helping with our boys' and girls' clubs and classes."

"Oh, I did n't mean that," said the minister; "I thought, in cases of death in their families, we might offer to read the burial service."

And he went away and did not see the humour of it!

Another minister made a similar proposition: he wanted to establish a Sunday School for coloured people. He asked Miss Bartholomew anxiously where he could hold it.

"Why not in your church in the afternoon?"

"Why, we could n't do that!" he exclaimed; "we should have to air all the cushions afterward!"

But to return to Boston. A proposition was recently made to organise for coloured people a separate Y. M. C. A., but the white members voted against any such discrimination. Yet a coloured man said to me hopelessly:

"It's only delayed. Next time we shall be put off with a separate institution."

Colour Line at Harvard

Even at Harvard where the Negro has always enjoyed exceptional opportunities, conditions are undergoing a marked change. A few years ago a large class of white students voluntarily chose a brilliant Negro student, R. C. Bruce, as valedictorian. But last year a Negro baseball player was the cause of so much discussion and embarrassment to the athletic association that there will probably never be another coloured boy on the university teams. The line has already been drawn, indeed, in the medical department. Although a coloured doctor only a few years ago was house physician at the Boston Lying-in-Hospital, coloured students are no longer admitted to that institution. One of them, Dr. Welker (an Iowa coloured man), cannot secure his degree because he hasn't had six obstetrical cases, and he can't get the six cases because he isn't admitted with his white classmates to the Lying-in-Hospital. It is a curious fact that not only the white patients but some Negro patients object to the coloured doctors. In a recent address which has awakened much sharp comment among Boston Negroes, President Eliot of Harvard indicated his sympathy with the general policy of separate education in the South by remarking that if Negro students were in the majority at Harvard, or formed a large proportion of the total number, some separation of the races might follow.

And this feeling is growing, notwithstanding the fact that no Negro student has ever disgraced Harvard and that no students are more orderly or law-abiding than the Negroes. On the other hand, Negro students have frequently made distinguished records for scholarship: last year one of them, Alain Leroy Locke,[2] who took the course in three years, won the first of the three Bowdoin prizes (the most important bestowed at Harvard) for a literary essay, and passed for his degree with a *magna cum laude*. Since then he has been accepted, after a brilliant competitive examination, for the Rhodes scholarship from the state of Pennsylvania.

Such feeling as that which is developing in the North comes

2. Locke became a distinguished scholar with a broad interest in Negro art and culture.

hard, indeed, upon the intelligent, educated, ambitious Negro — especially if he happens to have, as a large proportion of these Negroes do have, no little white blood. Many coloured people in Boston are so white that they cannot be told from white people, yet they are classed as Negroes.

Accompanying this change of attitude, this hesitation and withdrawal of the better class of white men, one finds crude sporadic outbreaks on the part of the rougher element of white men — who have merely a different way of expressing themselves.

White Gangs Attack Negroes

In Indianapolis the Negro comes in contact with the "bungaloo gangs," crowds of rough and lawless white boys who set upon Negroes and beat them frightfully, often wholly without provocation. Although no law prevents Negroes from entering any park in Indianapolis, they are practically excluded from at least one of them by the danger of being assaulted by these gangs.

The street cars are free in all Northern cities, but the Negro nevertheless sometimes finds it dangerous to ride with white people. Professor R. R. Wright, Jr., himself a Negro, and an acute observer of Negro conditions, tells this personal experience:

"I came out on the car from the University of Pennsylvania one evening in May about eight o'clock. Just as the car turned off Twenty-seventh to Lombard Street, a crowd of about one hundred little white boys from six to about fourteen years of age attacked it. The car was crowded, but there were only about a dozen Negroes on it, about half of them women. The mob of boys got control of the car by pulling off the trolley. They threw stones into the car, and finally some of them boarded the car and began to beat the Negroes with sticks, shouting as they did so, 'Kill the nigger!' 'Lynch 'em!' 'Hit that nigger!' etc. This all happened in Philadelphia. Doubtless these urchins had been reading in the daily papers the cry 'Kill the Negro!' and they were trying to carry out the injunction."

While I was in Indianapolis a clash of enough importance to be reported in the newspapers occurred between the races on a street car; and in New York, in the San Juan Hill district, one Sunday evening I saw an incident which illustrates the almost instinctive race antagonism which exists in Northern cities. The street was crowded. Several Negro boys were playing on the pavement. Stones were thrown. Instantly several white boys sided together and began to advance on the Negroes. In less time than it takes to tell it thirty or forty white boys and young men were chasing the Negroes down the street. At the next corner the Negroes were joined by dozens of their own race. Stones and sticks began to fly everywhere, and if it had n't been for the prompt action of two policemen there would have been a riot similar to those which have occurred not once but many times in New York City during the past two years. Of course these instances are exceptional, but none the less significant.

Bumptiousness as a Cause of Hatred

Some of the disturbances grow out of a characteristic of a certain sort of Negro, the expression of which seems to stir the deepest animosity in the city white boy. And that is the bumptiousness, the airiness, of the half-ignorant young Negro, who, feeling that he has rights, wants to be occupied constantly in using them. He mistakes liberty for licence. Although few in numbers among thousands of quiet coloured people, he makes a large showing. In the South they call him the "smart Negro," and an almost irresistible instinct exists among white boys of a certain class to take him down. I remember walking in Indianapolis with an educated Northern white man. We met a young Negro immaculately dressed; his hat-band was blue and white; his shoes were patent leather with white tops; he wore a flowered waistcoat, and his tread as he walked was something to see.

"Do you know," said my companion, "I never see that young fellow without wanting to step up and knock his head off. I know something about him. He is absolutely worthless: he does no work, but lives on the wages of a hard-working coloured woman and spends all he can get on his clothes. I know the instinct is childish, but I am just telling you how I feel. I 'm not sure it is racial prejudice; I presume I should feel much the same way toward a Frenchman

if he did the same thing.   And somehow I can't help believing
that a good thrashing would improve that boy's character."

I'm telling this incident just as it happened, to throw a
side-light on one of the manifestations of the growing prejudice.
One more illustration: Miss Eaton conducts a social settlement for Negroes in Boston.   One day a teacher said to one
of the little Negro boys in her class:

"Please pick up my handkerchief."

The boy did not stir; she again requested him to pick up
the handkerchief; then she asked him why he refused.

"The days of slavery are over," he said.

Now, this spirit is not common, but it exists, and it injures
the Negro people out of all proportion to its real seriousness.

In certain towns in Ohio, Indiana, and Illinois, on the
borders of the old South, the feeling has reached a stage still
more acute.   At Springfield, O.[3], two race riots have occurred,
in the first of which a Negro was lynched and in the second
many Negroes were driven out of town and a row of coloured
tenements was burned.   There are counties and towns where
no Negro is permitted to stop over night.   At Syracuse, O.,
Lawrenceburg, Ellwood, and Salem, Ind., for example,
Negroes have not been permitted to live for years.   If a Negro
appears he is warned of conditions, and if he does not leave
immediately, he is visited by a crowd of boys and men and
forced to leave.   A farmer who lives within a few miles of
Indianapolis told me of a meeting, held only a short time ago
by thirty-five farmers in his neighbourhood, in which an
agreement was passed to hire no Negroes, nor to permit
Negroes to live anywhere in the region.

Story of a Northern Race Riot

I stopped at Greensburg, Ind., on my way East and
found there a remarkable illustration showing just how feeling
arises in the North.   Greensburg is a comfortable, well-to-do,
conservative, church-going old town in eastern Indiana.
Many of the residents are retired farmers.   The population
of 7,000 is mostly of pure American stock, largely of Northern
origin.   And yet last April this quiet old town was shaken
by a race riot.   I made careful inquiries as to conditions there

3.   The race riots in Springfield, Ohio, occurred in March, 1904, and February,
1906.   They should not be confused with the most notorious northern race riot
of this period, which took place in Springfield, Illinois, in August, 1908.

and I was amazed to discover how closely this small disturbance paralleled the greater riot at Atlanta which I have already written about. Negroes had lived in Greensburg for many years, a group of self-respecting, decent, prosperous men and women. They were known to and highly regarded by their white neighbours. One of them, named Brooks, owned a barber shop and was janitor for the Presbyterian Church and for one of the banks. Another, George W. Edwards, whom I met, has been for years an employee in the Garland Mills.

"There is n't a better citizen in town than Edwards," a white lawyer told me; and I heard the same thing from other white men.

Another Negro, George Guess, is an engineer in the electric light plant. Of the local Negro boys, Robert Lewis, the first coloured graduate of the local schools, is now teaching engineering at Hampton Institute. Oscar Langston, another Negro boy, is a dentist in Indianapolis. These and other Negroes live in good homes, support a church and have a respectable society of their own. I found just such a body of good coloured people in Atlanta.

Well, progress brought an electric railroad to Greensburg. To work on this and on improvements made by the railroad hundreds of labourers were required. And they were Negroes of the ignorant, wandering, unlooked-after sort so common in similar occupations in the South. When the work was finished a considerable number of them remained in Greensburg. Now Greensburg, like other American cities, was governed by a mayor who was a "good fellow," and who depended on two influences to elect him: party loyalty and the saloon vote. He allowed a Negro dive to exist in one part of the town, where the idle and worthless Negroes congregated, where a murder was committed about a year before the riot. Exactly like Decatur Street in Atlanta! A rotten spot always causes trouble sooner or later. Good citizens protested and objected — to no purpose. They even organised a Good Citizenship League, the purpose of which was to secure a better enforcement of law. But the saloon interests were strong and wanted to sell whiskey and beer to the Negroes, and the city authorities were complaisant.

"Who cares," one of them asked, "about a few worthless Negroes?"

But in a democracy people *must* care for one another.

A Negro Crime in the North

One day last April a Negro labourer who had been working for Mrs. Sefton, a highly respected widow who lived alone, appeared in the house in broad daylight and criminally assaulted her. His name was John Green, a Kentucky Negro; he was not only ignorant, but half-witted; he had already committed a burglary and had not been punished. He was easily caught, convicted, and sentenced. But the town was angry. On April 30th a crowd of men and boys gathered, beat two or three Negroes, and drove many out of town. They never thought of mobbing the city officials who had allowed the Negro dives to exist. And, as in Atlanta, the decent Negroes suffered with the criminals: a crowd broke windows in the home of George Edwards, and threatened other respectable coloured men. As in Atlanta, the better white people were horrified and scandalised; but, as in Atlanta, the white men who made up the mob went unpunished (though Atlanta did mildly discipline a few rioters). As in Atlanta, the newspaper reports that were sent out made no distinction between the different sorts of Negroes. The entire Negro population of Greensburg was blamed for the crime of a single ignorant and neglected man. I have several different newspaper reports of the affair from outside papers, and nearly all indicate in the headlines that all the Negroes in Greensburg were concerned in the riot and were driven out of town, which was not, of course, true. As a matter of fact the respectable Negroes are still living in Greensburg on friendly terms with the white people.

Human Nature North and South

In fact, the more I see of conditions North and South, the more I see that human nature north of Mason and Dixon's line is not different from human nature south of the line.

Different degrees of prejudice, it is true, are apparent in the two sections. In the South the social and political prejudice,

the natural result of the memories of slavery and reconstruction, of the greater mass of Negro population and of the backward economic development, is stronger. In the North, on
the other hand, comparatively little social and political prejudice is apparent; but the Negro has a hard fight to get anything but the most subservient place in the economic machine.

Over and over again, while I was in the South, I heard
remarks like this:

"Down here we make the Negro keep his place socially,
but in the North you won't let him work."

This leads me to one of the most important phases of race-
relationship in the North — that is, the economic struggle
of the Negro, suddenly thrown, as he has been, into the swift-
moving, competitive conditions of Northern cities. Does he,
or can he, survive? Do the masses of Negroes now coming
North realise their ambitions? Is it true that the North will
not let the Negro work?

These questions must, perforce, be discussed in another
chapter.

CHAPTER VII

THE NEGROES' STRUGGLE FOR SURVIVAL IN NORTHERN CITIES

ONE of the questions I asked of Negroes whom I met both North and South was this:

"What is your chief cause of complaint?"

In the South the first answer nearly always referred to the Jim Crow cars or the Jim Crow railroad stations; after that, the complaint was of political disfranchisement, the difficulty of getting justice in the courts, the lack of good school facilities, and in some localities, of the danger of actual physical violence.

But in the North the first answer invariably referred to working conditions.

"The Negro isn't given a fair opportunity to get employment. He is discriminated against because he is coloured."

Professor Kelly Miller, one of the acutest of Negro writers, has said:

"The Negro (in the North) is compelled to loiter around the edges of industry."

Southern white men are fond of meeting Northern criticism of Southern treatment of the Negro with the response:

"But the North closes the doors of industrial opportunity to the Negro."

And yet, in spite of this complaint of conditions in the North, one who looks Southward can almost see the army of Negroes gathering from out of the cities, villages and farms, bringing nothing with them but a buoyant hope in a distant freedom, but tramping always Northward. And they come not alone from the old South, but from the West Indies, where the coloured population looks wistfully toward the heralded opportunities of America. A few are even coming from South Africa and South America. In New York, Boston, and Philadelphia, thousands of such foreign Negroes know nothing

A NEGRO CABIN WITH EVIDENCES OF ABUNDANCE

OFF FOR THE COTTON FIELDS

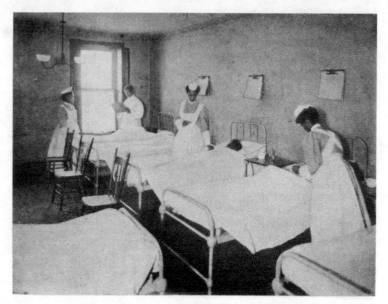

WARD IN A NEGRO HOSPITAL AT PHILADELPHIA

STUDIO OF A NEGRO SCULPTRESS

of America traditions; some of them do not even speak the English language.

And why do they come if their difficulties are so great? Is it true that there is no chance for them in industry? Are they better or worse off in the North than in the South?

In the first place, in most of the smaller Northern cities where the Negro population is not increasing rapidly, discrimination is hardly noticeable. Negroes enter the trades, find places in the shops, or even follow competitive business callings and still maintain friendly relationships with the white people.

But the small towns are not typical of the new race conditions in the North; the situation in the greater centres of population where Negro immigration is increasing largely, is decidedly different.

As I travelled in the North, I heard many stories of the difficulties which the coloured man had to meet in getting employment. Of course, as a Negro said to me, "there are always places for the coloured man at the bottom." He can always get work at unskilled manual labour, or personal or domestic service — in other words, at menial employment. He has had that in plenty in the South. But what he seeks as he becomes educated is an opportunity for better grades of employment. He wants to rise.

It is not, then, his complaint that he cannot get work in the North, but that he is limited in his opportunities to rise, to get positions which his capabilities (if it were not for his colour) would entitle him to. He is looking for a place where he will be judged at his worth as a man, not as a Negro: this he came to the North to find, and he meets difficulties of which he had not dreamed in the South.

At Indianapolis I found a great discussion going on over what to do with the large number of idle young coloured people, some of whom had been through the public schools, but who could not, apparently, find any work to do. As an able coloured man said to me: "What shall we do? Here are our young people educated in the schools, capable of doing good work in many occupations where skill and intelligence are required — and yet with few opportunities opening for them. They don't want to dig ditches or become porters or valets any more than intelligent white boys: they are human. The result is that some of them drop back into idle discouragement — or worse."

In New York I had a talk with William L. Bulkley, the coloured principal of Public School No. 80, attended chiefly by coloured children, who told me of the great difficulties and discouragements which confronted the Negro boy who wanted to earn his living. He relates this story:

"I received a communication the other day from an electric company stating that they could use some bright, clean, industrious boys in their business, starting them at so much a week and aiding them to learn the business. I suspected that they did not comprehend coloured boys under the generic term 'boys,' but thought to try. So I wrote asking if they would give employment to a coloured boy who could answer to the qualifications stated. The next mail brought the expected reply that no coloured boy, however promising, was wanted. I heaved a sigh and went on.

"The saddest thing that faces me in my work is the small opportunity for a coloured boy or girl to find proper employment. A boy comes to my office and asks for his working papers. He may be well up in the school, possibly with graduation only a few months off. I question him somewhat as follows: 'Well, my boy, you want to go to work, do you? What are you going to do?' 'I am going to be a door-boy, sir.' 'Well, you will get $2.50 or $3 a week, but after a while that will not be enough; what then?' After a moment's pause he will reply: 'I should like to be an office boy.' 'Well, what next?' A moment's silence, and, 'I should try to get a position as bell-boy.' 'Well, then, what next?' A rather contemplative mood, and then, 'I should like to climb to the position of head bell-boy.' He has now arrived at the top; further than this he sees no hope. He must face the bald fact that he must enter business as a boy and wind up as a boy."

And yet in spite of these difficulties, Negroes come North every year in increasing numbers, they find living expensive, they suffer an unusual amount of sickness and death, they meet more prejudice than they expected to meet, and yet they keep coming. Much as Negroes complain of the hardship

of Northern conditions, and though they are sometimes piti-
fully homesick for the old life in the South, I have yet to find
one who wanted to go back — unless he had accumulated
enough money to buy land.

"Why do they come?" I asked a Negro minister in
Philadelphia.

"Well, they're treated more like men up here in the
North," he said, "that's the secret of it. There's prejudice here, too, but the colour line isn't drawn in their faces at
every turn as it is in the South. It all gets back to a question of
manhood."

In the North prejudice is more purely economic than it is
in the South — an incident of industrial competition.

In the South the Negro still has the field of manual labour
largely to himself, he is unsharpened by competition; but
when he reaches the Northern city, he not only finds the work
different and more highly organised and specialised, but he
finds that he must meet the fierce competition of half a dozen
eager, struggling, ambitious groups of foreigners, who are
willing and able to work long hours at low pay in order to get
a foothold. He has to meet often for the first time the Italian,
the Russian Jew, the Slav, to say nothing of the white American
labourer. He finds the pace set by competitive industry
immensely harder than in most parts of the South. No life
in the world, perhaps, requires as much in brain and muscle
of all classes of men as that of the vast Northern cities in the
United States. I have talked with many coloured workmen
and I am convinced that not a few of them fail, not because of
their colour, nor because they are lazy (Negroes in the North
are of the most part hard workers — they *must* be, else they
starve or freeze), but for simple lack of speed and skill; they
haven't learned to keep the pace set by the white man.

A contractor in New York who employs large numbers of
men, said to me:

"It isn't colour so much as plain efficiency. I haven't
any sentiment in the matter at all. It's business. As a
general rule the ordinary coloured man can't do as much work
nor do it as well as the ordinary white man. The result, is, I
don't take coloured men when I can get white men. Yet I
have several coloured men who have been with me for years,

and I would n't part with them for any white man I know.
In the same way I would rather employ Italians than Russian
Jews: they 're stronger workers."

Not unnaturally the Negro charges these competitive difficulties which he has to meet in the North (as he has been
accustomed to do in the South) to the white man; he calls
it colour prejudice, when as a matter of fact, it is often only
the cold businesslike requirement of an industrial life which
demands tremendous efficiency, which in many lines of activity
has little more feeling than a machine, that is willing to use
Italians, or Japanese, or Chinese, or Negroes, or Hindus, or
any other people on the face of the earth.   On the other hand,
no doubt exists that many labour unions, especially in the
skilled trades, are hostile to Negroes, even though they may
have no rules against their admission.   I heard the experiences
of an expert Negro locomotive engineer named Burns who
had a run out of Indianapolis to the South.   Though he was
much in favour with the company, and indeed with many
trainmen who knew him personally, the general feeling was
so strong that by soaping the tracks, injuring his engine, and
in other ways making his work difficult and dangerous, he
was finally forced to abandon his run.   If there were space
I could give many accounts of strikes against the employment
of Negroes.   The feeling among union labour men has undoubtedly been growing more intense in the last few years owing
to the common use of Negroes as strike breakers.   With a
few thousand Negroes the employers broke the great stock-
yards strike in Chicago in 1904, and the teamsters' strike
in the following year.   Colour prejudice is used like any other
weapon for strengthening the monopoly of the labour union.
I know several unions which are practically monopolistic
corporations into which any outsider, white, yellow, or black,
penetrates with the greatest difficulty.   Such closely organised
unions keep the Negroes out in the South exactly as they do
in the North.   A Negro tile-setter, steam-fitter or plumber
can no more get into a union in Atlanta than in New York.
Of course these unions, like any other closely organised group
of men, employ every weapon to further their cause.   They
use prejudice as a competitive fighting weapon, they seize
upon the colour of the Negro, or the pig-tail and curious habits

of the Chinaman, or the low-living standard of the Hindu, to fight competition and protect them in their labour monopoly.

And yet, although I expected to find the Negro wholly ostracised by union labour, I discovered that where the Negro becomes numerous or skilful enough, he, like the Italian or the Russian Jew, begins to force his way into the unions. The very first Negro carpenter I chanced to meet in the North (from whom I had expected a complaint of discrimination) said to me:

"I 'm all right. I 'm a member of the union and get union wages."

And I found after inquiry that there are a few Negroes in most of the unions of skilled workers, carpenters, masons, iron-workers, even in the exclusive typographical union and in the railroad organisations — a few here and there, mostly mulattoes. They have got in just as the Italians get in, not because they are wanted, or because they are liked, but because by being prepared, skilled, and energetic, the unions have had to take them in as a matter of self-protection. In the South the Negro is more readily accepted as a carpenter, blacksmith, or bricklayer than in the North not because he is more highly regarded but because (unlike the North) the South has almost no other labour supply.

In several great industries North and South, indeed, the Negro is as much a part of labour unionism as the white man. Thousands of Negroes are members of the United Mine-Workers, John Mitchell's great organisation, and they stand on an exact industrial equality with the whites. Other thousands are in the cigar-makers' union, where, by virtue of economic pressure, they have forced recognition.

Indeed, in the North, in spite of the complaint of discrimination, I found Negroes working and making a good living in all sorts of industries — union or no union. A considerable number of Negro firemen have good positions in New York, a contracting Negro plumber in Indianapolis who uses coloured help has been able to maintain himself, not only against white competition, but against the opposition of organised white labour. I know of Negro paper-hangers and painters, not union men, but making a living at their trade and gradually getting hold. A good many Negro printers, pressmen, and the like are now found in Negro offices (over 200 newspapers and magazines are published by Negroes in this country) who are getting their training. I know of several girls (all mulattoes) who occupy responsible positions in offices in New York and Chicago. Not a few coloured nurses, seamstresses and milliners have found places in the life of the North which they seem capable of holding. It is not easy for them to make progress: each coloured man who takes a step ahead must prove, for his race, that a coloured man can after all, do his special work as well as a white man. The presumption is always against him.

Here is a little newspaper account of a successful skilled pattern maker in Chicago:

A few days ago a large box containing twenty-one large and small patterns was shipped to the Jamestown Exhibition by the McGuire Car Company of Paris, Illinois, one of the largest car companies in the West. Before the box was shipped scores of newspaper men, engineers and business men were permitted to inspect what is said to be the most complete and most valuable exhibit of the kind ever sent to an exhibition in this country. The contents of this precious box is entirely the work of a coloured man named George A. Harrison. Mr. Harrison is one of the highest salaried men on the pay-roll of the company. He makes all the patterns for all of the steel, brass, and iron castings for every kind of car made by this company. He graduated at the head of his class of sixty members in a pattern making establishment in Chicago.

Cases of this sort are exceptional among the vast masses of untrained Negro population in the cities, and yet it shows what can be done — and the very possibility of such advancement encourages Negroes to come North.

Trades Which Negroes Dominate

So much for the higher branches of industry. In some of the less skilled occupations, on the other hand, the Negro is not only getting hold, but actually becoming dominant.

The asphalt workers are nearly all coloured. In New York they have a strong union and although part of the membership is white (chiefly Italian), the chosen representative who sits with the Central Federated Union of the city is James H. Wallace, a coloured man.

In Indianapolis I found that the hod-carriers' industry was almost wholly in the hands of Negroes who have a strong union, with a large strike fund put aside. So successful have

they been that they now propose erecting a building of their
own as a club house. Although there are white men in the
union the officers are all coloured. Not long ago some of
the coloured members began to "rush" a white man at his
work. It was reported to the union and hotly discussed.
The coloured members finally decided that there should be
no discrimination against white men, and fined one of the
Negro offenders for his conduct. He could n't pay and had
to leave town.

Where the Negro workman gets a foothold in the North,
he often does very well indeed. R. R. Wright, Jr., calls attention to conditions in the Midvale Steel Company, which is
one of the largest, if not the largest employer of Negro labour
in Philadelphia. Charles J. Harrah, the president of this
company, said before the United States Industrial Commission
in 1900:

"We have fully 800 or 1,000 coloured men. The balance
are Americans, Irish and Germans. The coloured labour
we have is excellent . . . . They are lusty fellows; we
have some with shoulders twice as broad as mine, and with
chests twice as deep as mine. The men come up here ignorant
and untutored. We teach them the benefit of discipline. We
teach the coloured man the benefit of thrift, and coax him to
open a bank account; and he generally does it, and in a short
time has money in it, and nothing can stop him from adding
money to that bank account. We have no coloured men who
drink."

Asked as to the friction between the white and black workmen, Mr. Harrah replied:

"Not a bit of it. They work cheek by jowl with Irish, and
when the Irishman has a festivity at home he has coloured men
invited. We did it with trepidation. We introduced one man
at first to sweep up the yard, and we noticed the Irish and
Germans looked at him askance. Then we put in another.
Then we put them in the boiler-room, and then we got them
in the open hearth and in the forge, and gradually we got them
everywhere. They are intelligent and docile, and when they
come in as labourers, unskilled, they gradually become skilled,
and in the course of time we will make excellent foremen out
of them."

Mr. Harrah added that there was absolutely no difference in wages of Negroes and whites in the same grade of work.

I have pointed out especially in my last article how and where prejudice was growing in Northern cities, as it certainly is. On the other hand, where one gets down under the surface there are to be found many counteracting influences — those quiet constructive forces, which, not being sensational or threatening, attract too little attention. Northern people are able to help Negroes where Southern people are deterred by the intensity of social prejudice: for in most places in the South the teaching of Negroes still means social ostracism.

Help for Negroes in the North

Settlement work, in one form or another, has been instituted in most Northern cities, centres of enlightenment and hope. I have visited a number of these settlements and have seen their work. They are doing much, especially in giving a moral tone to a slum community: they help to keep the children off the streets by means of clubs and classes; they open the avenues of sympathy between the busy upper world and the struggling lower world. Such is the work of Miss Bartholomew, Miss Hancock, Miss Wharton in Philadelphia, Miss Eaton in Boston, Mrs. Celia Parker Woolley in Chicago, Miss Ovington in New York.[1] Miss Hancock, a busy, hopeful Quaker woman, has a "broom squad" of Negro boys which makes a regular business of sweeping several of the streets in the very worst slum district in Philadelphia; it gives them employment and it teaches them civic responsibility and pride.

But perhaps I can give the best idea of these movements by telling of the different forms of work in a single city — Indianapolis. In the first place, the Flanner Guild, projected by Mr. Flanner, a white man, is maintained largely by white contributions, but it is controlled wholly by coloured people. Millinery classes were opened for girls (of which there are now many practising graduates, eight of whom are giving lessons in Indianapolis and in other cities), and there are clubs and social gatherings of all sorts: it has been, indeed, a helpful social centre of influence.

1. Mary White Ovington, New York social worker and one of the organizers of the National Association for the Advancement of Colored People. Miss Ovington had visited the South and was vitally interested in race relations in

In the South, as I have shown, Negroes receive much offhand individual charity — food from the kitchen, gifts of old clothes and money; but it is largely personal and unorganised. In the North there is comparatively little indiscriminate giving, but an effort to reach and help Negro families by making them help themselves. One of the difficulties of the Negro is improvidence; but once given a start on the road to money saving, it is often astonishing to see him try to live up to cash in the bank. The Charity Organisation Society of Indianapolis has long maintained a dime savings and loan association which employs six women collectors, one coloured, who visit hundreds of homes every week. These form indeed a corps of friendly visitors, the work of collecting the savings furnishing them an opportunity of getting into the homes and so winning the confidence of the people that they can help them in many ways. Last year over 6,000 depositors were registered in the association, two-thirds of whom were Negroes, and over $25,000 was on deposit. Not less than twenty-five cents a week is accepted, but many Negroes save much more. As soon as they get into the habit of saving they usually transfer their accounts to the savings bank — and once with a bank book, they are on the road to genuine improvement.

Another work of great value which Mr. Grout of the Charity Organisation Society has organised is vacant lot cultivation. By securing the use of vacant land in and around the city many Negro families have been encouraged to make gardens, thus furnishing healthful and self-respecting occupation for the old or very young members of many Negro families, who otherwise might become public charges. The plots are ploughed and seeds are provided: the Negroes do their own work and take the crop. The work is supported by voluntary contributions from white people. A number of Negro women have raised enough vegetables not only to supply themselves but have had some to sell.

Negro children are closely looked after in Indianapolis. Compulsory education applies equally to both races. Every family thus comes also under the more or less active attention of the school authorities. An officer, Miss Sarah Colton Smith, is employed exclusively to visit and keep watch of the Negro children. Her work also is largely that of the friendly

the United States. Baker consulted her several times while gathering material for his book.

visitor, helping the various overworked mothers with suggestions, taking an interest in Negro organisations. For example, the Coloured Woman's Club, working with Miss Smith, has organised a day nursery which cares for some of the very young children of working Negro women, thereby allowing the older ones to go to school. Indianapolis (which has one of the most progressive and intelligent school systems, wholly non-political, in the country) is also thoroughly alive to the necessity of industrial education — for both races. Significantly enough, the Negro schools were first fitted with industrial departments, so that for a time the cost of education per capita in Indianapolis was higher for coloured children than for white. When I expressed my surprise at this unusual condition I was told:

"Of course, the immediate need of the Negro was greater."

Night schools are also held in the public school buildings from November to April — two schools for Negroes especially, where coloured people of all ages are at liberty to attend. It is a remarkable sight: Negroes fifty and sixty years old mingle there with mere children. The girls are taught sewing and cooking, the men carpentry — besides the ordinary branches. One old man from the South was found crying with joy over his ability to write his name. For the very young children, Negro equally with white, there is Mrs. Eliza Blaker's Kindergarten. For the aged coloured women a home is now supported principally by the coloured people themselves.

The Morals of Negro Women

I saw a good deal of these various lines of activity and talked with the people who come close in touch with the struggling masses of the Negro poor. I wish I had room to tell some of the stories I heard: the black masses of poverty, disease, hopeless ignorance, and yet everywhere shot through with hopeful tendencies and individual uplift and success. In Indianapolis, as in other Northern cities, I heard much to the credit of the Negro women.

"If the Negro is saved here in the North," Miss Smith told me, "it will be due to the women."

They gave me many illustrations showing how hard the

Negro women worked — taking in washing or going out every day to work, raising their families, keeping the home, sometimes supporting worthless husbands.

"A Negro woman of the lower class," one visitor said to me, "rarely expects her husband to support her. She takes the whole burden herself."

And the women, so the loan association visitors told me, are the chief savers: they are the ones who get and keep the bank accounts. I have heard a great deal South and North about the immorality of Negro women. Much immorality no doubt exists, but no honest observer can go into any of the crowded coloured communities of Northern cities and study the life without coming away with a new respect for the Negro women.

Another hopeful work in Indianapolis is the juvenile court. A boy who commits a crime is not immediately cast off to become a more desperate criminal and ultimately to take his revenge upon the society which neglected him. He comes into a specially organised court, where he meets not violence, but friendliness and encouragement. Mrs. Helen W. Rogers is at the head of the probation work in Indianapolis, and she has under her supervision a large corps of voluntary probation officers, thirty of whom are coloured men and women — the best in town. These coloured probation officers have an organisation of which George W. Cable, who is the foreman of the distributing department of the Indianapolis post-office, is the chairman. A Negro boy charged with an offence is turned over to one of these leading Negro men or women, required to report regularly, and helped until he gets on his feet again. Thus far the system has worked with great success. Boys whose offences are too serious for probation are sent, not to a jail or chain-gang, where they become habitual criminals, but to a reform school, where they are taught regular habits of work.

Why the Negro Often Fails

As I continued my inquiries I found that the leading coloured men in most cities, though they might be ever so discouraged over the condition of the ignorant, reckless masses of their people, were awakening to the fact that the Negro's difficulty in the North was not all racial, not all due to mere colour prejudice, but also in large measure to lack of training, lack of aggressiveness and efficiency, lack of organisation. In New York a "Committee for Improving the Industrial Condition of Negroes" has been formed. It is composed of both white and coloured men, and the secretary is S. R. Scottron, an able coloured man. The object of the committee is to study the condition of the Negroes in New York City, find out the causes of idleness, and try to help the Negro to better employment.

This committee has experienced difficulty not so much in finding openings for Negroes, as in getting reliable Negroes to fill them. Boys and girls, though educated in the public schools, come out without knowing how to do anything that will earn them a living. Although the advantages of Cooper Institute and other industrial training schools are open to Negroes, they have been little used, either from lack of knowledge of the opportunity, or because the Negroes preferred the regular literary courses of the schools. So many unskilled and untrained Negroes, both old and young, have discouraged many employers from trying any sort of Negro help. I shall not forget the significant remark of a white employer I met in Indianapolis: a broad-gauge man, known for his philanthropies.

"I 've tried Negro help over and over again, hoping to help out the condition of Negro idleness we have here. I have had two or three good Negro workers, but so many of them have been wholly undisciplined, irresponsible, and sometimes actually dishonest, that I 've given up trying. When I hear that an applicant is coloured, I don't employ him."

Upon this very point Professor Bulkley said to me:

"The great need of the young coloured people is practical training in industry. A Negro boy can't expect to get hold in a trade unless he has had training."

R. R. Wright, Jr., who has made a study of conditions in Philadelphia, says:

"It is in the skilled trades that the Negroes are at the greatest disadvantage. Negroes have been largely shut out of mechanical trades partly because of indifference and occasional active hostility of labour unions, partly because it has been difficult to overcome the traditional notion that a 'Negro's place' is in domestic service, but chiefly because there have been practically no opportunities for Negroes to learn trades. Those Negroes who know skilled trades and follow them are principally men from the South, who learned their trades there. The poorest of them fall into domestic service; the best have found places at their trades. For the Negro boy who is born in this city it is difficult to acquire a trade, and here, I say, the system has been weakest."

With the idea of giving more practical training School No. 80 in New York, of which Professor Bulkley is principal, is now opened in the evenings for industrial instruction. Last year 1,300 coloured people, young and old, were registered. In short, there is a recognition in the North as in the South of the need of training the Negro to work. And not only the Negro, but the white boy and girl as well — as Germany and other European countries have learned.

The Road from Slavery to Freedom

At Indianapolis I found an organisation of Negro women, called the Woman's Improvement Club. The president, Mrs. Lillian T. Fox, told me what the club was doing to solve the problem of the coloured girl and boy who could not get work. She found that, after all, white prejudice was not so much a bugaboo as she had imagined. The newspapers gave publicity to the work; the Commercial Club, the foremost business men's organisation of the city, offered to lend its assistance; several white employers agreed to try coloured help, and one, the Van Camp Packing Company, one of the great concerns of its kind in the country, even fitted up a new plant to be operated wholly by coloured people. Last fall, after the season's work was over, one of the officers of the company told me that the Negro plant had been a great success, that the girls had done their work faithfully and with great intelligence.

Just recently a meeting of coloured carpenters was held in New York to organise for self-help, and they found that, by bringing pressure to bear, the Brotherhood of Carpenters was perfectly willing to accept them as members of the union, on exactly the same basis as any other carpenters.

In short, the Negro is beginning to awaken to the fact that if he is to survive and succeed in Northern cities, it must be by his own skill, energy, and organisation. For, like any individual or any race, striving for a place in industry or in modern commercial life, the Negro must, in order to succeed, not only equal his competitor, but become more efficient. A Negro contractor said to me:

"Yes, I can get any amount of work, but they expect me to do it a little better and a little cheaper than my white competitors." Then he added:

"And I can do it, too!"

Those are the only terms on which success can be won.

For so long a time the Negro has been driven or forced to work, as in the South, that he learns only slowly, in an intense, impersonal, competitive life like that of the North, where work is at a premium, that he himself, not the white man, must do the driving. It is the lesson that raises any man from slavery into freedom.

Pullman Porters

So much for industry. The Negro in the North has also been going into business and into other and varied employment. The very difficulty of getting hold in the trades and in salaried employment has driven many coloured people into small business enterprises: grocery stores, tailor shops, real estate or renting agencies. If they are being driven out by white men as waiters and barbers, they enjoy, on the other hand, growing opportunities as railroad and Pullman porters and waiters — places which are often highly profitable, and lead, if the Negro saves his money, to better openings. A Negro banker whom I met in the South told me that he got his start as a Pullman porter. He had a good run, and by being active and accommodating, often made from $150 to $200 a month from his wages and tips.

But the same change is going on in the North that I found everywhere in the South. I mean a growing race consciousness among Negroes — the building up of a more or less independent Negro community life within the greater white civilisation. Every force seems to be working in that direction.

Business Among Boston and Philadelphia Negroes

As I have showed many Negroes in Boston (and indeed in other cities) have made a success in business enterprises which are patronised by white people — or rather by both races. Coloured doctors and lawyers in Boston have more or less white practice. Of course, coloured men who can succeed without reference to their colour and do business with both races, wish to continue to do so — but the tendency in the North, as in the South, is all against such development and toward Negro enterprises for the Negro population. Even in Boston numerous enterprises are conducted by Negroes for Negroes. I visited several small but prosperous grocery stores. A Negro named Basil F. Hutchins has built up a thriving undertaking and livery establishment for Negro trade. Charles W. Alexander has a print-shop with coloured workmen and publishes *Alexander's Magazine*. A new hotel called the Astor House, conducted by Negroes for Negroes, has 250 rooms with telephone service in each room, a large restaurant and many of the other attractions of a good hotel. But in this growth the North is far behind the South. Scores of Negro banks are to be found in the South, not one in the North. Cities like Richmond, Va., Jackson, Miss., Nashville, Tenn., have a really remarkable development of Negro business enterprises.

Perhaps I can convey a clearer idea of the great variety of employment of Negroes in Northern cities by outlining the condition in a single city, Philadelphia — information for which I am indebted to R. R. Wright, Jr. The census of 1900 shows that out of 28,940 Negro males (boys and men), 21,128 were at work, and out of 33,673 girls and women, 14,095 were wage-earners. Here are some of the more numerous occupations of Negro men:

Common labourers	7,690
Servants and waiters	4,378
Teamsters and hackmen	1,957
Porters and helpers in stores	921
Barbers and hairdressers	444
Messengers and errand boys	346
Brick and stone masons	308

Most of these are, of course, low-class occupations — the hard wage-work of the city in which the men often sink below the poverty line. On the other hand the census gives these figures:

Negro professional men (415) and women (170) including doctors, clergymen, dentists, teachers, electricians, architects, artists, musicians,
lawyers, journalists, civil engineers, actors, literary and scientific
persons, etc.   585
Retail merchants, men (297), women (22).   319
Hotel keepers   13

One Negro runs a men's furnishing store; another, a drug store; others, groceries, meats, etc. The beneficial society has grown to a regular insurance company, the renting agent has become a real estate dealer. Within the past twelve months Negroes have incorporated two realty companies, one land investment company, four building and loan associations, one manufacturing company, one insurance company, besides a number of other smaller concerns.

The civil service has proved of advantage to the Negro of Philadelphia, as of every other large Northern city. In the post-office there are about 150 clerks, carriers and other employees, on the police force about 70 patrolmen, and 40 school-teachers and about 200 persons in other municipal offices.

Wherein Lies Success for Negroes

I have thus endeavoured to present the conditions of the Negro in the North and show his relationship with white people. I have tried to exhibit every factor, good or bad, which plays a part in racial conditions. Many sinister influences exist: the large increase of ignorant and unskilled Negroes from the South; the growing prejudice in the North, both social and industrial, against the Negro; the high death-rate and low birth-rate among the Negro population, which is due to poverty, ignorance, crime, and an unfriendly climate. On the other hand, many encouraging and hopeful tendencies are perceptible. Individual Negroes are forcing recognition in nearly all branches of human activity, entering business life and the professions. A new racial consciousness is growing up leading to organisations for self-help; and while white preju-

A NEGRO MAGAZINE EDITOR'S OFFICE IN PHILADELPHIA

A "BROOM SQUAD" OF NEGRO BOYS

Which makes a regular business of sweeping several of the streets in the very worst slum district in Philadelphia; it gives them employment and it teaches them civic responsibility and pride. Miss Hancock at the right.

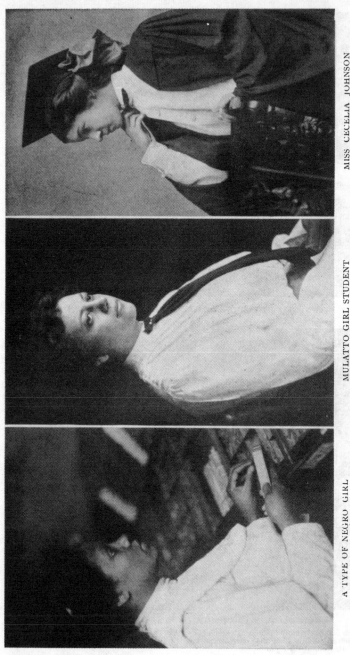

A TYPE OF NEGRO GIRL

Typesetter in Atlanta. Many Negro girls are entering stenography, bookkeeping, dressmaking, millinery and other occupations.

MULATTO GIRL STUDENT

At Clark University, Atlanta. At the completion of her studies this young woman will take up missionary work in Africa.

MISS CECELIA JOHNSON

A mulatto who could be easily taken for a white person. She was a leader in her class in Chicago University.

dice is increasing, so is white helpfulness as manifested in social settlements, industrial schools, and other useful philanthropies.

All these forces and counter forces — economic, social, religious, political — are at work. We can all see them plainly, but we cannot judge of their respective strength. It is a tremendous struggle that is going on — the struggle of a backward race for survival within the swift-moving civilisation of an advanced race. No one can look upon it without the most profound fascination for its interests as a human spectacle, nor without the deepest sympathy for the efforts of 10,000,000 human beings to surmount the obstacles which beset them on every hand.

And what a struggle it is! As I look out upon it and see this dark horde of men and women coming up, coming up, a few white men here and there cheering them on, a few bitterly holding them back, I feel that Port Arthur and the battles of Manchuria, bloody as they were, are not to be compared with such a conflict as this, for this is the silent, dogged, sanguinary, modern struggle in which the combatants never rest upon their arms. But the object is much the same: the effort of a backward race for a foothold upon this earth, for civilised respect and an opportunity to expand. And the Negro is not fighting Russians, but Americans, Germans, Irish, English, Italians, Jews, Slavs — all those mingling white races (each, indeed, engaged in the same sort of a struggle) which make up the nation we call America.

The more I see of the conflict the more I seem to see that victory or defeat lies with the Negro himself. As a wise Negro put it to me:

"Forty years ago the white man emancipated us: but we are only just now discovering that we must emancipate ourselves."

Whether the Negro can survive the conflict, how it will all come out, no man knows. For this is the making of life itself.

PART THREE

THE NEGRO IN THE NATION

CHAPTER VIII

THE MULATTO: THE PROBLEM OF RACE MIXTURE

I HAD not been long engaged in the study of the race problem when I found myself face to face with a curious and seemingly absurd question:

"What is a Negro?"

I saw plenty of men and women who were unquestionably Negroes, Negroes in every physical characteristic, black of countenance with thick lips and kinky hair, but I also met men and women as white as I am, whose assertion that they were really Negroes I accepted in defiance of the evidence of my own senses. I have seen blue-eyed Negroes and golden-haired Negroes; one Negro girl I met had an abundance of soft straight red hair. I have seen Negroes I could not easily distinguish from the Jewish or French types; I once talked with a man I took at first to be a Chinaman but who told me he was a Negro. And I have met several people, passing everywhere for white, who, I knew, had Negro blood.

Nothing, indeed, is more difficult to define than this curious physical colour line in the individual human being. Legislatures have repeatedly attempted to define where black leaves off and white begins, especially in connection with laws prohibiting marriage between the races. Some of the statutes define a Negro as a "person with one-eighth or more of Negro blood." Southern people, who take pride in their ability to distinguish the drop of dark blood in the white face, are themselves frequently deceived. Several times I have heard police judges in the South ask concerning a man brought before them: "Is this man coloured or white?"

Just recently a case has arisen at Norfolk, Va., in which a Mrs. Rosa Stone sued the Norfolk & Western Railroad Company for being compelled by the white conductor, who thought her a Negro, to ride in a "Jim Crow" car. Having been forced into the Negro compartment, it remained for a real coloured woman, who knew her personally, to draw the line against her. This coloured woman is reported as saying:

"Lor, Miss Rosa, this ain't no place for you; you b'long in the cars back yonder."

It appears that Mrs. Stone was tanned.

Curious Story of a White Man Who Was Expelled as a Negro

Here is a story well illustrating the difficulties sometimes encountered by Southerners in deciding who is white and who is coloured. On March 6, 1907, the Atlanta *Georgian* published this account of how a man who, it was said, was a Negro passing for a white man, was expelled by a crowd of white men from the town of Albany, Ga.:

Peter Zeigler, a Negro, was last night escorted out of town by a crowd of white men. Zeigler had been here for a month and palmed himself off as a white man. He has been boarding with one of the best white families in the city and has been associating with some of Albany's best people. A visiting lady recognised him as being a Negro who formerly lived in her city, and her assertion was investigated and found to be correct. Last night he was carried to Forester's Station, a few miles north of here, and ordered to board an outgoing train.

Zeigler has a fair education and polished manners, and his colour was such that he could easily pass for a white man where he was not known.

Immediately after suffering the indignity of being expelled from Albany, Mr. Zeigler communicated with his friends and relatives, a delegation of whom came from Charleston, Orangeburg, and Summerville, S. C. and proved to the satisfaction of everyone that Mr. Zeigler was, in reality, a white man connected with several old families of South Carolina. Of this return of Mr. Zeigler the Albany *Herald* says:

The *Herald* yesterday contained the account of the return to Albany of Peter B. Zeigler, the young man who was forced to leave Albany between suns on the night of March 4th. The young man upon his return was accompanied by a party composed of relatives and influential friends from his native state of South Carolina.

Nothing surely could throw a more vivid light on colour line confusions in the South than this story.

Another extraordinary case is that of Mrs. Elsie Massey, decided in Tipton County, Tenn., after years of litigation, in which one side tried to prove that Mrs. Massey was a Negro, the daughter of a cotton planter named "Ed"

Barrow, and a quadroon slave, and the other side tried to prove that she was of pure Caucasian blood. On June 13, 1907, a jury of white men finally declared that Mrs. Massey was white and that she and her children might inherit $250,000 worth of property. Such instances as these, a few among almost innumerable cases, will indicate how difficult it often is to decide who is and who is not a Negro — the definition of Negro here being that used in the South, a person having any Negro blood, no matter how little.

How Many Mulattoes There Are

Few people realise how large a proportion of the so-called Negro race in this country is not really Negro at all, but mulatto or mixed blood, either half white, or quadroon, or octoroon, or some other combination. In the last census (1900) the government gave up the attempt in discouragement of trying to enumerate the mulattoes at all, and counted all persons as Negroes who were so classed in the communities where they resided. The census of 1870 showed that one-eighth (roughly) of the Negro population was mulatto, that of 1890 showed that the proportion had increased to more than one-seventh. But these statistics are confessedly inaccurate: the census report itself says:

"These figures are of little value. Indeed, as an indication of the extent to which the races have mingled, they are misleading."

From my own observation, and from talking and corresponding with many men who have had superior opportunities for investigation, I think it safe to say that between one-fourth and one-third of the Negroes in this country at the present time have a *visible* admixture of white blood. At least the proportion is greater than the census figures of 1870 and 1890 would indicate. It is probable that 3,000,000 persons out of the 10,000,000 population are visibly mulattoes. It will be seen, then, how very important a matter it is, in any careful survey of the race problem, to consider the influence of the mixed blood. In the North, indeed, the race problem may almost be called a mulatto problem rather than a Negro problem, for in not a few places the mixed bloods are in excess of the darker types.

Many mulattoes have a mixed ancestry reaching back to the beginning of civilisation in North America; for the Negro slave appeared practically as soon as the white colonist. Many Negroes mixed (and are still mixing in Oklahoma) with the Indians, and one is to-day often astonished to see distinct Indian types among them. I shall never forget a woman I saw in Georgia — as perfect of line as any Greek statue — erect, lithe, strong, with sleek straight hair, the high cheek-bones of the Indian, but the lips of the Negro. She was plainly an Indian type — but had no memory of anything but Negro ancestry. A strain of Arab blood from Africa runs in the veins of many Negroes, in others flows the blood of the Portuguese slave-traders or of the early Spanish adventurers or of the French who settled in New Orleans, to say nothing of every sort of American white blood. In my classification I have estimated 3,000,000 persons who are "visibly" mulattoes: the actual number who have some strain of blood — Arab, Portuguese, Spanish, French, Indian — other than Negro, must be considerably larger.

It is a curious problem, this of colour. Several times, in different parts of the country, I have been told by both white and coloured observers that Negroes, even without the admixture of white blood, were gradually growing lighter — the effect of a cold climate, clothing and other causes. A tendency toward such a change, an adaptation to new environment, is certainly in accord with the best scientific beliefs, but whether a mere century or two in America has really operated to whiten the blackness of thousands of years of jungle life, must be left for the careful scientist to decide. It is certain that the darkest American Negro is far superior to the native African Negro.

Story of a Real African Woman

At Montgomery, Ala., Mr. Craik took me to see a real African woman, one of the very few left who were captured in Africa and brought to this country as slaves. She came in the *Wanderer*, long after the slave trade was forbidden by law, and was secretly landed at Mobile about 1858. She is a stocky, vigorous old woman. She speaks very little English, and I could not understand even that little. She asserts, I am told, that she is the daughter of a king in Africa, and she tells yet of the hardships and alarms of the ocean voyage. Her daughter is married to a respectable-looking Negro farmer. Mr. Craik succeeded, in spite of her superstitious terrors, in getting her to submit to having a picture taken.

And yet all these strange-blooded people are classed roughly together as Negroes. I remember sitting once on the platform at a great meeting at the People's Tabernacle in Atlanta. An audience of some 1,200 coloured people was present. A prominent white man gave a brief address in which he urged the Negroes present to accept with humility the limitations imposed upon them by their heredity, that they were Negroes and that therefore they should accept with grace the place of inferiority. Now as I looked out over that audience, which included the best class of coloured people in Atlanta, I could not help asking myself:

"What is this blood he is appealing to, anyway?"

For I saw comparatively few men and women who could really be called Negroes at all. Some were so light as to be indistinguishable from Caucasians. A bishop of the African Methodist Episcopal Church who sat near me on the platform was a nephew of Robert Toombs, one of the great men of the South, a leader of the Confederacy. Another man present was a grandson of a famous senator of South Carolina. Several others that I knew of were half-brothers or sisters or cousins of more or less well-known white men. And I could not hear this appeal to heredity without thinking of the not at all humble Southern blood which flowed in the veins of some of these men and women. How futile such advice really was, and how little it got into the hearts of the audience, was forcibly impressed on me afterward by the remark of a mulatto I met.

"They've given us their blood, whether we wanted it or not," he said, "and now they ask us not to respond to the same ambitions and hopes that they have. They have given us fighting blood and expect us not to struggle."

Attitude of the Mixed Blood Toward the Black Negroes

In the cities of the South no inconsiderable communities of mulattoes have long existed, many of them highly prosperous.

Even before the war thousands of "free persons of colour" resided in Charleston, Richmond, and New Orleans. In places like Charleston they had (and still have to some extent) an exclusive society of their own which looked down on the black Negro with a prejudice equal to that of the white man. The census of 1860 shows a population of 3,441 "free persons of colour" in Charleston alone, of whom 2,554 were mulattoes. In New Orleans in the same year lived 9,084 free Negroes, of whom 7,357 were mulattoes; and they were so far distant in sympathy from the slave population that they even tendered their support to the Confederacy at the beginning of the war.

But with the Emancipation Proclamation the aristocratic "free person of colour" who had formed a sort of third class as between the white above and the black below, lost his unique position: the line was drawn against him. When I went South I expected to find a good deal of aloofness between the mulatto and the black man. It does exist, but really less to-day in the South than in Boston! The very first mulatto, a preacher in Atlanta, with whom I raised the question, surprised me by denying that the mulatto was in any degree potentially superior to the real Negro: that if the black man were given the same advantages and environment as the mulatto, he would do as well, that the prominence of the mulatto is the result of the superior advantages he has long enjoyed, being the house servant in slavery times, with opportunities for education and discipline that the black man never possessed. This was his argument, and to support it he gave me a long list of black Negroes who had achieved success or leadership. I found Booker T. Washington and Professor Du Bois (themselves both mulattoes) arguing along the same lines. In other words, the prejudice of white people has forced all coloured people, light or dark, together, and has awakened in many ostracised men and women who are nearly white a spirit which expresses itself in the passionate defence of everything that is Negro.

And yet, with what pathos! What is this race? The spirit and the ideals are not Negro: for the people are not Negro, even the darkest of them, in the sense that the inhabitants of the jungles of Africa are Negroes. The blackest of black American Negroes is far ahead of his naked cousin in Africa. But neither are they white!

One evening last summer I attended a performance at Philadelphia of a Negro play called the "Shoo-Fly Regiment." It was written, both words and music, by two clever mulattoes, Cole and Johnson;[1] and it was wholly presented by Negroes. The audience was large, mostly composed of coloured people, and the laughter was unstinted. The point that impressed me was this, that the writers had chosen a distinct Negro subject. The play dealt with two questions of much interest among coloured people: the matter of industrial education, and the Negro soldier. That, it seemed to me, was significant: it was an effort to appeal to the class consciousness of the Negro.

And yet as I sat and watched the play I could not help being impressed with the essential tragedy of the so-called Negro people. The players of the company were of every colour, from the black African type to the mulatto with fair hair and blue eyes. In spite of this valiant effort to emphasise certain racial interests, one who saw the play could not help asking: "What, after all, is this Negro race? What is the Negro spirit? Is it in this black African or in this white American with the drop of dark blood?"

In a recent address a coloured minister of San Francisco, J. Hugh Kelley, said:

"My father's father was a Black Hawk Indian, seven feet tall. My father's mother was an Irishwoman. My mother's father was an American white man. Her mother was a full-blooded African woman. What am I?"

Pathetic Desire of Negroes to Be Like White Men

Even among those Negroes who are most emphatic in defence of the race there is, deep down, the pathetic desire to be like the dominant white man. It is not unreasonable, nor unnatural, for all outward opportunity of development lies open to the white man. To be coloured is to be handicapped in the race for those things in life which men call desirable. I remember discussing the race question one evening with a group of intelligent coloured men. They had made a strong case for the

1. Bob Cole and J. Rosamond Johnson were two notable musical-comedy composers.

Negro spirit, and the need of the race to stand for itself, but one of them said in a passing remark (what the investigator overhears is often of greater significance than what he hears), speaking of a mulatto friend of his:

"His hair is *better* than mine."

He meant *straighter*, more like that of the white man.

The same evening, another Negro, referring to a light-complexioned coloured man, said:

"Thank God, he is passing now for white."

At Philadelphia a dark Negro made this comment on one of the coloured churches where mulattoes are in the ascendancy:

"You can't have a good time when you go there unless you have straight hair."

This remark indicated not only the ideal held by the speaker, but showed the line drawn by the light-coloured man against his darker brother.

In the same way it is almost a universal desire of Negroes to "marry whiter;" that is, a dark man will, if possible, marry a mulatto woman, the lighter the better.   The ideal is whiteness: for whiteness stands for opportunity, power, progress.

Give a coloured man or woman white blood, educate him until he has glimpses of the greater possibilities of life and then lock him forever within the bars of colour, and you have all the elements of tragedy.   Dr. DuBois in his remarkable book, "The Souls of Black Folk,"[2] has expressed more vividly than any other writer the essential significance of this tragedy.   I read the book before I went South and I thought it certainly overdrawn, the expression of a highly cultivated and exceptional Mulatto, but after meeting many Negroes I have been surprised to find how truly it voices a wide experience.

Experience of a Highly Educated Mulatto

DuBois tells in this book how he first came to realise that he was really a Negro.   He was a boy in school near his home in Massachusetts.

"Something," he writes, "put it into the boys' and girls' heads to buy gorgeous visiting cards — ten cents a package — and exchange.   The exchange was merry, till one girl, a tall

2. *The Souls of Black Folk* (Chicago, 1903).

newcomer, refused my card — refused it peremptorily, with a glance. Then it dawned upon me with a certain suddenness that I was different from the others; or like, mayhap, in heart and life and longing, but shut out from their world by a vast veil. I had thereafter no desire to tear down that veil, to creep through; I held all beyond it in common contempt, and lived above it in a region of blue sky and great wandering shadows. That sky was bluest when I could beat my mates at examination time, or beat them at a foot-race, or even beat their stringy heads. Alas, with the years all this fine contempt began to fade; for the worlds I longed for, and all their dazzling opportunities, were theirs not mine. . . . With other black boys the strife was not so fiercely sunny; their youth shrunk into tasteless sycophancy or into silent hatred of the pale world about them and mocking distrust of everything white; or wasted itself in a bitter cry, Why did God make me an outcast and a stranger in mine own house? The shades of the prison-house closed round about us all: walls strait and stubborn to the whitest, but relentlessly narrow, tall and unscalable to sons of night who must plod darkly on in resignation, or beat unavailing palms against the stone, or steadily, half-hopelessly, watch the streak of blue above."

If space permitted I could tell many stories illustrative of the daily tragedy which many mulattoes are meeting in this country, struggles that are none the less tragic for being inarticulate. Here is a letter which I received not long ago from a mulatto professor in a Western Negro college:

"I wonder how you will treat that point to which you have thus far only referred in your studies, 'Where does the colour line really begin?' What is to become of that large class of which I am a part, that class which is neither white nor black and yet both? There are millions of us who have the blood of both races, and, if heredity means anything, who have the traditions, feelings, and passions of both. Yet we are black in name, in law, in station, in everything save face and figure, despite the overwhelming white blood. And why? Certainly not because we have to be. America is a big country: it is easy to get lost, even in a neighbouring state. Some of us do, and the process has been going on so long in certain large cities of the North until we cease to think about it. But the majority of us stay and live and work out our destiny among the people into whom we were born, living ofttimes side by side with our white brothers and sisters.   When I go back to Atlanta after an absence of two years, I can, if I wish, go back in a Pullman, go out of the main entrance of the station, get my dinner at the Piedmont Hotel, and when I am tired of being Mr. Hyde, I can stroll down Auburn Avenue with my friends in the full glory of Dr. Jekyll.   As a matter of fact I shall doubtless avail myself of the privilege of a sleeper, sneak out the side entrance, get on the last seat of the car, despite the conductor's remonstrance, go on to my friends at once and be myself all the time I am there.   I would n't be a white man if I had to.   I want to be black.   I want to love those who love me.   I want to help those who need my help.   And I know hundreds just like me: I know others who are not.

"I wonder if you can decide: 'Where does the colour line really — end ?'"

A Negro Who Lived First as a White Man, Then as a Negro

When I was in Philadelphia I met an intelligent Negro named A. L. Manley, who is at present the janitor of a large apartment house. He has been connected with the good-government movement in Philadelphia, being the leader of a club of coloured men who have supported the reform party. When I first met him I should not have known him for a Negro, he is so white. His white grandfather was a famous governor of North Carolina — Charles Manley. He was educated at Wilmington, N. C., and at Hampton Institute. For a time he published a Negro newspaper at Wilmington, but during the race riot in that city a number of years ago he was driven out and his property was destroyed, his office being burned to the ground.[3] After a year or two in Washington he came to Philadelphia, where he endeavoured to get work at his trade as a painter and decorator, but the moment he informed employers that he was a coloured man they refused to hire him — usually excusing themselves on the ground that union labour would refuse to work with him.

"So I tried being white," he said: "that is, I did not reveal the fact that I had coloured blood, and I immediately got work

3. Alex Manly had been editor of the Wilmington *Record,* which Democratic leaders in North Carolina attacked during the white supremacy campaign of 1898 for allegedly advocating social equality. Soon after the November election

in some of the best shops in Philadelphia. I joined the union and had no trouble at all."

But during all this time he had to live, as he says, "the life of a sneak." He had to sneak out of his home in the morning and return to it only after nightfall, lest someone discover that his family (he has a wife and two children) was coloured.

"The thing finally became unbearable," he said; "no decent man could stand it. I preferred to be a Negro and hold up my head rather than to be a sneak."

So he dropped his trade and became a janitor. In other words, he stepped back, as so many Negroes in the North are forced to do, into a form of domestic service, although in his case the position is one of responsibility and good pay.

Such stories of the problem of the mulatto are innumerable; and yet I do not wish to imply that the life is all shadow, for it is n't. The Negro blood, wherever it is, supplies an element of light-heartedness which will not be wholly crushed. It is this element, indeed, that accounts in no small degree for the survival of the Negro in this country. Where the Indian perished for want of adaptability, the Negro has survived by sheer elasticity of temperament: it is perhaps the highest natural gift of the Negro race. One hears much of the unfavourable traits of the Negro, but certainly, judging from any point of view, the power of adaptability displayed by the Negro in a wholly foreign environment, under the harshest conditions, and his ability to thrive and increase in numbers, even meeting the competition of the dominant race, and to keep on laughing at his work, is a power which in any race would be regarded as notable.

Why Some Light Mulattoes do not "Cross over to White"

I once asked a very light mulatto why he did not "cross the line," as they call it (or "go over to white") and quit his people. His answer surprised me; it was so distinctly an unexpected point of view.

"Why," he said, "white people don't begin to have the good times that Negroes do. They 're stiff and cold. They are n't sociable. They don't laugh."

Here certainly was a criticism of the white man! And it was corroborated by a curious story I heard at Memphis, of a

in 1898, a terrible riot in Wilmington took the lives of eleven Negroes and wounded many more.

mulatto well known among the coloured people of Tennessee. A number of years ago it came to him suddenly one day that he was white enough to pass anywhere for white, and he acted instantly on the inspiration. He went to Memphis and bought a first-class ticket on a Mississippi River boat to Cincinnati. No one suspected that he was coloured; he sat at the table with white people and even occupied a state-room with a white man. At first he said he could hardly restrain his exultation, but after a time, although he said he talked and smoked with the white men, he began to be lonesome.

"It grew colder and colder," he said.

In the evening he sat on the upper deck and as he looked over the railing he could see, down below, the Negro passengers and deck hands talking and laughing. After a time, when it grew darker, they began to sing — the inimitable Negro songs.

"That finished me," he said, "I got up and went downstairs and took my place among them. I've been a Negro ever since."

An ordinary community of middle or working class white people is often singularly barren of any social or intellectual interest: it is often sombre, sodden, uninteresting. Not so the Negro community. In several cities I have tried to trace out the social life of various cliques, especially among the mulattoes, and I have been astonished to find how many societies there are, often with high-sounding names, how many church affairs must be attended to, how many suppers and picnics are constantly under way, how many clubs and secret societies are supported.

Forced upon themselves, every point of contact with the white race becomes to the Negro a story of peculiar human interest. The view they get from the outside or underneath of white civilisation is not, to say the least, altogether *our* view. Once, in a gathering of mulattoes I heard the discussion turn to the stories of those who had "gone over to white" — friends or acquaintances of those who were present. Few such cases are known to white people, but the Negroes know many of them. It developed from this conversation (and afterward I got the same impression many times) that there is a sort of conspiracy of silence to protect the Negro who "crosses the line" and takes his place as a white man. Such cases even awaken glee among them, as though the Negro, thus, in some way, was getting even with the dominant white man.

Stories of Negroes Who Have Crossed the Colour Line

I don't know how many times I have heard mulattoes speak of the French novelist Dumas as having Negro blood, and they also claim Robert Browning and Alexander Hamilton (how truly I do not know). But the cases which interest them most are those in this country; and there must be far more of them than white people imagine. I know of scores of them. A well-known white actress, whose name, of course, I cannot give, when she goes to Boston, secretly visits her coloured relatives. A New York man who holds a prominent political appointment under the state government and who has become an authority in his line, is a Negro. Not long ago he entered a hotel in Baltimore and the Negro porter who ran to take his bag said discreetly:

"Hello, Bob."

As boys they had gone to the same Negro school.

"Let me carry your bag," said the porter, "I won't give you away."

In Philadelphia there lives a coloured woman who married a rich white man. Of course, no white people know she is coloured, but the Negroes do, and do not tell. Occasionally she drives down to a certain store, dismisses her carriage and walks on foot to the home of her mother and sisters.

Only a few years ago the newspapers were filled for a day or two with the story of a girl who had been at Vassar College, and upon graduation by merest accident it was discovered that she was a Negro. A similar case arose last year at Chicago University, that of Miss Cecelia Johnson, who had been a leader in her class, a member of the Pi Delta Phi Sorority and president of Englewood House, an exclusive girls' club. She was the sister of a well-known Negro politician of Chicago.

The Chicago *Tribune*, after publishing a story to the effect that Miss Johnson had kept her parentage secret apologised for the publicity in these words:

The *Tribune* makes this reparation spontaneously and as a simple act of justice.

There is not the slightest mystery about Miss Johnson. Her life has been an open book. She has won distinction at high school, and university, and her career appears to have been free from any blemish that should lessen the love of her intimate friends or the respect in which she is held by her acquaintances.

Some mulattoes I know of, one a prominent Wall Street broker, have "crossed the line" by declaring that they are Mexicans, Brazilians, Spanish or French; one says he is an Armenian. Under a foreign name they are readily accepted among white people where, as Negroes, they would be instantly rejected. No one, of course, can estimate the number of men and women with Negro blood who have thus "gone over to white"; but it must be large.

Does Race Amalgamation Still Continue?

One of the first questions that always arises concerning the mulatto is whether or not the mixture of blood still continues and whether it is increasing or decreasing. In other words, is the amalgamation of the races still going on and to what extent ?

Intermarriage between the races is forbidden by law in all the Southern states and also in the following Northern and Western states: Arizona, California, Colorado, Delaware, Idaho, Indiana, Missouri, Nebraska, Nevada, Oklahoma, Oregon, and Utah. In all other Northern and Western states marriage between the races is lawful.

And yet, the marriage laws, so far as they affect the actual problem of amalgamation, mean next to nothing at all. No legal marriage existed between the races in slavery times and yet there was a widespread mixture of blood. Concubinage was a common practice: a mulatto was worth more in cash than a black man. The great body of mulattoes now in the country trace their origin to such relationships.

And such practice of slavery days no more ceased instantly with a paper Emancipation Proclamation than many other customs and habits which had grown up out of centuries of slave relationships. It is a slow process, working out of slavery, both for white men and black.

I made inquiries widely in every part of the South among both white and coloured people and I found a strong and rapidly growing sentiment against what the South calls "miscegenation." For years white men in many communities, often prominent judges, governors, wealthy planters, made little or no secret of the fact that they had a Negro family as well as a white family.

And the practice is far from dead yet. Every Southern town knows of such cases, often many of them: and a large number of mulatto children to-day are the sons and daughters of Southern white men, often men of decided importance in their communities. In one town I visited I heard a white man expressing with great bitterness his feeling against the Negro race, arguing that the Negro must be kept down, else it would lead to the mongrelisation of the white race. The next morning as chance would have it, another white man with whom I was walking pointed out to me a neat cottage, the home of the Negro family of the white man who had talked with me on the previous evening. And I saw this man's coloured children in the yard!

The better class of Southern people know perfectly well of these conditions and are beginning to attack them boldly. At a meeting in the Court Street Methodist Church in Montgomery, Ala., in 1907, Dr. J. A. Rice, the pastor, made this statement, significant in its very fearlessness, of changing sentiment:

"I hesitate before I make another statement which is all too true. I hesitate, because I fear that in saying it I shall be charged with sensationalism. But even at the risk of such a charge I will say, for it must be said, that there are in the city of Montgomery, four hundred Negro women supported by white men."

The next morning this statement was reported in the Montgomery *Advertiser*.

It may be said also, that these 400 cases in a city of 35,000 people do not represent a condition of mere vice. Many of the women are comfortably provided for and have families of children. Vice is wholly distinct from this system of concubinage; for there are in Montgomery thirty-two Negro dives operated for white patronage — also the statement of Dr. Rice, quoted in the Montgomery *Advertiser*.

The proportion of such cases in some of the less progressive Southern towns even to-day, is almost appalling: and at the same time that speakers and writers are railing at the mulatto for his disturbing race leadership and his restless desire for political and other rights, and while they are declaiming against amalgamation and mongrelisation, the mulatto population is increasing. Striving to keep the Negro in his place as a Negro, the South is making him more and more a white man.

Attempt to Stop Miscegenation

Among Southern women, not unnaturally, the feeling aroused by these practices has been especially bitter. Here is a remarkable plea, published in the *Times-Democrat* on June 21, 1907, signed "A woman."

Will you kindly publish the following without attaching my signature or divulging it in any way? I have several brothers who are old-maidish enough to have nervous prostration if they should see my name signed to such an unmaidenly, immodest letter, but I do my thinking without any assistance from them, and hope for the sake of peace in my family that they will not recognise me in print.

I am a resident of a large town in the Yazoo-Mississippi Delta, where miscegenation is common — where, if a man isolates himself from feminine society, the first and only conclusion reached is, "he has a woman of his own" in saddle, of duskier shade. This conclusion is almost without exception true. If some daring woman, not afraid of being dubbed a Carrie Nation, were to canvass the delta counties of Mississippi taking the census, she would find so many cases of miscegenation, and their resultant mongrel families, that she would bow her head in shame for the "flower of Southern chivalry" — gone to seed.

Awakened by a sense of the fearfulness of these conditions, such a strong paper as the New Orleans *Times-Democrat* has been conducting a campaign for laws which shall punish the white man who maintains illicit relations with Negroes. For years attempts have been made in the legislatures of several states (in part successfully) to enact such legislation, but the practice has been so firmly entrenched that many of the efforts have failed. On February 15, 1906, the *Times-Democrat* put the case in stronger language than I would dare to do:

It is a public scandal that there should be no law of this kind (against miscegenation) on the statute book of Louisiana, and that it should be left to mobs to break up the miscegenatious couples. The failure to pass a law of this kind is attributed to white degenerates, men who denounce social equality yet practice it, men who are more dangerous to their own race than the most inflammatory Negro orator and social equality preacher, and who have succeeded by some sort of legislative trickery in pigeon-holing or killing the bills intended to protect Louisiana from a possible danger. Such men should be exposed before the people of the state in their true colours.

It will thus be seen how deep-seated the difficulty is. And yet, as I have followed the editorial expression of many Southern newspapers, I have been astonished to see how people are beginning to talk out. Here is an editorial from the *Star* of Monroe, La.:

DESTRUCTIVE CRIME OF MISCEGENATION

There can be no greater wrong done the people of any community than for public sentiment to permit and tolerate this growing and destructive crime of miscegenation, yet in many towns and cities of Louisiana, especially, there are to-day white men cohabiting with Negro women, who have sweet and lovable families. This is a crime that becomes almost unbearable, and should bring the blush of shame to every man's cheek who dares to flaunt his debased and degrading conceptions of morality in the eyes of self-respecting men and women.

In January, 1907, District Attorney J. H. Currie, in Judge Cochran's[4] court at Meridian, Miss., addressed a jury on what he called "the curse of miscegenation." In the course of his speech he said:

"The accursed shadow of miscegenation hangs over the South to-day like a pall of hell. We talk much of the Negro question and all of its possible ramifications and consequences, but, gentlemen, the trouble is not far afield. Our own people, our white men with their black concubines, are destroying the integrity of the Negro race, raising up a menace to the white race, lowering the standard of both races and preparing the way for riot, mob, criminal assaults, and, finally, a death struggle for racial supremacy. The trouble is at our own door. We have tolerated this crime long enough, and if our country is not run by policy rather than by law, then it is time to rise up and denounce this sin of the earth."

Anti-Miscegenation League is Formed

Strong men and women, indeed, in several states have begun to organise against the evil. At Francisville, La., in May (1907), a meeting was called to organise against what one of the speakers, Mr. Wickliffe, called the "yellow peril" of the South. He said that "every man familiar with conditions in our midst knows that the enormous increase in persons of mixed blood is due to men of the white race openly keeping

4. Judge R. F. Cochran of the tenth Mississippi judicial district.

Negro women as concubines." Out of this meeting grew an organisation to help stamp out the evil. About the same time, a mass meeting was held in Vicksburg, Miss., and an Anti-Miscegenation League was formed.

The hatred and fear of such relationships have grown most rapidly, of course, among the better classes of white people. The class of white men who consort with Negro women at the present time is of a much lower sort than it was five or ten years ago, or than it was in slavery times.

And the Negroes on their part are also awakening to the seriousness of this problem. I found in several Negro communities women's clubs and other organisations which are trying, feebly enough, but significantly trying, to stem the evil from their side. It is a terrible slough to get out of. Negro women, and especially the more comely and intelligent of them, are surrounded by temptations difficult indeed to meet. It has been and is a struggle in Negro communities, especially village communities, to get a moral standard established which will make such relationships with white men unpopular. In some places to-day, the Negro concubines of white men are received in the Negro churches and among the Negroes generally, and honoured rather than ostracised. They are often among the most intelligent of the Negro women, they often have the best homes and the most money to contribute to their churches. They are proud of their light-coloured children. And yet, as the Negroes begin to be educated, they develop an intense hatred of these conditions: and the utter withdrawal of the best sort of Negro families from any white associations is due in part to the dread of such temptations. I shall never forget the bitterness in the reply of a coloured blacksmith who had a number of good-looking girls. I said to him jokingly:

"I suppose you are going to send them to college."

"Why should I?" he asked. "What good will it do? Educate them to live with some white man!"

The Tragedy of the Negro Girl

A friend of mine, Southern by birth, told me a story of an experience he had at Nashville, where he went to deliver an address at Fisk University, a Negro college. On his way home in the dark, he chanced to walk close behind two mulatto girls who had been at the lecture. They were discussing it. One of them said:

"Well, it's no use. There is no chance down here for a yellow girl. It's either get away from the South — or the usual thing."

In that remark lay a world of bitter knowledge of conditions.

It is remarkable, indeed, that the Negroes should have begun to develop moral standards as rapidly as they have. For in the South few people *expect* the coloured girl to be moral: everything is against her morality. In the first place, the home life of the great mass of Negroes is still primitive. They are crowded together in one or two rooms, they get no ideas of privacy, or of decency. The girls are the prey not only of white men but of men of their own race. The highest ideal before their eyes in many cases is the finely dressed, prosperous concubine of a white man. Moreover, in nearly all Southern towns, houses of prostitution are relegated to the Negro quarter. At Montgomery, Ala., I saw such places in respectable Negro neighbourhoods, against which the Negro people had repeatedly and bitterly objected to the city authorities, to no purpose. The example of such places of vice on Negro children is exactly what it would be on white children. In the same way, although it seems unbelievable, Negro schools in several cities have been built in vice districts. I saw a fine new brick school for coloured children at Louisville placed in one of the very nastiest streets of the city. The same conditions surround at least one coloured school which I saw at New Orleans.

And yet the South, permitting such training in vice, wonders at Negro immorality and is convulsed over the crime of rape. Demanding that the Negro be self-restrained, white men set the example in every way from concubinage down, of immorality and lack of restraint. They sow the whirlwind and look for no crop!

When the coloured girl grows up, she goes to service in a white family, where she either sleeps in an outbuilding (the survival of the old system of Negro "quarters") or goes home at night. In either event the mistress rarely pays the slightest attention to her conduct in this particular. I talked with a woman, a fine type of the old gentlefolk, who expressed with frankness a common conviction in the South.

"We don't consider," she said, "that the Negroes have any morals. Up North where I was visiting this summer I was amazed to find women with coloured servants looking after them, trying to keep them in at night and prevent mischief. We never do that; we know it is n't any use."

It may be imagined how difficult it is in such an atmosphere for Negroes to build up moral standards, or to live decently. If there ever was a human tragedy in this world it is the tragedy of the Negro girl.

Relations Between White Men and Negro Women

Illicit relationships between the races have not gone on without causing many a troubled conscience. Nor has a difference in colour always deadened the deeper feelings of the human heart. In spite of laws and colour lines, human nature, wherever found, is profoundly alike. In making my inquiries among coloured colleges I found to my astonishment that in nearly all of them mulatto boys and girls are being educated, and well educated, by their white fathers. A number of them are at Atlanta University, Tuskegee, Hampton, Fisk — indeed, at all of the colleges. And Wilberforce College, next after Lincoln University of Chester County, Pa., the oldest Negro institution of learning in the country, founded in 1856, was largely supported in slavery times by Southern white men who felt a moral obligation to educate their coloured sons and daughters. Large farms around Wilberforce (near Xenia) which I have visited were originally bought by Southern slave-owners for their mulatto children, where they could get away from the South and grow up in a free state. Some of these mulatto children, educated in Latin and Greek, with too much money and little to do, went straight to the devil, while others conserved their property, and it is to-day in the hands of their descendants.

Thus the relations between white men and Negro women even to-day, though marriage is forbidden by law, are sometimes remarkable in their expression of the deepest emotions of the human heart. I shall never forget the story of one such case among many that I heard in the South. I withhold the names in this case although the story is widely known among the people in that part of Alabama. At —— lives a planter of prominence who was formerly on the staff of the governor of the state. He had no white family, but everyone knew that he lived with a mulatto woman and was raising a coloured family. When the boys and girls were old enough, he sent them to Atlanta University, to Tuskegee, and to Spellman Seminary, providing them plentifully with money. He also paid for his wife's sister's schooling.

A year or so ago his mulatto "wife" died; and he was heart-broken. He sent for his boys to come from college and let it be known that he would have something to say at the funeral. Many white and coloured people, therefore, attended and followed the body of the Negro woman to the cemetery. At the grave, General —— stepped forward and raised his hand.

"I have just one word to say here to-day. These children who are here have always gone by their mother's name. I want to acknowledge them now in front of all these people as my children; and henceforth they will bear my name. I wish also to say that this woman who lies here was my wife, not by law, but in the sight of God. I here acknowledge her. This is a duty I have to do not only to this woman but to God. When I leave my property I shall leave it to those children, and shall see that they get it."

Intermarriage of the Races in the North

So much for Southern conditions. How is it in the North where intermarriage is not forbidden by law?

In 1903, during a heated political campaign in Mississippi, United States Senator Money⁵ repeatedly made the assertion that in Massachusetts in the previous year, because there were no laws to separate the Negro and prevent intermarriage, 2,000 white women had married Negro men. I heard echoes of Senator Money's statistics in several places in the South.

I have made a careful investigation of the facts in several northern cities, and I have been surprised to discover how little intermarriage there really is.

If intermarriage in the North were increasing largely, Boston,

5. Hernando De Soto Money, United States representative 1875-1885, 1893-1897, United States senator 1897-1911.

being the city where the least race prejudice exists and where the proportion of mulattoes is largest, would show it most plainly. As a matter of fact, in the year 1902, when according to Senator Money, 2,000 white women married coloured men, there were in Boston, which contains the great bulk of the Negro population of Massachusetts, just twenty-nine inter-racial marriages.

Although the Negro population of Boston has been steadily increasing, the number of marriages between the races, which remained about stationary from 1875 to 1890, has since 1900 been rapidly decreasing. Here are the exact figures as given by the registry department:

RACIAL INTERMARRIAGES IN BOSTON

	Groom Coloured Bride White	Groom White Bride Coloured	Total Mixed Marriages		Groom Coloured Bride White	Groom White Bride Coloured	Total Mixed Marriages
1900	32	3	35	1903	27	2	29
1901	30	1	31	1904	27	1	28
1902	25	4	29	1905	17	2	19

At Boston and in other Northern towns I made inquiries in regard to the actual specific instances of intermarriage.

There are two classes of cases, first, what may be called the intellectuals; highly educated mulattoes who marry educated white women. I have the history of a number of such inter-marriages, but there is not space here to relate the really interesting life stories which have grown out of them. One of the best-known Negro professors in the country has a white wife. I saw the home where they live under almost ideal surroundings. A mulatto doctor of a Southern town married a white girl who was a graduate of Wellesley College; they had trouble in the South and have "gone over to white" and are now living in the North. They have two children. A Negro business man of Boston has a white wife; they celebrated recently the twenty-fifth anniversary of their marriage.

But such cases as these are rare. In the great majority of intermarriages the white women belong to the lower walks of life. They are German, Irish, or other foreign women, respectable, but ignorant. As far as I can see from investigating a number of such cases, the home life is as happy as that of other people in the same stratum of life. But the white woman who thus marries a Negro is speedily declassed: she is ostracised by the white people, and while she finds a certain place among the Negroes, she is not even readily accepted as a Negro. In short, she is cut off from both races. When I was at Xenia, O., I was told of a case of a white man who was arrested for living with a Negro woman. The magistrate compelled him to marry the Negro woman as the worst punishment he could invent!

For this reason, although there are no laws in most Northern states against mixed marriages, and although the Negro population has been increasing, the number of intermarriages is not only not increasing, but in many cities, as in Boston, it is decreasing. It is an unpopular institution!

No one phase of the race question has aroused more acrimonious discussion than that of the Mulatto, especially as to the comparative physical strength and intelligence of the black Negro and the mulatto, a subject which cannot be here entered into.

Most Leaders of the Negro Race are Mulattoes

This much I know from my own observation: most of the leading men of the race to-day in every line of activity are mulattoes. Both Booker T. Washington and Dr. DuBois are mulattoes. Frederick Douglass was a mulatto. The foremost literary men, Charles W. Chesnutt and William Stanley Braithwaite, are mulattoes; the foremost painter of the race, H. O. Tanner, whose pictures have been in the Luxembourg, and who has been an honour to American art, is a mulatto. Both Judge Terrell[6] and his wife, Mary Church Terrell, who is a member of the School Board of Washington, are mulattoes. On the other hand, there are notable exceptions to the rule. W. T. Vernon, Register of the United States Treasury, and Professor Kelly Miller of Washington, D. C., one of the ablest men of his race, both have the appearance of being full-blooded Negroes. Paul Lawrence Dunbar, the poet, was an undoubted Negro; so was J. C. Price, a brilliant orator; so is M. C. B. Mason, secretary of the Southern Aid Society of the Methodist Church.

6. Robert H. Terrell was appointed justice of the peace in the District of Columbia by President Theodore Roosevelt. He later served as a municipal judge in the District.

Full-blooded Negroes often make brilliant school and college records, even in comparison with white boys. It is the judgment of Hampton Institute, after years of careful observation, that there is no difference in ability between light and dark Negroes. I quote from the *Southern Workman*, published at Hampton:

The question as to the comparative intelligence of light and dark Negroes is one that is not easily settled. After long years of observation Hampton's records show that about an equal number of mulattoes and pure blacks have made advancement in their studies and at their work. While it is probable that the lighter students are possessed of a certain quickness which does not belong to the darker, there is a power of endurance among the blacks that does not belong to their lighter brethren.

As to the comparative accomplishment of light and dark Negroes after leaving school, the evidence is so confusing that I would not dare to enter upon a generalisation: that question must be left to the great scientific sociologist who will devote a lifetime to this most interesting problem in human life.

MRS. BOOKER T. WASHINGTON   MRS. ROBERT H. TERRELL

TWO OF THE LEADING WOMEN OF THE NEGRO RACE

PAUL REED   WILL CATO

Negroes lynched by being burned alive at Statesboro, Georgia

NEGROES OF THE CRIMINAL TYPE

Pictures taken in the Atlanta Jail

Will Johnson, arrested, charged with the Camp assault.   Lucius Frazier, who entered a home in the residence district of Atlanta.

CHAPTER IX

LYNCHINGS, SOUTH AND NORTH

MOST of the studies for this book were made in 1906, 1907, and 1908, but I investigated the subject of lynching, South and North, in the fall of 1904. Since that time the feeling against mob-vengeance has been gaining strength throughout the country and the number of lynchings has been steadily decreasing. But the number is still appalling and many recent cases, especially in the black belt, have been accompanied by brutal excesses. My studies made four years ago are typical of present conditions; I have, indeed, confirmed them by a somewhat careful examination made last year (1907) of two or three recent cases.

Lynch-law reached its height in the late eighties and early nineties. In the sixteen years from 1884 to 1900 the number of persons lynched in the United States was 2,516. Of these 2,080 were in the Southern states and 436 in the North; 1,678 were Negroes and 801 were white men; 2,465 were men and 51 were women. I am here using the accepted (indeed the only) statistics — those collected by the Chicago *Tribune*.[1] As showing the gradual growth of the sentiment against mob-law I can do no better than to give the record of lynchings for a number of successive years:

1891	192	1900	116
1892	235	1901	135
1893	200	1902	96
1894	190	1903	104
1895	171	1904	87
1896	131	1905	66
1897	166	1906	73
1898	127	1907	56
1899	107		

Before I take up the account of specific cases an analysis of the lynchings for the years 1906 and 1907 will help to show in what states mob rule is most often invoked and for what

[1]. These figures are generally in line with those later compiled for this period by Tuskegee Institute and the N.A.A.C.P.

offences lynchings are most common. Mississippi, Alabama, Louisiana and Georgia — the black belt states — are thus seen to have the worst records, and the figures here given do not include the men killed in the Atlanta riot which would add twelve to the Georgia record for 1906:

Following is the comparative number of lynchings for the two years.

State	1907	1906
Alabama	13	5
Arkansas	3	4
Colorado	—	1
Florida	—	6
Georgia	6	9
Indian Territory	2	1
Iowa	1	—
Kentucky	1	3
Louisiana	8	9
Maryland	2	1
Mississippi	12	13
Missouri	—	3
Nebraska	1	—
North Carolina	—	5
Oklahoma	2	—
South Carolina	1	2
Tennessee	1	5
Texas	3	6
Totals	**56**	**73**

Of those lynched in 1907, 49 were Negro men, three Negro women and four white men. By methods:

Hanging	31
Shot to death	17
Hanged and shot	3
Shot and burned	2
Beaten to death	1
Kicked to death	1

The offences for which these men and woman were lynched range from stealing seventy-five cents and talking with white girls over the telephone, to rape and murder. Here is the list:

For being father of boy who jostled white women	1
For being victor over white man in fight	1
Attempted murder	5
Murder of wife	1
Murder of husband and wife	1
Murder of wife and stepson	1
Murder of mistress	1

Manslaughter	.	.	.	.	.	.	.	.	.	10
Accessory to murder	.	.	.	.	.	.	.	.	.	1
Rape	.	.	.	.	.	.	.	.	.	8
Attempted rape	.	.	.	.	.	.	.	.	.	11
Raping own stepdaughter	.	.	.	.	.	.	.	.	1
For being wife and son of a raper	.	.	.	.	.	.	2
Protecting fugitive from posse	.	.	.	.	.	.	.	1
Talking to white girls over telephone	.	.	.	.	.	.	1
Expressing sympathy for mob's victim	.	.	.	.	.	.	3
Three-dollar debt	.	.	.	.	.	.	.	.	.	2
Stealing seventy-five cents	.	.	.	.	.	.	.	.	1
Insulting white man	.	.	.	.	.	.	.	.	.	1
Store burglary	.	.	.	.	.	.	.	.	.	3

In making my study I visited four towns where lynchings had taken place, two in the South, Statesboro in Ga. and Huntsville in Ala.; and two in the North, Springfield, O., and Danville, Ill.

I.—LYNCHING IN THE SOUTH

Statesboro, Ga., where two Negroes were burned alive under the most shocking circumstances, on August 16, 1904, is a thrifty county seat located about seventy miles from Savannah.

For a hundred years a settlement has existed there, but it was not until the people discovered the wealth of the turpentine forests and of the sea-island cotton industry that the town became highly prosperous. Since 1890 it has doubled in population every five years, having in 1904 some 2,500 people. Most of the town is newly built. A fine, new court-house stands in the city square, and there are new churches, a large, new academy, a new water-works system and telephones, electric lights, rural free delivery — everywhere the signs of improvement and progress. It is distinctly a town of the New South, developed almost exclusively by the energy of Southerners and with Southern money. Its population is pure American, mostly of old Carolina, Georgia, and Virginia stock. Fully 70 per cent of the inhabitants are church members — Baptists, Presbyterians, and Methodists — and the town has not had a saloon in twenty-five years and rarely has a case of drunkenness. There are no beggars and practically no tramps. A poorhouse, built several years ago, had to be sold because no one would go to it. The farms are small, for the most part, and owned by the farmers themselves; only 8 per cent. of them are mortgaged. There are schools for both white and coloured children, though the school year is short and education not compulsory.

In short, this is a healthy, temperate, progressive American town — a country city, self-respecting, ambitious, with a good future before it — the future of the New South.

Character of the Negro Population

About 40 per cent. of the population of the county consists of Negroes. Here as elsewhere there are to be found two very distinct kinds of Negroes — as distinct as the classes of white men. The first of these is the self-respecting, resident Negro. Sometimes he is a land-owner, more often a renter; he is known to the white people, employed by them, and trusted by them. In Statesboro, as in most of the South, a large proportion of the Negroes are of this better class. On the other hand, one finds everywhere many of the so-called "worthless Negroes," perhaps a growing class, who float from town to town, doing rough work, having no permanent place of abode, not known to the white population generally. The turpentine industry has brought many such Negroes to the neighbourhood of Statesboro. Living in the forest near the turpentine-stills, and usually ignorant and lazy, they and all their kind, both in the country districts and in the city, are doubly unfortunate in coming into contact chiefly with the poorer class of white people, whom they often meet as industrial competitors.

Danger from the Floating Negro

In all the towns I visited, South as well as North, I found that this floating, worthless Negro caused most of the trouble. He prowls the roads by day and by night; he steals; he makes it unsafe for women to travel alone. Sometimes he has gone to school long enough to enable him to read a little and to write his name, enough education to make him hate the hard work of the fields and aspire to better things, without giving him the determination to earn them. He has little or no regard for the family relations or home life, and when he commits a crime or is tired of one locality, he sets out, unencumbered, to seek new fields, leaving his wife and children without the slightest compunction.

About six miles from the city of Statesboro lived Henry Hodges, a well-to-do planter. He had a good farm, he ran three ploughs, as they say in the cotton country, and rumour reported that he had money laid by. Coming of an old family, he was widely related in Bulloch County, and his friendliness and kindness had given him and his family a large circle of acquaintances. Family ties and friendships, in old-settled communities like those in the South, are influences of much greater importance in fixing public opinion and deciding political and social questions than they are in the new and heterogeneous communities of the North.

The South is still, so far as the white population is concerned, a sparsely settled country. The farmers often live far apart; the roads are none too good. The Hodges home was in a lonely place, the nearest neighbours being Negroes, nearly half a mile distant. No white people lived within three-quarters of a mile. Hodges had been brought up among Negroes, he employed them, he was kind to them. To one of the Negroes suspected of complicity in the subsequent murder, he had loaned his shotgun; another, afterward lynched, called at his home the very night before the murder, intending then to rob him, and Hodges gave him a bottle of turpentine to cure a "snake-graze."

Story of the Murder

On the afternoon of July 29, 1904, Mr. Hodges drove to a neighbour's house to bring his nine-year-old girl home from school. No Southern white farmer, especially in thinly settled regions like Bulloch County, dares permit any woman or girl of his family to go out anywhere alone, for fear of the criminal Negro.

"You don't know and you can't know," a Georgian said to me, "what it means down here to live in constant fear lest your wife or daughter be attacked on the road, or even in her home. Many women in the city of Statesboro dare not go into their backyards after dark. Every white planter knows that there is always danger for his daughters to visit even the nearest neighbour, or for his wife to go to church without a man to protect her."

It is absolutely necessary to understand this point of view before one can form a true judgment upon conditions in the South.

When Hodges arrived at his home that night, it was already dark. The little girl ran to join her mother; the father drove to the barn. Two Negroes — perhaps more — met him there and beat his brains out with a stone and a buggy brace. Hearing the noise, Mrs. Hodges ran out with a lamp and set it on the gate-post. The Negroes crept up — as nearly as can be gathered from the contradictory stories and confessions — and murdered her there in her doorway with peculiar brutality. Many of the crimes committed by Negroes are marked with almost animal-like ferocity. Once aroused to murderous rage, the Negro does not stop with mere killing; he bruises and batters his victim out of all semblance to humanity. For the moment, under stress of passion, he seems to revert wholly to savagery.

The Negroes went into the house and ransacked it for money. The little girl, who must have been terror-stricken beyond belief, hid behind a trunk; the two younger children, one a child of two years, the other a mere baby, lay on the bed. Finding no money, the Negroes returned to their homes. Here they evidently began to dread the consequences of their deed, for toward midnight they returned to the Hodges home. During all this time the little girl had been hiding there in darkness, with the bodies of her father and mother in the doorway. When the Negroes appeared, she either came out voluntarily, hoping that friends had arrived, or she was dragged out.

"Where's the money?" demanded the Negroes.

The child got out all she had, a precious five-cent piece, and offered it to them on condition that they would not hurt her. One of them seized her and beat her to death.

I make no excuse for telling these details; they *must be told*, else we shall not see the depths or the lengths of this problem.

Burning of the Hodges Home

The Negroes then dragged the bodies of Mr. and Mrs. Hodges into their home and set the house afire. As nearly as can be made out from the subsequent confessions, the two younger children were burned alive.

When the neighbours reached the scene of the crime, the house was wholly consumed, only the great end chimney left standing, and the lamp still burning on the gate-post.

Well, these Southerners are warm-hearted, home-loving people. Everybody knew and respected the Hodges — their friends in the church, their many relatives in the county — and the effect of this frightful crime described in all its details, may possibly be imagined by Northern people living quietly and peacefully in their homes. When two of the prominent citizens of the town told me, weeks afterward, of the death of the little girl, they could not keep back their tears.

The murder took place on Friday night; on Saturday the Negroes, Paul Reed and Will Cato, were arrested with several other suspects, including two Negro preachers. Both Reed and Cato were of the illiterate class; both had been turpentine workers, living in the forest, far from contact with white people. Cato was a floater from South Carolina. Reed was born in the county, but he was a good type of the worthless and densely ignorant Negro.

It is a somewhat common impression that a whole town loses itself in a passion of anarchy, and is not satisfied until the criminals are killed. But in spite of the terrible provocation and the intense feeling, there yet existed in Statesboro exactly such a feeling for the sacredness of law, such intelligent Americanism, as exists in your town or mine. Not within the present generation had a lynching taken place in the town, and the people were deeply concerned to preserve the honour and good name of their community. In the midst of intense excitement a meeting of good citizens, both white and black, was called in the court-house. It was presided over by J. A. Brannan, one of the foremost citizens. Speeches were made by Mayor Johnstone, by the ministers of the town, and by other citizens, including a Negro, all calling for good order and the calm and proper enforcement of the law.

Attempts to Prevent the Lynching

And the regular machinery of justice was put in motion with commendable rapidity. Fearing a lynching, the Negroes who had been arrested were sent to Savannah and there lodged in jail. A grand jury was immediately called, indictments were found, and in two weeks — the shortest possible time under the law — the Negroes were brought back from Savannah for trial. To protect them, two military companies, one from Statesboro, one from Savannah, were called out. The proof of guilt was absolutely conclusive, and, although the Negroes were given every advantage to which they were entitled under the law, several prominent attorneys having been appointed to defend them, they were promptly convicted and sentenced to be hanged.

In the meantime great excitement prevailed. The town was crowded for days with farmers who came flocking in from every direction. The crime was discussed and magnified; it was common talk that the " niggers of Bulloch County are getting too bigoty" — that they would n't "keep their places." Fuel was added to the flame by the common report that the murderers of the Hodges family were members of a Negro society known as the "Before Day Club," and wild stories were told of other murders that had been planned, the names of intended victims even being reported.

On the Sunday night before the trial, two Negro women, walking down the street are said to have crowded two respectable white girls off the sidewalk. A crowd dragged the women from a church where they had gone, took them to the outskirts of the town, whipped them both violently, and ordered them to leave the county.

"Let the law take its course," urged the good citizen. "The Negroes have been sentenced to be hanged, let them be hanged legally; we want no disgrace to fall on the town."

How the Lynchers Themselves Defend a Lynching

But as the trial progressed and the crowd increased, there were louder and louder expressions of the belief that hanging was too good for such a crime. I heard intelligent citizens argue that a Negro criminal, in order to be a hero in the eyes of his people, does not mind being hanged! Another distinct feeling developed — a feeling that I found in other lynching towns: that somehow the courts and the law were not to be trusted to punish the criminals properly. Although Reed and Cato were sentenced to be hanged, the crowd argued that "the lawyers would get them off," that "the case would be appealed, and they would go free."

Members of the mob tried to get Sheriff Kendrick to promise not to remove the Negroes to Savannah, fearing that in some way they would be taken beyond the reach of justice.

In other words, there existed a deep-seated conviction that justice too often miscarried in Bulloch County and that murderers commonly escaped punishment through the delays and technicalities of the law.

A Habit of Man-killing

And there is, unfortunately, a foundation for this belief. In every lynching town I visited I made especial inquiry as to the prevalence of crime, particularly as to the degree of certainty of punishment for crime. In all of them property is safe; laws looking to the protection of goods and chattels are executed with a fair degree of precision; for we are a business-worshipping people. But I was astounded by the extraordinary prevalence in all these lynching counties, North as well as South, of crimes of violence, especially homicide, accompanied in every case by a poor enforcement of the law. Bulloch County, with barely twenty-five thousand inhabitants, had thirty-two homicides in a little more than five years before the lynching — an annual average of one to every four thousand five hundred people (the average in the entire United States being one to nine thousand). Within eight months prior to the Hodges lynching, no fewer than ten persons (including the Hodges family) were murdered in Bulloch County. In twenty-eight years, notwithstanding the high rate of homicides, only three men, all Negroes, have been legally hanged, while four men — three Negroes and one white man — have been lynched.

It is well understood that if the murderer has friends or a little money to hire lawyers, he can, especially if he happens to be white, nearly always escape with a nominal punishment. These facts are widely known and generally commented upon. In his subsequent charge to the grand jury, Judge Daley said that the mob was due in part to "delays in the execution of law and to the people becoming impatient."

I am not telling these things with any idea of excusing or palliating the crime of lynching, but with the earnest intent of setting forth all the facts, so that we may understand just what the feelings and impulses of a lynching town really are, good as well as bad. Unless we diagnose the case accurately, we cannot hope to discover effective remedies.

Psychology of the Mob

In the intense, excited crowd gathered around the court-house on this Tuesday, the 16th of August, other influences were also at work, influences operating in a greater or less degree in every lynching mob. We are accustomed to look upon a mob as an entity, the expression of a single concrete feeling; it is not; it is itself torn with dissensions and compunctions, swayed by conflicting emotions. Similarly, we look upon a militia company as a sort of machine, which, set in operation, automatically performs a certain definite service. But it is not. It is made up of young men, each with his own intense feelings, prejudices, ideals; and it requires unusual discipline to inculcate such a sense of duty that the individual soldier will rise superior to the emotions of the hour. Most of these young men of Statesboro and Savannah really sympathised with the mob; among the crowd the Statesboro men saw their relatives and friends. Some of the officers were ambitious men, hoping to stand for political office. What would happen if they ordered the troops to fire on their neighbours?

And "the nigger deserved hanging," and "why should good white blood be shed for nigger brutes?" At a moment of this sort the clear perception of solemn abstract principles and great civic duties fades away in tumultuous excitement. Yet these soldier boys were not cowards; they have a fighting history; their fathers made good soldiers; they themselves would serve bravely against a foreign enemy, but when called upon for mob service they failed utterly, as they have failed repeatedly, both North and South.

Up to the last moment, although the crowd believed in lynch-

ing and wanted to lynch, there seemed to be no real and
general determination to forestall the law. The mob had no
centre, no fixed purpose, no real plan of action. One determined man, knowing his duty (as I shall show in another story),
and doing it with common sense, could have prevented trouble,
but there was no such man. Captain Hitch, of the Savannah
Company, a vacillating commander, allowed the crowd to pack
the court-house, to stream in and out among his soldiers; he
laid the responsibility (afterward) on the sheriff, and the sheriff
shouldered it back upon him. In nearly all the cases I investigated, I found the same attempt to shift responsibility, the same
lack of a responsible head. Our system too often fails when
mob stress is laid upon it — unless it happens that some
strong man stands out, assumes responsibility, and becomes
a momentary despot.

How the Soldiers Were Overpowered

A mob, no matter how deeply inflamed, is always cowardly.
This mob was no exception. It crowded up, crowded up,
testing authority. It joked with the soldiers, and when it found
that the jokes were appreciated, it took further liberties; it
jostled the soldiers — good-humouredly. "You don't dare
fire," it said, and the soldiers made no reply. "Your guns
are n't loaded," it said, and some soldier confessed that they
were not. In tender consideration for the feelings of the mob,
the officers had ordered the men not to load their rifles. The
next step was easy enough; the mob playfully wrenched away
a few of the guns, those behind pushed forward — those behind
always do push forward, knowing they will not be hurt — and
in a moment the whole mob was swarming up the stairs, yelling
and cheering.

In the court-room, sentence had been passed on Reed and
Cato, and the judge had just congratulated the people on
"their splendid regard for the law under very trying conditions."
Then the mob broke in. A brother of the murdered Hodges,
a minister from Texas, rose magnificently to the occasion.
With tears streaming down his face, he begged the mob to let
the law take its course.

"We don't want religion, we want blood," yelled a voice.

The mob was now thoroughly stirred; it ceased to hesitate; it was controlled wholly by its emotions. The leaders plunged down the court-room and into the witness chamber, where the Negroes sat with their wives, Reed's wife with a young baby. The officers of the law accommodatingly indicated the right Negroes, and the mob dragged them out. Hanging was at first proposed, and a man even climbed a telegraph-pole just outside the court-house, but the mob, growing more ferocious as it gathered volume and excitement, yelled its determination:

"Burn them! burn them!"

They rushed up the road, intending to take the Negroes to the scene of the crime. But it was midday in August, with a broiling hot sun overhead and a dusty road underfoot. A mile from town the mob swerved into a turpentine forest, pausing first to let the Negroes kneel and confess. Calmer spirits again counselled hanging, but some one began to recite in a high-keyed voice the awful details of the crime, dwelling especially on the death of the little girl. It worked the mob into a frenzy of ferocity.

"They burned the Hodges and gave them no choice; burn the niggers!"

"Please don't burn me," pleaded Cato. And again: "Hang me or shoot me; please don't burn me!"

Burning of the Negroes

Some one referred the question to the father-in-law of Hodges. He said Hodges's mother wished the men burned. That settled it. Men were sent into town for kerosene oil and chains, and finally the Negroes were bound to an old stump, fagots were heaped around them, and each was drenched with oil. Then the crowd stood back accommodatingly, while a photographer, standing there in the bright sunshine, took pictures of the chained Negroes. Citizens crowded up behind the stump and got their faces into the photograph. When the fagots were lighted, the crowd yelled wildly. Cato, the less stolid of the two Negroes, partly of white blood, screamed with agony; but Reed, black and stolid, bore it like a block of wood. They threw knots and sticks at the writhing creatures, but always left room for the photographer to take more pictures.

And when it was all over, they began, in common with all mobs, to fight for souvenirs. They scrambled for the chains before they were cold, and the precious links were divided among the populace. Pieces of the stump were hacked off, and finally one young man — it must be told — gathered up a few charred remnants of bone, carried them uptown, and actually tried to give them to the judge who presided at the trial of the Negroes, to the utter disgust of that official.

After Effects of Mob-law

This is the law of the mob, that it never stops with the thing it sets out to do. It is exactly like any other manifestation of uncontrolled human passion — given licence it takes more licence, it releases that which is ugly, violent, revengeful in the community as in the individual human heart. I have heard often of a "quiet mob," an "orderly mob," which "went about its business and hanged the nigger," but in all the cases I have known about, and I made special inquiries upon this particular point, not one single mob stopped when the immediate work was done, unless under compulsion. Even good citizens of Statesboro will tell you that "the niggers got only what they deserved," and "it was all right if the mob had only stopped there." But it did not stop there; it never does.

All the stored-up racial animosity came seething to the surface; all the personal grudges and spite. As I have already related, two Negro women were whipped on the Sunday night before the lynching. On the day following the lynching the father of the women was found seeking legal punishment for the men who whipped his daughters, and he himself was taken out and frightfully beaten. On the same day two other young Negroes, of the especially hated "smart nigger" type, were caught and whipped — one for riding a bicycle on the sidewalk, the other, as several citizens told me, "on general principles." But this was not the worst. On Wednesday night an old Negro man and his son — Negroes of the better class — were sitting in their cabin some miles from Statesboro, when they were both shot at through the window and badly wounded. Another respectable Negro, named McBride,² was visited in his home by a white mob, which first whipped his wife, who was confined with a baby three days old, and then beat, kicked, and shot McBride himself so horribly that he died the next day. The better class of citizens, the same men who would, perhaps, condone the burning of Reed and Cato, had no sympathy with this sort of thing. Some of them took McBride's dying statement, and four white men were arrested charged with the murder; but never punished.

Indeed, the mob led directly to a general increase of crime in Bulloch County. As Judge Daley said in his charge to a subsequent grand jury:

"Mob violence begets crime. Crime has been more prevalent since this lynching than ever before. In the middle circuit the courts have been so badly crowded with murder trials that it has been almost impossible to attend to civil business."

Another evil result of the lynching was that it destroyed valuable evidence. The prosecutors had hoped to learn from the convicted Reed and Cato whether or not they had any companions and thereby bring to justice all the other Negroes suspected of complicity in the murder of the Hodges. If the Before Day Club ever existed and had a criminal purpose (which is doubtful) most of the members who composed it were left at large, awaiting the next opportunity to rob and murder.

Mob Justice and the Cotton Crop

Mob-law has not only represented a moral collapse in this community, but it struck, also, at the sensitive pocket of the business interests of the county. Frightened by the threatening attitude of the whites, the Negroes began to leave the county. It was just at the beginning of the cotton-picking season, when labour of every sort was much needed, Negro labour especially. It would not do to frighten away all the Negroes. On Thursday some of the officials and citizens of Statesboro got together, appointed extra marshals, and gave notice that there were to be no more whippings, and the mob spirit disappeared — until next time.

2. Sebastian McBride.

But what of the large Negro population of Statesboro during all this excitement? The citizens told the "decent Negroes": "We don't want to hurt you; we know you; you are all right; go home and you won't be hurt." Go home they did, and there was not a Negro to be seen during all the time of the lynching. From inquiry among the Negroes themselves, I found that many of them had no voice to raise against the burning of Reed and Cato. This was the grim, primitive eye-for-an-eye logic that they used, in common with many white men:

"Reed and Cato burned the Hodges; they ought to be burned."

Even Cato's wife used this logic.

But all the Negroes were bitter over the indiscriminate whippings which followed the lynching. These whippings widened the breach between the races, led to deeper suspicion and hatred, fertilised the soil for future outbreaks. In the same week that I visited Statesboro, no fewer than three cotton-gins in various parts of Bulloch County were mysteriously burned at night, and while no one knew the exact origin of the fires, it was openly charged that they were caused by revengeful Negroes. None of these terrible after-effects would have taken place if the law had been allowed to follow its course.

A Fighting Parson

The overwhelming majority of the people of Bulloch County undoubtedly condoned the lynching, even believed in it heartily and completely. And yet, as I have said, there was a strong dissenting opposition among the really thoughtful, better-class citizens. All the churches of Statesboro came out strongly for law and order. The Methodist church, led by a fighting parson, the Rev. Whitely Langston, expelled two members who had been in the mob — an act so unpopular that the church lost twenty-five members of its congregation. Of course, the members of the mob were known, but none of them was ever punished. The judge especially charged the grand jury to investigate the lynching, and this was its report:

"We deplore the recent lawlessness in our city and community, specially referred to by his Honour, Judge A. F. Daley, in his able charge. We have investigated the matter in the light of information coming under our personal knowledge and obtained by the examination of a number of witnesses, but we have been unable to find sufficient evidence to warrant indictments. We tender thanks to his Honour, Judge Daley, for his able and comprehensive charge."

A feeble attempt was made to discipline the military officers who allowed the populace to walk over them and take away their guns. A court-martial sat for days in Savannah and finally recommended the dismissal of Captain Hitch from the service of the state; but the Governor let him off with half the penalty suggested. Two lieutenants were also disciplined.

In the state election which followed the lynching, numerous voters in Bulloch County actually scratched the name of Governor Terrell, of Georgia, because he ordered the troops to Statesboro, and substituted the name of Captain Hitch. Sheriff Kendrick, who failed to protect Reed and Cato, was re-elected without opposition.

It was in a tone of deep discouragement that Mayor G. S. Johnstone, of Statesboro, said to me:

"If our grand jury won't indict these lynchers, if our petit juries won't convict, and if our soldiers won't shoot, what are we coming to?"

Revolution of Opinion in the South on Lynching

Conditions at Statesboro are, perhaps, typical of those in most Southern towns. In most Southern towns a lynching would be conducted much as it was in Statesboro; there would be the same objecting but ineffective minority of good citizens, the troops would refuse their duty, and the lynchers would escape in much the same way. And yet, if we were to stop with the account of the Statesboro affair, we should overlook some of the greatest influences now affecting the lynching problem in the South. No one who visits the South can escape the conviction that, with its intensified industrial life, and the marvelous development and enrichment of the whole country, other equally momentous, if less tangible, changes are taking place. Public opinion is developing along new lines, old, set prejudices are breaking up, and there is, among other evident influences, a marked revolution in the attitude of the Southern people and the Southern newspapers on the lynching question. I turn now to the lynching at Huntsville, Ala., which reveals in a striking manner some of the features of the new revolt in the South against mob-law.

A Negro Crime at Huntsville, Ala.

One evening in September, 1904, a Negro of Huntsville, Ala., asked an old peddler named Waldrop for a ride. Waldrop was a kindly old man, well known and respected throughout Madison County; he drove into the city two or three times a week with vegetables and chickens to sell, and returned with the small product of his trade in his pocket.

Waldrop knew the Negro, Maples,³ and, although Maples was of the worthless sort, and even then under indictment for thieving, the peddler made room for him in his waggon, and they rode out of the town together. They drove into a lonely road. They crossed a little bridge. Tall trees shaded and darkened the place. Night was falling. The Negro picked up a stone and beat out the brains of the inoffensive old man, robbed him, and left him lying there at the roadside, while the horse wandered homeward.

How a murder cries out! The murderer fled in the darkness but it was as if he left great footprints. The next day, in Huntsville, the law laid its hand on his shoulder.

Now, Huntsville is one of the best cities in Alabama. No other city, perhaps, preserves more of the aristocratic habiliments of the older South. It was the first capital of the state. Seven governors lie buried in its cemetery; its county house, its bank, some of its residences are noble examples of the architecture of the ante-bellum South. And while preserving these evidences of the wealth and refinement of an older civilisation, few cities in the South have responded more vigorously to the new impulses of progress and development. Its growth during the last few years has been little short of amazing. Northern capital has come in; nine cotton-mills have been built, drawing a large increase of population, and stimulating the development of the country in every direction.

3. Horace Maples.

It is a fine, orderly, progressive city — intensely American, ambitious, self-respecting.

Relation of Lynching to Business Success

Huntsville has had its share of lynchings in the past. Within twenty years seven Negroes and one white man had been the victims of mobs in Madison County. The best citizens knew what a lynching meant; they knew how the mob began, and what invariably followed its excesses, and they wanted no more such horrors. But this revolt was not wholly moral. With awakening industrial ambition the people realised that disorder had a tendency to frighten away capital, stop immigration, and retard development generally. Good business demands good order. This feeling has been expressed in various forms and through many channels. It existed in Statesboro, but it was by no means as vigorous as in this manufacturing city of Huntsville. We find, for instance, Congressman Richardson[4] of Alabama, a citizen of Huntsville, saying in a speech on the floor of the House of Representatives:

"Why, Mr. Chairman, we have more reason in the South to observe the law and do what is right than any other section of this Union."

The Atlanta *Constitution* presents the same view in vigorous language:

Aside entirely from the consideration of the evil effects of the mob spirit in breeding general disrespect for the law, and aside from the question of the inevitable brutalising effect of lynching upon those who are spectators — and the effect goes even further — the practical question arises: Can we at the South afford it?

Is there any use blinding ourselves to the fact, patent to everybody, that it is this sort of thing that has kept hundreds of thousands of desirable immigrants from coming to the Southern states?

Story of a Bold Judge

When the murderer of the peddler Waldrop was arrested, therefore, the thoughtful and progressive people of the city — the kind who are creating the New South — took immediate steps to prevent mob disturbance. The city was fortunate in having an able, energetic young man as its circuit judge — a judge, the son of a judge, who saw his duty clearly, and who was not afraid to act, even though it might ruin his immediate political

4. William Richardson, member of the United States House of Representatives 1900-1914.

future, as, indeed, it did. Rare qualities in these days! The murder was committed Tuesday, September 6th, the Negro was arrested Wednesday, Judge Speake[5] impanelled a special grand jury without waiting a moment, and that very afternoon, within six hours after the Negro's arrest and within twenty hours after the crime was committed, the Negro was formally indicted. Arrangements were then made to call a special trial jury within a week, in the hope that the prospect of immediate punishment would prevent the gathering of a mob.

A Record of Homicide as a Cause of Lynching

But, unfortunately, we find here in Madison County not only a history of lynching — a habit, it may be called — but there existed the same disregard for the sacredness of human life which is the common characteristic of most lynching communities, South or North. I made a careful examination of the records of the county. In the five years preceding this lynching, no fewer than thirty-three murder and homicide cases were tried in the courts, besides eight murderers indicted, but not arrested. This is the record of a single county of about forty thousand people. Notwithstanding this record of crime, there had not been a legal hanging in the county, even of a Negro, for nineteen years. It was a fact — well known to everybody in the county — that it was next to impossible to convict a white man for killing. Murderers employed good lawyers, they appealed their cases, they brought political friendships to bear, and the relationships between the old families were so far extended that they reached even into the jury room. As a consequence, nearly every white murderer went free. Only a short time before the lynching, Fred Stevens a white man, who shot a white man in a quarrel over a bucket of water, was let out with a fine of $50, costs, and thirty days in jail. This for a *killing*. And the attorney for Stevens actually went into court afterward and asked to have the costs cut down. Negroes who committed homicide, though more vigorously punished than white murderers, yet frequently escaped with five or ten years in the penitentiary — especially if they had money or a few white friends. All this had induced a contempt of the courts of justice — a fear that, after all, through the delays and techni-

5. Judge Paul Speake of the sixteenth Alabama judicial circuit.

calities of the law and the compassion of the jury, the murderer of Waldrop would not be punished as he deserved. This was the substance of the reasoning I heard repeatedly: "That Negro, Maples, ought to have been hanged; we were not sure the jury would hang him; we hanged him to protect ourselves."

I met an intelligent farmer during a drive through Madison County. Here are some of the things he said, and they voiced closely what I heard in one form or another from many people in all walks of life:

"Life is cheap in Madison County. If you have a grudge against a man, kill him; don't wound him. If you wound him, you'll likely be sent up; if you kill him, you can go free. They often punish more severely for carrying concealed weapons or even for chicken stealing in Madison County than they do for murder."

So strong was the evidence in one murder case in an adjoining circuit that Judge Kyle[6] instructed the jury to find the murderer guilty; the jury deliberately returned a verdict, "Not guilty." The Alabama system of justice is cursed by the professional juror chosen by politicians, and often open to political influences. This, with the unlimited right of appeal and the great number of peremptory challenges allowed to the defence in accepting jurymen, gives such power to the lawyers for the defendant that convictions are exceedingly difficult. Oftentimes, also, the prosecuting attorney is a young, inexperienced lawyer, ill-paid, who is no match for the able attorneys employed by the defendant.

No, it is not all race prejudice that causes lynchings, even in the South. One man in every six lynched in this country in 1903 — the year before the lynching I am describing — was a white man. It is true that a Negro is often the victim of mob-law where a white man would not be, but the chief cause certainly seems to lie deeper, in the widespread contempt of the courts, and the unpunished subversion of the law in this country, both South and North. This, indeed, would probably be the sole cause of lynching, were it not for the crime of rape, of which I wish to speak again a little later.

Composition of the Mob at Huntsville

Well, a mob began gathering in Huntsville before the grand jury had ceased its labours. It was chiefly composed of the

6. Judge Osceola Kyle of the eighth Alabama judicial circuit.

workmen from the cotton-mills. These are of a peculiar class — pure American stock, naturally of high intelligence, but almost wholly illiterate — men from the hills, the descendants of the "poor white trash," who never owned slaves, and who have always hated the Negroes. The poor whites are and have been for a long time in certain lines the industrial competitors of the Negroes, and the jealousy thus engendered accounts in no small degree for the intensity of the race feeling.

Anticipating trouble, Judge Speake ordered the closing of all the saloons — there were then only fifteen to a population of some twenty-one thousand — and called out the local military company. But the mob ran over the militiamen as though they were not there, broke into the jail, built a fire in the hallway, and added sulphur and cayenne pepper. Fearing that the jail would be burned and all the prisoners suffocated, the sheriff released the Negro, Maples, and he jumped out of a second-story window into the mob. They dragged him up the street to the square in the heart of the city. Here, on the pleasant lawn, the Daughters of America were holding a festival, and the place was brilliant with Japanese lanterns. Scattering the women and children, the mob jostled the Negro under the glare of an electric light, just in front of the stately old court-house.

Here impassioned addresses were made by several prominent young lawyers — J. H. Wallace, Jr., W. B. Bankhead, and Solicitor Pettus[7] — urging the observance of law and order. A showing of hands afterward revealed the fact that a large proportion of those present favoured a legal administration of justice. But it was too late now.

A peculiarly dramatic incident fired the mob anew. The Negro was suddenly confronted by the son of the murdered peddler. "Horace," he demanded, "did you kill my old dad ?"

Quivering with fright, the Negro is said to have confessed the crime. He was instantly dragged around the corner, where they hanged him to an elm-tree, and while he dangled there in the light of the gala lanterns, they shot him full of holes. Then they cut off one of his little fingers and parts of his trousers for souvenirs. So he hung until daylight, and crowds of people came out to see.

7. Erle Pettus, solicitor of the sixteenth Alabama judicial circuit.

Effort to Punish the Lynchers

But the forces of law and order here had vigour and energy. Judge Speake, communicating with the Governor, had troops sent from Birmingham, and then, without shilly-shallying or delaying or endeavouring to shift responsibility, he ordered a special grand jury to indict the lynchers the very next day and he saw to it that it was composed of the best citizens in town. When it met, so deep and solemn was its feeling of responsibility that it was opened with prayer, an extraordinary evidence of the awakened conscience of the people. More than this, the citizens generally were so aroused that they held a mass meeting, and denounced the lynching as a "blot upon our civilisation," and declared that "each and every man taking part" with the mob was "guilty of murder." Bold words, but no bolder than the editorials of the newspapers of the town or of the state. Every force of decency and good order was at work. Such strong newspapers as the Birmingham *Age-Herald*, the *Ledger*, and the *News*, the Montgomery *Advertiser*, the Chattanooga *News*, and, indeed, prominent newspapers all over the South united strongly in their condemnation of the lynchers and in their support of the efforts to bring the mob to justice.

Southern Newspapers on Lynching

The Huntsville *Mercury* spoke of the "deep sense of shame felt by our good citizens in being run over by a few lawless spirits."

"There is no justification," said the Birmingham *News*, "for the mob who, in punishing one murderer, made many more."

"This lynching," said the Birmingham *Ledger*, "is a disgrace to our state. The *Ledger* does n't put its ear to the ground to hear from the North, nor does it care what Northern papers say. The crime is our own, and the disgrace falls on us."

"Where, in fact," said the *Age-Herald*, "does such business lead to? The answer is summed up in a word — anarchy!"

It would be well if every community in this country could read the full report of Judge Speake's grand jury. It is a work of the sort struck off only by men stirred to high things by what they feel to be a great crisis; it is of the same metal as the Declaration of Independence. Here is a single paragraph:

Realising that this is a supreme moment in our history; that we must either take a stand for the law to-day or surrender to the mob and to the anarchists for all time; that our actions shall make for good or evil in future generations; forgetting our personal friendships and affiliations, and with malice toward none, but acting only as sworn officers of the state of Alabama, we, the grand jury of Madison County, state of Alabama, find ——

Ten members of the mob were indicted — and not for mere rioting or for breaking into the jail, but for *murder*. The jury also charged Sheriff Rodgers, Mayor Smith, and Chief of Police Overton with wilful neglect and incompetence, and advised their impeachment. No one not understanding the far-reaching family and political relationships in these old-settled Southern communities, and the deep-seated feeling against punishment for the crime of lynching, can form any adequate idea of what a sensation was caused by the charges of the grand jury against the foremost officials of the city. It came like a bolt from a clear sky; it was altogether an astonishing procedure, at first not fully credited. When the utter seriousness of Judge Speake came to be fully recognised, a good many men hurriedly left town. The Birmingham soldiers, led by a captain with backbone, arrested a number of those who remained. Judge Speake ordered a special trial jury, and appointed an able lawyer to assist Prosecutor Pettus in bringing the lynchers to justice. The very next week the trials were begun.

Difficulty of Breaking the Lynching Habit

By this time, however, the usual influences had begun to work; the moral revulsion had carried far, and the rebound had come. The energetic judge and his solicitors found themselves face to face with the bad old jury system, with the deep-seated distrust of the courts, with the rooted habit of non-punishment for lynchers. Moreover, it was found that certain wild young men, with good family connections, had been mixed up in the mob — and all the strong family and political machinery of the county began to array itself against conviction. A community has exactly as hard a road to travel in breaking a bad habit as an individual. The New South is having a struggle to break the habits of the Old South. It was found, also, that the great mass of people in the country, as well as the millworkers in the city, were still strongly in favour of punishment by lynching. One hundred and ten veniremen examined for jurors to try the lynchers were asked this question; "If you were satisfied from the evidence beyond a reasonable doubt that the defendant took part with or abetted the mob in murdering a Negro, would you favour his conviction?" And seventy-six of them answered, "No."

In other words, a large majority believed that a white man should not be punished for lynching a Negro. And when the juries were finally obtained, although the evidence was conclusive, they acquitted the lynchers, one after another. Only one man in one jury stood out for conviction — a young clerk named S. M. Blair, a pretty good type of the modern hero. He hung the jury, and so bitter was the feeling against him among the millworkers that they threatened to boycott his employer.

Relation of Lynching to the "Usual Crime"

This is the reasoning of many of the men chosen as jurors; I heard it over and over again, not only in Huntsville but, in substance, everywhere that I stopped in the South:

"If we convict these men for lynching the Negro, Maples, we shall establish a precedent that will prevent us from lynching for the crime of rape."

Every argument on lynching in the South gets back sooner or later to this question of rape. Ask any high-class citizen — the very highest — if he believes in lynching, and he will tell you roundly, "No." Ask him about lynching for rape, and in ninety-nine cases out of a hundred he will instantly weaken.

"If my sister or my daughter — look here, if your sister or your daughter ——"

Lynching, he says, is absolutely necessary to keep down this crime. You ask him why the law cannot be depended upon, and he replies:

"It is too great an ordeal for the self-respecting white woman to go into court and accuse the Negro ravisher and withstand a public cross-examination. It is intolerable. No woman will do it. And, besides, the courts are uncertain. Lynching is the only remedy."

Yet the South is deeply stirred over the prevalence of lynching. The mob spirit, invoked to punish such a crime as rape, is defended by some people in the North as well as in the South; but once invoked, it spreads and spreads, until to-day lynching for rape forms only a very small proportion of the total number of mob hangings. It spreads until a Negro is lynched for chicken stealing, or for mere "obnoxiousness." In the year 1903, out of 104 lynchings, only 11 were for rape and 10 for attempted rape, while 47 were for murder, 15 for complicity in murderous assault, 4 for arson, 5 for mere "race prejudice," 2 for insults to whites, 1 for making threats, 5 for unknown offenses, 1 for refusing to give information, and 3 were wholly innocent Negroes, lynched because their identity was mistaken. It is probable that lynching in the South would immediately be wiped out, if it were not for the question of rape. You will hear the problem put by thinking Southerners very much in this fashion:

"We must stop mob-law; every month we recognise that fact more clearly. But can we stop mob-law unless we go to the heart of the matter and stop lynching for rape? Is there not a way of changing our methods of legal procedure so that the offender in this crime can be punished without subjecting the victim to the horrible publicity of the courts?"

Governor Cunningham — A Real Leader

But I have wandered from my story. In Acting-Governor Cunningham,[8] the people of Alabama had a leader who was not afraid to handle a dangerous subject like lynching. He sent a court of inquiry to Huntsville, which found the local military company "worthless and inefficient," because it had failed to protect the jail. Immediately, upon the receipt of this report, the Governor dismissed the Huntsville company from the service, every man in it. Quite a contrast from the action at Statesboro! The Governor then went a step further: he ordered the impeachment of the sheriff. A little later Federal Judge Jones[9] took up the case, charged his jury vigorously, and some of the mob rioters were indicted in the federal courts.

8. Dr. Russell M. Cunningham, lieutenant governor of Alabama 1903-1907, and acting governor for several months during that period because of the illness of Governor William D. Jelks.

9. Thomas Goode Jones, governor of Alabama, 1890-1894, was appointed a

Governor Cunningham took a bold stand against mob-law everywhere and anywhere in the state:

"I am opposed to mob-law," he said, "of whatsoever kind, for any and all causes. If lynching is to be justified or extenuated for any crime, be it ever so serious, it will lead to the same method of punishment for other crimes of a less degree of depravity, and through the operation of the process of evolution, will enlarge more and more the field of operation for this form of lawlessness."

It means something also when citizens, in support of their institutions and out of love of their city, rise above politics. Judge Speake had been nominated by the Democrats to succeed himself. A Democratic nomination in Alabama means election. After his vigorous campaign against the lynchers, he became exceedingly unpopular among the majority of the people. They resolved to defeat him. A committee waited on Shelby Pleasants, a prominent Republican lawyer, and asked him to run against Judge Speake, assuring him a certain election.

"I will not be a mob's candidate," he said. "I indorse every action of Judge Speake."

The committee approached several other lawyers, but not one of them would run against the judge, and the Republican newspaper of the town came out strongly in support of Judge Speake, even publishing his name at the head of its editorial columns. Before he could be elected, however, a decision of the State Supreme Court, unconnected in any way with the lynching, followed like fate, and deprived Madison County of his services![10] He was now a private citizen, and even if he had come up for nomination to any political office, he would undoubtedly have been defeated. The New South is not yet strong enough to defy the Old South politically.

Influences Tending to Prevent Future Lynchings in the South

The influences against lynching in the South are constantly growing stronger. With most (not all) of the newspapers, the preachers and the best citizens united against it, the outlook is full of hope. And rural free delivery and country telephones, spreading in every direction, are inestimable influences in the quickening of public opinion. Better roads

judge of the federal district court in Alabama by President Roosevelt in 1901.

10. The act creating Judge Speake's office was ruled unconstitutional by the state supreme court in the fall of 1904.

are being built, the country is settling up with white people, schools are improving and the population generally, after a series of profitable cotton crops, is highly prosperous — all influences working toward the solution of this problem.

When I went South I shared the impression of many Northerners that the South was lawless and did not care — an impression that arises from the wide publication of the horrible details of every lynching that occurs, and the utter silence regarding those deep, quiet, and yet powerful moral and industrial forces which are at the work of rejuvenation beneath the surface — an account of which I have given.   I came away from the South deeply impressed with two things:

That the South is making fully as good progress in overcoming its peculiar forms of lawlessness as the North is making in overcoming *its* peculiar forms.

II.—LYNCHING IN THE NORTH

Having looked, into two Southern lynching towns, let us now see what a Northern lynching is like.   The comparison is highly interesting and illuminating.

Springfield, O., is one of the most prosperous of the smaller cities of the state.   It is a beautiful town having, in 1904, some 41,000 people.   It has fine streets, fine buildings, busy factories, churches, an imposing library.   Some of the older families have resided there for nearly a century.   It is the seat of government of one of the most fertile and attractive counties in the state: an altogether progressive, enlightened city.   Of its population in 1904 over 6,000 were Negroes (about one-seventh), a considerable proportion of whom are recent settlers.   Large numbers of Negroes, as I have shown in former chapters, have been migrating from the South, and crowding into Northern towns located along the Ohio or in those portions of Indiana, Illinois, Ohio, Pennsylvania, Kansas, and other states, which border on the Old South.   Many of the Negroes in Springfield came from Kentucky.   We discover in these Northern towns exactly as in the South, the two classes of Negroes: the steady, resident class, more or less known to the whites, and a restless, unstable, ignorant class, coming to one neighbourhood to-day to help build a bridge, and going elsewhere to-morrow to dig a canal. For years no such thing as race prejudice existed in Springfield; but with the growth of Negro population it increased with rapidity. For instance, a druggist in Springfield refused to sell soda-water to a Negro college professor, the typesetters in a publishing house compelled the discharge of Negro workmen, a Negro physician visited the high-school, found the half-dozen Negro pupils sitting by themselves and, angrily charging discrimination, ordered his child to sit among the white children. This feeling of race repulsion was especially noticeable between the working class of white men and the Negroes who come more or less into industrial competition with them. The use of Negroes for breaking strikes in the coalfields and elsewhere has been a fertile source of discord, kindling the fire of race prejudice in places where it never before existed.

How the Negroes Sold Their Votes

In Springfield there were about 1,500 Negro voters, many of whom were bought at every election. The Democrats and the Republicans were so evenly divided that the city administration was Democratic and the county administration Republican. The venal Negro vote went to the highest bidder, carried the elections, and, with the whiskey influence, governed the town. Springfield, enlightened, educated, progressive, highly American, had 145 saloons — or one to every 285 people. Before the lynching, nine of these were Negro saloons — some of them indescribably vile. A row of houses along the railroad tracks, not three blocks from the heart of the city, was known as the Levee. It was a Negro row composed of saloons and disorderly houses, where the lowest of the low, Negro men and both Negro and white women, made a general rendezvous. Just back of it was one of the foremost Catholic churches in town; hardly a block away were the post-office, the public library, and the foremost club of the city, and within three or four hundred yards were the back doors of some of the city's most aristocratic residences. For years, the ineffective good citizen had protested against these abominable resorts, but when the Republicans wanted to win they needed the votes from these places, and when the Democrats wanted to win *they* needed them. Burnett, the Democratic boss, said in a tone of real injury to a gentleman — a Democrat — who protested against the protection of the Levee:

"Don't you want the party to win? We 've got to have those sixty or eighty votes from Hurley" — Hurley being the notorious Negro proprietor of a dive called the Honky Tonk.

Corrupt Politics and the Negro Question

So these vile places remained open, protected by the police, breeding crime, and encouraging arrogance, idleness, and vice among the Negroes.

And yet one will hear good citizens of Springfield complaining that the Negroes make themselves conspicuous and obnoxious at primaries and elections, standing around, waiting, and refusing to vote until they receive money in hand.

"To my mind," one of these citizens said to me, "the conspicuousness of the Negro at elections is one of the chief causes of race prejudice."

But who is to blame? The Negro who accepts the bribe, or the white politician who is eager to give it, or the white business man who, desiring special privileges, stands behind the white politician, or the ordinary citizen who does n't care? Talk with these politicians on the one hand, and the impractical reformers on the other, and they will tell you in all seriousness of the sins of the South in disfranchising the Negro.

"Every Negro in Springfield," I was told, "exercises his right to vote."

If you were to tell these men that the Negroes of Springfield are disfranchised as absolutely as they are anywhere in the South, they would stare at you in amazement. But a purchased voter is a disfranchised voter. The Negroes have no more real voice in the government of Springfield than they have in the government of Savannah or New Orleans. In the South the Negro has been disfranchised by law or by intimidation: in the North by cash. Which is worse?

Story of the Crime that Led to the Lynching

A few months before the lynching a Negro named Dixon[11] arrived in Springfield from Kentucky. He was one of the

11. Richard Dixon.

illiterate, idle, floating sort. He had with him a woman not his wife, with whom he quarrelled. He was arrested and brought into court.

I am profoundly conscious of the seriousness of any charge which touches upon our courts, the last resort of justice, and yet it was a matter of common report that "justice was easy" in Clark County, that laws were not enforced, that criminals were allowed to escape on suspended sentence. I heard this talk everywhere, often coupled with personal accusations against the judges, but I could not discover that the judges were more remiss than other officials. They were afflicted with no other disease.

Even in a serious sociological study of Clark County by Professor E. S. Todd, I find this statement:

In Springfield, one of the chief faults of the municipal system has been and is the laxity and discrimination in the enforcement of the law. Many of the municipal ordinances have been shelved for years. The saloon closing ordinances are enforced intermittently, as are those concerning gambling.

When the Negro Dixon was brought into court he was convicted and let out on suspended sentence. He got drunk immediately and was again arrested, this time serving several weeks in jail. The moment he was free he began quarrelling with his "wife," in a house directly across the street from police headquarters. An officer named Collis tried to make peace and Dixon deliberately shot him through the stomach, also wounding the woman.

This was on Sunday. Dixon was immediately placed in the county jail. Collis died the next morning.

Human Life Cheap in Clark County

I have called attention to the fact that the lynching town nearly always has a previous bad record of homicide. Disregard for the sacredness of human life seems to be in the air of these places. Springfield was no exception. Between January 1, 1902, and March 7, 1904, the day of the lynching, a little more than two years, no fewer than ten homicides were committed in the city of Springfield. White men committed five of these crimes and Negroes five. Three of the cases were decided within a short time before the lynching and the punishment administered was widely criticised. Bishop, a coloured man who had killed a coloured man, was fined $200 and sentenced to six months in the workhouse. This was for *killing a man*. O'Brien, a white man, who killed a white man, got one year in the penitentiary. And only a week before the lynching, Schocknessy, a white man who killed a white man, but who had influential political friends, went scott-free!

On the morning after the Collis murder, the *Daily Sun* published a list of the recent homicides in Springfield in big type on its first page and asked editorially:

"What are you going to do about it?"

It then answered its own question:

"Nothing."

The following morning, after the lynching, the same paper printed in its headlines:

AWFUL REBUKE TO THE COURTS

They Have Temporised With the Criminal Classes Until Patience was Exhausted

I cite these facts to show the underlying conditions in Springfield; a soil richly prepared for an outbreak of mob law — with corrupt politics, vile saloons, the law paralysed by non-enforcement against vice, a large venal Negro vote, lax courts of justice.

Gathering of the Lynching Mob

Well, on Monday afternoon the mob began to gather. At first it was an absurd, ineffectual crowd, made up largely of lawless boys of sixteen to twenty — a pronounced feature of every mob — with a wide fringe of more respectable citizens, their hands in their pockets and no convictions in their souls, looking on curiously, helplessly. They gathered hooting around the jail, cowardly, at first, as all mobs are, but growing bolder as darkness came on and no move was made to check them. The murder of Collis was not a horrible, soul-rending crime like that at Statesboro, Ga.; these men in the mob were not personal friends of the murdered man; it was a mob from the back rooms of the swarming saloons of Springfield; and it included also the sort of idle boys "who hang around cigar stores," as one observer told me. The newspaper reports are fond of describing lynching mobs as "made up of the foremost citizens of the town." In few cases that I know of, either South or North, except in back country neighbourhoods, has a mob been made up of what may be called the best citizens; but the best citizens have often stood afar off "decrying the mob" — as a Springfield man told me — and letting it go on. A mob is the method by which good citizens turn over the law and the government to the criminal or irresponsible classes.

And no official in direct authority in Springfield that evening, apparently, had so much as an ounce of grit within him. The sheriff came out and made a weak speech in which he said he "did n't want to hurt anybody." They threw stones at him and broke his windows. The chief of police sent eighteen men to the jail but did not go near himself. All of these policemen undoubtedly sympathised with the mob in its efforts to get at the slayer of their brother officer; at least, they did nothing effective to prevent the lynching. An appeal was made to the Mayor to order out the engine companies that water might be turned on the mob. He said he did n't like to; *the hose might be cut.* The local militia company was called to its barracks, but the officer in charge hesitated, vacillated, doubted his authority, and objected finally because he had no ammunition *except* Krag-Jorgenson cartridges, which, if fired into a mob, would kill too many people! The soldiers did not stir that night from the safe and comfortable precincts of their armoury.

A sort of dry rot, a moral paralysis, seems to strike the administrators of law in a town like Springfield. What can be expected of officers who are not accustomed to enforce the law, or of a people not accustomed to obey it — or who make reservations and exceptions when they do enforce it or obey it?

Threats to Lynch the Judges

When the sheriff made his speech to the mob, urging them to let the law take its course they jeered him. The law! When, in the past, had the law taken its proper course in Clark County? Some one shouted, referring to Dixon:

"He 'll only get fined for shooting in the city limits."

"He 'll get ten days in jail and suspended sentence."

Then there were voices:

"Let's go hang Mower and Miller"—the two judges.

This threat indeed, was frequently repeated both on the night of the lynching and on the day following.

So the mob came finally, and cracked the door of the jail with a railroad rail. This jail is said to be the strongest in Ohio, and having seen it, I can well believe that the report is true. But steel bars have never yet kept out a mob; it takes something a good deal stronger: human courage backed up by the consciousness of being right.

They murdered the Negro in cold blood in the jail doorway; then they dragged him to the principal business street and hung him to a telegraph-pole, afterward riddling his lifeless body with revolver shots.

Lesson of a Hanging Negro

That was the end of that! Mob justice administered! And there the Negro hung until daylight the next morning—an unspeakably grizzly, dangling horror, advertising the shame of the town. His head was shockingly crooked to one side, his ragged clothing, cut for souvenirs, exposed in places his bare body: he dripped blood. And, with the crowds of men both here and at the morgue where the body was publicly exhibited, came young boys in knickerbockers, and little girls and women by scores, horrified but curious. They came even with baby carriages! Men made jokes: "A dead nigger is a good nigger." And the purblind, dollars-and-cents man, most despicable of all, was congratulating the public:

"It'll save the county a lot of money!"

Significant lessons, these, for the young!

But the mob was n't through with its work. Easy people imagine that, having hanged a Negro, the mob goes quietly about its business; but that is never the way of the mob. Once released, the spirit of anarchy spreads and spreads, not subsiding until it has accomplished its full measure of evil.

Mob Burning of Negro Saloons

All the following day a rumbling, angry crowd filled the streets of Springfield, threatening to burn out the notorious Levee, threatening Judges Mower and Miller, threatening the "niggers." The local troops — to say nothing of the police force — which might easily have broken up the mob, remained sedulously in their armouries, vacillating, doubtful of authority, knowing that there were threats to burn and destroy, and making not one move toward the protection of the public. One of the captains was even permitted to go to a neighbouring city to a dance! At the very same time the panic-stricken officials were summoning troops from other towns. So night came on, the mob gathered around the notorious dives, some one touched a match, and the places of crime suddenly disgorged their foul inhabitants. Black and white, they came pouring out and vanished into the darkness where they belonged — from whence they did not return. Eight buildings went up in smoke, the fire department deliberating — intentionally, it is said — until the flames could not be controlled. The troops, almost driven out by the county prosecutor, McGrew, appeared after the mob had completed its work.

Good work, badly done, a living demonstration of the inevitability of law — if not orderly, decent law, then of mob-law.

For days following the troops filled Springfield, costing the state large sums of money, costing the county large sums of money. They chiefly guarded the public fountain; the mob had gone home — until next time.

Efforts to Punish the Mob

What happened after that? A perfunctory court-martial, that did absolutely nothing. A grand jury of really good citizens that sat for weeks, off and on; and like the mountain that was in travail and brought forth a mouse, they indicted two boys and two men out of all that mob, not for murder, but for "breaking into jail." And, curiously enough, it developed — how do such things develop? — that every man on the grand jury was a Republican, chosen by Republican county officers, and in their report they severely censured the police force (Democratic), and the mayor (Democratic), and had not one word of disapproval for the sheriff (Republican). Curiously enough, also, the public did not become enthusiastic over the report of that grand jury.

But the worst feature of all in this Springfield lynching was the apathy of the public. No one really seemed to care. A "nigger" had been hanged: what of it? But the law itself had been lynched. What of that? I had just come from the South, where I had found the people of several lynching towns in a state of deep excitement — moral excitement if you like, thinking about this problem, quarrelling about it, expelling men from the church, impeaching sheriffs, dishonourably discharging whole militia companies. Here in Springfield, I found cold apathy, except for a few fine citizens, one of whom, City Solicitor Stewart L. Tatum, promptly offered his services to the sheriff and assisted in a vain effort to remove the Negro in a closed carriage and afterward at the risk of personal assault earnestly attempted to defeat the purposes of the mob. Another of these citizens, the Rev. Father Cogan, pleaded with the mob on the second night of the rioting at risk to himself; another withdrew from the militia company because it had not done its duty. And afterward the city officials were stirred by the faintest of faint spasms of righteousness: some of the Negro saloons were closed up, but within a month, the most notorious of all the dive-keepers, Hurley, the Negro political boss, was permitted to open an establishment — through the medium of a brother-in-law!

If there ever was an example of good citizenship lying flat on its back with political corruption squatting on its neck, Springfield furnished an example of that condition. There was no reconstructive movement, no rising and organisation of the better sort of citizens. Negro dives gradually reopened, the same corrupt politics continued: and the result was logical and inevitable. About two years later, in February, 1906, another race riot broke out in Springfield — worse in some ways than the first. On February 26th, Martin M. Davis, a white brakeman, was shot in the railroad yards near a row of notorious Negro houses, by Edward Dean, a coloured man. The Negro was at once removed from the city and a mob which had gathered in anticipation of another lynching, when it was cheated of its victim, set fire to a number of houses in the Negro settlement. The militia was at once called out, but the following night the mob gathered as before and visiting the Negro settlement, tried to set fire to other buildings.

It is significant that on the very night that this riot occurred the city council had under consideration an ordinance prohibiting the use of screens or other obstructions to the view of the interior of saloons after closing hours on week days or during Sundays.   A committee of the council, favourable to the saloon interests, had recommended that the ordinance be not acted upon by council but referred to the people at a distant election, a proposition wholly illegal.   While Stewart L. Tatum, the city solicitor to whom I have already referred, argued to the council the illegality of the proposal made by the committee the noise of the mob reached the council chamber and the friends of the ordinance seized the opportunity to adjourn and delay action that would evidently result in the defeat of the ordinance.

Finally, as a result of both these riots, the city was mildly stirred; a Civic League was formed by prominent citizens and the *attack on property* vigorously deprecated; the passage of the screen ordinance was recommended and at the next meeting of the council this ordinance, which had been vetoed by the mayor of the previous administration and had excited considerable public interest during a period of two years, was passed and has proved of great assistance to the police department in controlling the low saloons where the riot spirit is bred.

I turn with pleasure from the story of this lynching to another Northern town, where I found as satisfying an example of how to deal with a mob as this country has known.

In Springfield we had an exhibition of nearly complete supineness and apathy before the mob; in Statesboro, Ga., we discovered a decided law-and-order element, not strong enough, however, to do much; in Huntsville, Ala., we had a tremendous moral awakening.   In Danville, Ill., we find an example of law vindicated, magnificently and completely, through the heroism of a single man, backed up later by wholesome public opinion.

Character of Danville, Ill.

Danville presented many of the characteristics of Springfield, O.   It had a growing Negro population and there had been an awakening race prejudice between the white workingmen and the Negroes, especially in the neighbouring coal mines.

As in other places where lynchings have occurred, I found that Vermilion County, of which Danville is the seat, had also a heavy record of homicide and other crime. They counted there on a homicide every sixty days; at the term of court preceding the lynching seven murder trials were on the docket; and in all its history the county never had had a legal hanging, though it had suffered two lynchings. The criminal record of Vermilion County was exceeded at that time only by Cook County (Chicago), and St. Clair County (East St. Louis), where the horrible lynching of a Negro schoolmaster took place (at Belleville) in the preceding summer.

Story of a Starved Negro

The crime which caused the rioting was committed by the familiar vagrant Negro from the South — in this case a Kentucky Negro named Wilson — a miserable, illiterate, half-starved creature who had been following a circus. He had begged along the road in Indiana and no one would feed him. He came across the line into Illinois, found a farmhouse door open, saw food on the table, and darted in to steal it. As he was leaving, the woman of the house appeared. In an animal-like panic, the Negro darted for the door, knocking the woman down as he escaped. Immediately the cry went up that there had been an attempted criminal assault, but the sheriff told me that the woman never made any such charge and the Negro bore all the evidence of the truthfulness of the assertion that he was starving; he was so emaciated with hunger that even after his arrest the sheriff dared not allow him a full meal.

Hot Weather and Mobs

But it was enough to stir up the mob spirit. It was Saturday night, July 25th,[12] and the usual crowd from all over the county had gathered in the town. Among the crowd were many coal miners, who had just been paid off and were drinking. As in Springfield, the town had a very large number of saloons, ninety-one within a radius of five miles, to a population of

12. 1903.

some 25,000. Most Northern towns are far worse in this
respect than the average Southern town. It was a hot night;
mobs work best in hot weather. Statistics, indeed, show that
the great majority of lynchings take place in the summer,
particularly in July and August.

It was known that the sheriff had brought his Negro prisoner
to the jail, and the crime was widely discussed. The whole
city was a sort of human tinder-box, ready to flare up at a
spark of violence.

Well, the spark came — in a saloon. Metcalf,[13] a Negro,
had words with a well-known white butcher named Henry
Gatterman. Both had been drinking. The Negro drew
a revolver and shot Gatterman dead. Instantly the city
was in a furor of excitement. The police appeared and arrested
Metcalf, and got him finally with great difficulty to the police
station, where he was locked up. A mob formed instantly.
It was led, at first, by a crowd of lawless boys from sixteen to
eighteen years old. Rapidly gathering strength, it rushed
into the city hall, and although the mayor, the chief of police,
and nearly the entire police force were present, they got the
Negro out and hanged him to a telegraph-pole in the main
street of the town, afterward shooting his body full of holes.

Intoxicated by their swift success and, mob-like, growing
in recklessness and bloodthirstiness, they now turned upon
the jail determined to lynch the Negro Wilson. It was a
much uglier mob than any I have hitherto described; it was
a drunken mob, and it had already tasted blood. It swarmed
around the jail, yelling, shooting, and breaking the windows
with stones.

A "Strict" Sheriff

Sheriff Hardy H. Whitlock of Vermilion County had never
been looked upon as an especially remarkable man — except,
as I was told everywhere, he had a record as *a strict sheriff*, as a
man who did his best to enforce the law in times of peace. He
and the state's attorney were so industrious that they caught
and punished four times as many criminals in proportion to
population as were convicted in Chicago. The sheriff was
a big, solid, deliberate man with gray eyes. He was born
in Tennessee. His father was an itinerant Presbyterian

13. John D. Metcalf.

preacher, always poor, doing good for everybody but himself, and stern in his conceptions of right and wrong. His mother, as the sheriff related, made him obey the law with peach-tree switches. His history was the commonest of the common; not much education, had to make his living, worked in a livery stable. He was faithful at that, temperate, friendly. They elected him constable, an office that he held for seven years. He was faithful at that. They elected him sheriff of the county. He went at the new task as he had at all his other work, with no especial brilliancy, but steadily doing his duty, catching criminals. He found a great deal to learn and he learned. The extradition laws of the states troubled him when he wanted to bring prisoners home. There was no compilation of the laws on the subject. Here was work to be done. Although no lawyer, he went at it laboriously and compiled a book of five hundred pages, containing all the extradition laws of the country, and had it published at his own expense.

Defending a Jail With a Riot-gun

And when the crisis came that night with the mob howling around his jail, Hardy Whitlock had become so accustomed to doing his duty that he did n't know how to do anything else. Here was the jail to be protected: he intended to protect it. He sent for no troops — there was no time anyhow — nor for the police. He had a couple of deputies and his wife. Though the mob was breaking the windows of the house and the children were there, his wife said:

"Give me a gun, Hardy, and I 'll stay by you."

The sheriff went out on the porch, unarmed, in his shirt-sleeves, and made them a little speech. They yelled at him, threw stones, fired revolvers. They brought a railroad rail to break in the door. He went out among them, called them Bill, and Jim, and Dick, and persuaded them to put it down; but others took it up willingly.

"Are you going to open the door?" they yelled.

"No!" said the sheriff.

Then he went in and got his riot-gun, well loaded with duck-shot. He was one man against two thousand. They began battering on the iron door, yelling and shooting. It was not

an especially strong door, and it began to give at the bottom,
and finally bent inward enough to admit a man's body. The
crucial moment had come: and the sheriff was there to meet
it. He stuck his riot-gun out of the opening and began firing.
The mob fell back but came charging forward again, wild
with passion. The sheriff fired again, seven times in all, and
one of his deputies opened with a revolver. For a time
pandemonium reigned; they attempted the house entrance
of the jail; the sheriff was there also with his riot-gun; they
threatened dynamite and fire. They cut down the Negro,
Metcalf, brought him in front of the jail, piled straw on the
body and attempted to burn it. Part of the time they were
incited to greater violence by a woman who stood in a waggon-
box across the street. So they raged all night, firing at the
jail, but not daring to come too near the man with the riot-gun.

"On Sunday," the sheriff told me. "I realised I was up
against it. I knew the tough element in town had it in for me."

How a Real Sheriff Punished a Mob

They even threatened him on the street. A large number
of men had been wounded by the firing, some dangerously,
though no one, fortunately, was killed. The sheriff stood
alone in the town. A lesser man might still have failed
ignominiously. But Whitlock went about the nearest duty:
punishing the rioters. He had warrants issued and arrested
every man he could find who was streaked or speckled with
shot — indubitable evidence of his presence in the mob at the
jail door. Many fled the city, but he got twenty or thirty.

Vermilion County also had a prosecuting attorney who
knew his duty — J. W. Keeslar. Judge Thompson called
a grand jury, Attorney Keeslar pushed the cases with great
vigour, and this was the result: thirteen men and one woman
(the disorderly woman of the waggon-box) were sent to the
penitentiary, eight others were heavily fined. At the same
time the Negro, Wilson, came up for trial, pleaded guilty, and
was legally punished by a term in the penitentiary.

And the people came strongly to the support of their officers.
Hardy Whitlock became one of the most popular men in the
county. Keeslar, coming up for reëlection the following fall,

COURT HOUSE AND BANK IN THE PUBLIC SQUARE AT HUNTSVILLE, ALABAMA

The Negro, Maples, was lynched by being hung to the elm tree at the corner of the court house, near the extreme right of the picture

Photographed by Collins & Son

Photograph by Edmondson

CHARLES W. CHESNUTT

The well-known novelist, author of "The Colonel's Dream," "The House Behind the Cedars,"
"The Conjure Woman," etc. Mr. Chesnutt is a lawyer in Cleveland, Ohio

with mob-law for the essential issue, was returned to his office with an overwhelming majority. The sheriff told me that, in his opinion, the success of the officers in convicting the lynchers was due largely to a thoroughly awakened public opinion, the strong attitude of the newspapers, especially those of Chicago, the help of the governor, and the feeling, somehow, that the best sentiment of the county was behind them.

Conclusions Regarding Lynching in This Country

And finally, we may, perhaps venture upon a few general conclusions.

Lynching in this country is peculiarly the white man's burden. The white man has taken all the responsibility of government; he really governs in the North as well as in the South, in the North disfranchising the Negro with cash, in the South by law or by intimidation. All the machinery of justice is in his hands. How keen is the need, then, of calmness and strict justice in dealing with the Negro! Nothing more surely tends to bring the white man down to the lowest level of the criminal Negro than yielding to those blind instincts of savagery which find expression in the mob. The man who joins a mob, by his very acts, puts himself on a level with the Negro criminal: both have given way wholly to brute passion. For, if civilisation means anything, it means self-restraint; casting away self-restraint the white man becomes as savage as the criminal Negro.

If the white man sets an example of non-obedience to law, of non-enforcement of law, and of unequal justice, what can be expected of the Negro? A criminal father is a poor preacher of homilies to a wayward son. The Negro sees a man, white or black, commit murder and go free, over and over again in all these lynching counties. Why should he fear to murder? Every passion of the white man is reflected and emphasised in the criminal Negro.

CHAPTER X

AN OSTRACISED RACE IN FERMENT

THE CONFLICT OF NEGRO PARTIES AND NEGRO LEADERS OVER METHODS OF DEALING WITH THEIR OWN PROBLEM

ONE of the things that has interested me most of all in studying Negro communities, especially in the North, has been to find them so torn by cliques and divided by such wide differences of opinion.

No other element of our population presents a similar condition; the Italians, the Jews, the Germans and especially the Chinese and Japanese are held together not only by a different language, but by ingrained and ancient national habits. They group themselves naturally. But the Negro is an American in language and customs; he knows no other traditions and he has no other conscious history; a large proportion, indeed, possess varying degrees of white American blood (restless blood!) and yet the Negro is not accepted as an American. Instead of losing himself gradually in the dominant race, as the Germans, Irish, and Italians are doing, adding those traits or qualities with which Time fashions and modifies this human mosaic called the American nation, the Negro is set apart as a peculiar people.

With every Negro, then, an essential question is: "How shall I meet this attempt to put me off by myself?"

That question in one form or another — politically, industrially, socially — is being met daily, almost hourly, by every Negro in this country. It colours his very life.

"You don't know, and you can't know," a Negro said to me, "what it is to be a problem, to understand that everyone is watching you and studying you, to have your mind constantly on your own actions. It has made us think and talk about ourselves more than other people do. It has made us self-conscious and sensitive."

It is scarcely surprising, then, that upon such a vital question there should be wide differences of opinion among Negroes. As a matter of fact, there are almost innumerable points of view and suggested modes of conduct, but they all group themselves into two great parties which are growing more distinct in outline and purpose every day. Both parties exist in every part of the country, but it is in the North that the struggle between them is most evident. I have found a sharper feeling and a bitterer discussion of race relationships among the Negroes of the North than among those of the South. If you want to hear the race question discussed with fire and fervour, go to Boston!

For two hundred and fifty years the Negro had no thought, no leadership, no parties; then suddenly he was set free, and became, so far as law could make him, an integral and indistinguishable part of the American people. But it was only in a few places in the North and among comparatively few individuals that he ever approximately reached the position of a free citizen, that he ever really enjoyed the rights granted to him under the law. In the South he was never free politically, socially, and industrially, in the sense that the white man is free, and is not so to-day.

But in Boston, and in other Northern cities in lesser degree, a group of Negroes reached essentially equal citizenship. A few families trace their lineage back to the very beginnings of civilisation in this country, others were freemen long before the war, a few had revolutionary war records of which their descendants are intensely and justly proud. Some of the families have far more white blood than black; though the census shows that only about 40 per cent. of the Negroes of Boston are mulattoes, the real proportion is undoubtedly very much higher.

In abolition times these Negroes were much regarded. Many of them attained and kept a certain real position among the whites; they were even accorded unusual opportunities and favours. They found such a place as an educated Negro might find to-day (or at least as he found a few years ago) in Germany. In some instances they became wealthy. At a time when the North was passionately concerned in the abolition of slavery the colour of his skin sometimes gave the Negro special advantages, even honours.

For years after the war this condition continued; then a stream of immigration of Southern Negroes began to appear, at first a mere rivulet, but latterly increasing in volume, until to-day all of our Northern cities have swarming coloured colonies. Owing to the increase of the Negro population and for other causes which I have already mentioned, sentiment in the North toward the Negro has been undergoing a swift change.

How Colour Lines Are Drawn

Now the tragedy of the Negro is the colour of his skin: he is easily recognisable. The human tendency is to class people together by outward appearances. When the line began to be drawn it was drawn not alone against the unworthy Negro, but against the Negro. It was not so much drawn by the highly intelligent white man as by the white man. And the white man alone has not drawn it, but the Negroes themselves are drawing it — and more and more every day. So we draw the line in this country against the Chinese, the Japanese, and in some measure against the Jews (and they help to draw it). So we speak with disparagement of "dagoes" and "square heads." Right or wrong, these lines, in our present state of civilisation, are drawn. They are here; they must be noted and dealt with.

What was the result? The Northern Negro who has been enjoying the free life of Boston and Philadelphia has protested passionately against the drawing of a colour line: he wishes to be looked upon, and not at all unnaturally, for he possesses human ambitions and desires, solely for his worth as a man, not as a Negro.

In Philadelphia I heard of the old Philadelphia Negroes, in Indianapolis of the old Indianapolis families, in Boston a sharp distinction was drawn between the "Boston Negroes" and the recent Southern importation. Even in Chicago, where there is nothing old, I found the same spirit.

In short, it is the protest against separation, against being deprived of the advantages and opportunities of a free life. In the South the most intelligent and best educated Negroes are, generally speaking, the leaders of their race, but in Northern cities some of the ablest Negroes will have nothing to do with the masses of their own people or with racial movements;

DR. BOOKER T. WASHINGTON

Photograph by Dimock

DR. W. E. B. DU BOIS
of Atlanta University

they hold themselves aloof, asserting that there is no colour line, and if there is, there should not be. Their associations and their business are largely with white people and they cling passionately to the fuller life.

"When I am sick," one of them said to me, "I don't go to a Negro doctor, but to a doctor. Colour has nothing to do with it."

In the South the same general setting apart of Negroes as Negroes is going on, of course, on an immeasurably wider scale. By disfranchisement they are being separated politically, the Jim Crow laws set them apart socially and physically, the hostility of white labour in some callings pushes them aside in the industrial activities. But the South presents no such striking contrasts as the North, because no Southern Negroes were ever really accorded a high degree of citizenship.

Two Great Negro Parties

Now, the Negroes of the country are meeting the growing discrimination against them in two ways, out of which have grown the two great parties to which I have referred. One party has sprung, naturally, from the thought of the Northern Negro and is a product of the freedom which the Northern Negro has enjoyed; although, of course, it finds many followers in the South.

The other is the natural product of the far different conditions in the South, where the Negro cannot speak his mind, where he has never realised any large degree of free citizenship. Both are led by able men, and both are backed by newspapers and magazines. It has come, indeed, to the point where most Negroes of any intelligence at all have taken their place on one side or the other.

The second-named party, which may best, perhaps, be considered first, is made up of the great mass of the coloured people both South and North; its undisputed leader is Booker T. Washington.

The Rise of Booker T. Washington

Nothing has been more remarkable in the recent history of the Negro than Washington's rise to influence as a leader, and the spread of his ideals of education and progress. It is noteworthy that he was born in the South, a slave, that he knew intimately the common struggling life of his people and the attitude of the white race toward them. He worked his way to education in Southern schools and was graduated at Hampton — a story which he tells best himself in his book, "Up From Slavery."[1] He was and is Southern in feeling and point of view. When he began to think how he could best help his people the same question came to him that comes to every Negro:

"What shall we do about this discrimination and separation?"

And his was the type of character which answered, "Make the best of it; overcome it with self-development."

The very essence of his doctrine is this:

"Get yourself right, and the world will be all right."

His whole work and his life have said to the white man:

"You've set us apart. You don't want us. All right; we'll be apart. We can succeed as Negroes."

It is the doctrine of the opportunist and optimist: peculiarly, indeed, the doctrine of the man of the soil, who has come up fighting, dealing with the world, not as he would like to have it, but as it overtakes him. Many great leaders have been like that: Lincoln was one. They have the simplicity and patience of the soil, and the immense courage and faith. To prevent being crushed by circumstances they develop humour; they laugh off their troubles. Washington has all of these qualities of the common life: he possesses in high degree what some one has called "great commonness." And finally he has a simple faith in humanity, and in the just purposes of the Creator of humanity.

Being a hopeful opportunist Washington takes the Negro as he finds him, often ignorant, weak, timid, surrounded by hostile forces, and tells him to go to work at anything, anywhere, but go to work, learn how to work better, save money, have a better home, raise a better family.

What Washington Teaches the Negro

The central idea of his doctrine, indeed, is work. He teaches that if the Negro wins by real worth a strong economic

1. Booker T. Washington, *Up from Slavery: An Autobiography* (New York, 1901).

position in the country, other rights and privileges will come to him naturally. He should get his rights, not by gift of the white man, but by earning them himself.

"I noticed," he says, "when I first went to Tuskegee to start the Tuskegee Normal and Industrial Institute, that some of the white people about there looked rather doubtfully at me. I thought I could get their influence by telling them how much algebra and history and science and all those things I had in my head, but they treated me about the same as they did before. They did n't seem to care about the algebra, history, and science that were in my head only. Those people never even began to have confidence in me until we commenced to build a large three-story brick building; and then another and another, until now we have eighty-six buildings which have been erected largely by the labour of our students, and to-day we have the respect and confidence of all the white people in that section.

"There is an unmistakable influence that comes over a white man when he sees a black man living in a two-story brick house that has been paid for."

In another place he has given his ideas of what education should be:

"How I wish that, from the most cultured and highly endowed university in the great North to the humblest log cabin schoolhouse in Alabama, we could burn, as it were, into the hearts and heads of all that usefulness, that service to our brother is the supreme end of education."

It is, indeed, to the teaching of service in the highest sense that Washington's life has been devoted. While he urges every Negro to reach as high a place as he can, he believes that the great masses of the Negroes are best fitted to-day for manual labour; his doctrine is that they should be taught to do that labour better: that when the foundations have been laid in sound industry and in business enterprise, the higher callings and honours will come of themselves.

His emphasis is rather upon duties than upon rights. He does not advise the Negro to surrender a single right: on the other hand, he urges his people to use fully every right they have or can get — for example, to vote wherever possible, and vote thoughtfully. But he believes that some of the rights given the Negro have been lost because the Negro had neither the wisdom nor the strength to use them properly.

Washington's Influence on His People

I have not said much thus far in these articles about Booker T. Washington, but as I have been travelling over this country, South and North, studying Negro communities, I have found the mark of him everywhere in happier human lives. Wherever I found a prosperous Negro enterprise, a thriving business place, a good home, there I was almost sure to find Booker T. Washington's picture over the fireplace or a little framed motto expressing his gospel of work and service. I have heard bitter things said about Mr. Washington by both coloured people and white. I have waited and investigated many of these stories, and I am telling here what I have seen and known of his influence among thousands of common, struggling human beings. Many highly educated Negroes, especially, in the North, dislike him and oppose him, but he has brought new hope and given new courage to the masses of his race. He has given them a working plan of life. And is there a higher test of usefulness? Measured by any standard, white or black, Washington must be regarded to-day as one of the great men of this country: and in the future he will be so honoured.

Dr. Du Bois and the Negro

The party led by Washington is made up of the masses of the common people; the radical party, on the other hand, represents what may be called the intellectuals. The leading exponent of its point of view is unquestionably Professor W. E. B. Du Bois of Atlanta University — though, like all minority parties, it is torn with dissension and discontent. Dr. Du Bois was born in Massachusetts of a family that had no history of Southern slavery.[2] He has a large intermixture of white blood. Broadly educated at Harvard and in the universities of Germany, he is to-day one of the able sociologists of this country. His economic studies of the Negro made for the United States Government and for the Atlanta University conference (which he organised) are works of sound scholarship and furnish the

2. For a fuller treatment of Du Bois' ideas and influence, see his *Dusk of Dawn: An Essay toward an Autobiography of a Race Concept* (New York, 1940) ; Francis L. Broderick, *W. E. B. Du Bois: Negro Leader in a Time of*

student with the best single source of accurate information regarding the Negro at present obtainable in this country. And no book gives a deeper insight into the inner life of the Negro, his struggles and his aspirations, than "The Souls of Black Folk."

Dr. Du Bois has the temperament of the scholar and idealist — critical, sensitive, unhumorous, impatient, often covering its deep feeling with sarcasm and cynicism. When the question came to him:

"What shall the Negro do about discrimination?" his answer was the exact reverse of Washington's: it was the voice of Massachusetts:

"Do not submit! agitate, object, fight."

Where Washington reaches the hearts of his people, Du Bois appeals to their heads. Du Bois is not a leader of men, as Washington is: he is rather a promulgator of ideas. While Washington is building a great educational institution and organising the practical activities of the race, Du Bois is the lonely critic holding up distant ideals. Where Washington cultivates friendly human relationships with the white people among whom the lot of the Negro is cast, Du Bois, sensitive to rebuffs, draws more and more away from white people.

A Negro Declaration of Independence

Several years ago Du Bois organised the Niagara movement for the purpose of protesting against the drawing of the colour line[3] It is important, not so much for the extent of its membership, which is small, but because it represents, genuinely, a more or less prevalent point of view among many coloured people. Its declaration of principles says:

We refuse to allow the impression to remain that the Negro-American assents to inferiority, is submissive under oppression and apologetic before insults. Through helplessness we may submit, but the voice of protest of ten million Americans must never cease to assail the ears of their fellows, so long as America is unjust.

Any discrimination based simply on race or colour is barbarous, we care not how hallowed it be by custom, expediency, or prejudice. Differences made on account of ignorance, immorality, or disease are legitimate methods of fighting evil, and against them we have no word of protest, but discriminations based simply and solely on physical peculiarities, place of birth, colour of skin, are relics of that unreasoning human savagery of which the world is, and ought to be, thoroughly ashamed."

Crisis (Stanford, 1959); and Elliott M. Rudwick, *W. E. B. Du Bois: A Study in Minority Leadership* (Philadelphia, 1960).

3. Du Bois and a group of other young Negroes met at Niagara Falls, Canada,

The object of the movement is to protest against disfranchisement and Jim Crow laws and to demand equal rights of education, equal civil rights, equal economic opportunities, and justice in the courts. Taking the ballot from the Negro they declare to be only a step to economic slavery; that it leaves the Negro defenceless before his competitor — that the disfranchisement laws in the South are being followed by all manner of other discriminations which interfere with the progress of the Negro.

"Persistent manly agitation is the way to liberty," says the declaration, "and toward this goal the Niagara movement has started."

The annual meeting of the movement was held last August in Boston, the chief gathering being in Faneuil Hall. Every reference in the speeches to Garrison, Phillips, and Sumner was cheered to the echo. "It seemed," said one newspaper report, "like a revival of the old spirit of abolitionism — with the white man left out."

Several organisations in the country, like the New England Suffrage League, the Equal Rights League of Georgia, and others, take much the same position as the Niagara movement.

The party led by Dr. Du Bois is, in short, a party of protest which endeavours to prevent Negro separation and discrimination against Negroes by agitation and political influence.

Two Negro Parties Compared

These two points of view, of course, are not peculiar to Negroes; they divide all human thought. The opportunist and optimist on the one hand does his great work with the world as he finds it: he is resourceful, constructive, familiar. On the other hand, the idealist, the agitator, who is also a pessimist, performs the function of the critic; he sees the world as it should be and cries out to have it instantly changed.

Thus with these two great Negro parties. Each is working for essentially the same end — better conditions of life for the Negro — each contains brave and honest men, and each is sure, humanly enough, that the other side is not only wrong, but venally wrong, whereas both parties are needed and both perform a useful function.

in June, 1905, and formulated a platform for aggressive action. The National Association for the Advancement of Colored People grew out of the Niagara Movement.

The chief, and at present almost the only, newspaper exponent of the radical Negro point of view is the Boston *Guardian*, published by William Monroe Trotter. Mr. Trotter is a mulatto who was graduated a few years ago with high honours from Harvard. His wife, who is active with him in his work, has so little Negro blood that she would ordinarily pass for white. Mr. Trotter's father fought in the Civil War and rose to be a lieutenant in Colonel Hallowell's Massachusetts regiment. He was one of the leaders of the Negro soldiers who refused to accept $8 a month as servants when white soldiers received $13. He argued that if a Negro soldier stood up and stopped a bullet, he was as valuable to the country as the white soldier. Though his family suffered, he served without pay rather than accept the money. It was the uncompromising spirit of Garrison and Phillips.

A Negro Newspaper of Agitation

The *Guardian* is as violent and bitter in some of its denunciations as the most reactionary white paper in the South. It would have the North take up arms again and punish the South for its position on the Negro question! It breathes the spirit of prejudice. Reading it sometimes, I am reminded of Senator Tillman's speeches. It answers the white publicity given in the South to black crime against white women by long accounts of similar crimes of white men. One of its chief points of conflict is the position of President Roosevelt regarding the Brownsville riot and the discharge of Negro soldiers; the attack on Roosevelt is unceasing, and in this viewpoint, at least, it is supported undoubtedly by no small proportion of the Negroes of the country.[4] Another leading activity is its fight on Booker T. Washington and his work. Denouncing Washington as a "notorious and incorrigible Jim Crowist," it says that he "dares to assert that the best way to get rights is not to oppose their being taken away, but to get money." Two or three years ago, when Mr. Washington went to Boston to address a coloured audience in Zion Church, Mr. Trotter and his friends scattered cayenne pepper on the rostrum and created a disturbance which broke up the meeting. Mr. Trotter went to jail for the offence. From the *Guardian*

4. In August, 1906, three companies of Negro soldiers were involved in a riot at Brownsville, Texas. When President Roosevelt subsequently dismissed the entire battalion without honor, many Negroes and other Americans thought

of September 2d[5] I cut part of the leading editorial which will show its attitude:

PROPHET OF SLAVERY AND TRAITOR TO RACE

As another mark of the treacherous character of Booker Washington in matters concerning the race, come his discordant notes in support of Secretary Taft for President of the United States in spite of the fact that every Negro organisation of any note devoted to the cause of equal rights and justice have condemned President Roosevelt for his unpardonable treatment of the soldiers of the 25th Infantry, U. S. A., and Secretary Taft for his duplicity, and declared their determination to seek the defeat of either if nominated for the office of President of these United States, or anyone named by them for said office. Booker Washington, ever concerned for his own selfish ambitions, indifferent to the cries of the race so long as he wins the approval of white men who do not believe in the Negro, defies the absolutely unanimous call of all factions of the race for Foraker? Leader of the self-seekers, he has persistently, but thank heaven unsuccessfully, sought to entangle the whole race in the meshes of subordination.   Knowing the race could only be saved by fighting cowardice, we have just as persistently resisted every attempt he has made to plant his white flag on the domains of equal manhood rights and our efforts have been rewarded by the universal denunciation of his doctrines of submission and his utter elimination as a possible leader of his race.

Generally speaking, the radical party has fought every movement of any sort that tends to draw a colour line.

Boston Hotel for Coloured People

One of the enterprises of Boston which interested me deeply was a Negro hotel, the Astor House, which is operated by Negroes for Negro guests.   It has 200 rooms, with a telephone in each room, a restaurant, and other accommodations.   It struck me that it was a good example of Negro self-help that Negroes should be proud of.   But upon mentioning it to a coloured man I met I found that he was violently opposed to it.

"Why hotels for coloured men?" he asked.   "I believe in hotels for men.   The coloured man must not draw the line himself if he does n't want the white man to do it.   He must demand and insist constantly upon his rights as an American citizen."

I found in Boston and in other Northern cities many Negroes who took this position.   A white woman, who sought to establish a help and rescue mission for coloured girls similar to those conducted for the Jews, Italians, and other nationalities in other cities, was violently opposed, on the ground that it set up

---

he had acted hastily and on the basis of inadequate evidence to warrant such drastic action. Roosevelt later made some amends for his action.

5. Issue of September 2, 1907.

a precedent for discrimination. In the same way separate settlement work (though there is a separate settlement for Jews in Boston) and the proposed separate Y. M. C. A. have met with strong protests. Everything that tends to set the Negro off as a Negro, whether the white man does it or the Negro does it, is bitterly opposed by this party of coloured people.

They fought the Jamestown Exposition because it had a Negro Building, which they called the "Jim Crow Annex," and they fought the National Christian Endeavour Convention because the leaders could not assure Negro delegates exactly equal facilities in the hotels and restaurants. Of course the denunciation of the white South is continuous and bitter. It is noteworthy, however, that even the leaders of the movement not only recognise and conduct separate newspapers and ask Negroes to support them, but that they urge Negroes to stand together politically.

Boston Negroes Seen by a New York Negro Newspaper

But the large proportion of coloured newspapers in the country, the strongest and ablest of which is perhaps the New York *Age*, are supporters of Washington and his ideals. The Boston correspondent of the *Age* said recently:

It is unfortunate in Boston that we have a hall which we can get free of charge: we refer to Faneuil Hall. They work Faneuil Hall for all it is worth. Scarcely a month ever passes by that does not see a crowd of Afro-Americans in Faneuil Hall throwing up their hats, yelling and going into hysterics over some subject usually relating to somebody a thousand miles away, never in relation to conditions right at home. The better element of Negroes and the majority of our white friends in this city have become disgusted over the policy that is being pursued and has been pursued for several months in Boston. Your correspondent can give you no better evidence of the disgust than to state that a few days ago there was one of these hysterical meetings held in Faneuil Hall and our people yelled and cried and agitated for two hours and more. The next day not one of the leading papers, such as the *Herald* and the *Transcript*, had a single line concerning this meeting. A few years ago had a meeting been held in Faneuil Hall under the leadership of safe and conservative Afro-Americans, both of these newspapers and papers of similar character would have devoted from two to three columns to a discussion of it. Now, in Boston, they let such meetings completely alone.

If there ever was a place where the Negro seems to have more freedom than he seems to know what to do with, it is in this city.

In spite of the agitation against drawing the colour line by the radical party, however, the separation is still going on.

6. Joseph B. Foraker, Republican senator from Ohio 1897-1909, was the leading congressional critic of President Roosevelt in the Brownsville affair.

And it is not merely the demand of the white man that the Negro step aside by himself, for the Negro himself is drawing the colour line, and drawing it with as much enthusiasm as the white man. A genuine race-spirit or race-consciousness is developing. Negroes are meeting prejudice with self-development.

It is a significant thing to find that many Negroes who a few years ago called themselves "Afro-Americans," or "Coloured Americans," and who winced at the name Negro, now use Negro as the race name with pride. While in Indianapolis I went to a Negro church to hear a speech by W. T. Vernon, one of the leading coloured men of the country, who was appointed Register of the United States Treasury by President Roosevelt. On the walls of the church hung the pictures of coloured men who had accomplished something for their race, and the essence of the speaker's address was an appeal to racial pride and the demand that the race stand up for itself, encourage Negro business and patronise Negro industry. All of which, surely, is significant.

How Negroes Themselves Draw the Colour Line

The pressure for separation among the Negroes themselves is growing rapidly stronger. Where there are mixed schools in the North there is often pressure by Negroes for separate schools. The Philadelphia *Courant*, a Negro newspaper, in objecting to this new feeling, says:

> Public sentiment, so far as the white people are concerned, does not object to the mixed school system in vogue in our city half as much as the Afro-American people seem to be doing themselves. We find them the chief objectors.

One reason why the South to-day has a better development of Negro enterprise, one reason why Booker T. Washington believes that the South is a better place for the Negro than the North, and advises him to remain there, is this more advanced racial spirit. Prejudice there, being sharper, has forced the Negro back upon his own resources.

Dr. Frissell[7] of Hampton is always talking to his students of the "advantages of disadvantages."

I was much struck with the remark of a Negro business man I met in Indianapolis:

7. Hollis B. Frissell succeeded General Samuel C. Armstrong as principal of Hampton Institute in 1893.

"The trouble here is," he said, "that there is not enough prejudice against us."

"How is that?" I inquired.

"Well, you see we are still clinging too much to the skirts of the white man. When you hate us more it will drive us together and make us support coloured enterprises."

When in Chicago I heard of an interesting illustration of this idea. With the increasing number of Negro students prejudice has increased in the Chicago medical schools, until recently some of them have, by agreement, been closed to coloured graduate students. Concerning this condition, the Chicago *Conservator*, a Negro newspaper, says: "The cause of this extraordinary announcement is that the Southern students object to the presence of Negroes in the classes. Now it is up to the Negro doctors of the country to meet this insult by establishing a post-graduate school of their own. They can do it if they have the manhood, self-respect, and push. Let Doctors Hall, Williams,[8] Boyd and others get busy."

To this the New York *Age* adds:

"Yes; let us have a school of that sort of our own."

And this is no idle suggestion. Few people have any conception of the growing progress of Negroes in the medical profession. In August, 1907, the Coloured National Medical Association held its ninth annual session at Baltimore. Over three hundred delegates and members were in attendance from thirty different states. Graduates were there not only from Harvard, Yale, and other white colleges, but from coloured medical schools like Meharry and Howard University. Negro hospitals have been opened and are well supported in several cities.

National Negro Business League

All over the country the Negro is organised in business leagues and these leagues have formed a National Business League which met last August in Topeka, Kansas. I can do no better in interpreting the spirit of this work, which is indeed the practical spirit of the Southern party, than in quoting briefly from the address of Booker T. Washington, who is the president of the league:

Despite much talk, the Negro is not discouraged, but is going forward. The race owns to-day an acreage equal to the combined acreage of Holland and

8. Dr. Daniel Hale Williams became the foremost Negro surgeon in the United States.

Belgium. The Negro owns more land, more houses, more stores, more banks, than has ever been true in his history. We are learning that no race can occupy a soil unless it gets as much out of it as any other race gets out of it. Soil, sunshine, rain, and the laws of trade have no regard for race or colour. We are learning that we must be builders if we would succeed. As we learn this lesson we shall find help at the South and at the North. We must not be content to be tolerated in communities, we must make ourselves needed. The law that governs the universe knows no race or colour. The force of nature will respond as readily to the hand of the Chinaman, the Italian, or the Negro as to any other race. Man may discriminate, but nature and the laws that control the affairs of men will not and cannot. Nature does not hide her wealth from a black hand."

All along the line one finds this spirit of hopeful progress. A vivid picture of conditions, showing frankly both the weakness and strength of the Negro, is given by a coloured correspondent of the Indianapolis *Freeman*. He begins by telling of the organisation at Carbondale, Ill., of a joint stock company composed of thirty-nine coloured men to operate a dry goods store. The correspondent writes:

The question is, "Will the coloured people support this enterprise with their patronage?" It is a general cry all over the country that coloured people pass by the doors of our merchants and trade with any other concerns — Jews, Dagoes, Polacks, and what not. This is a very unfortunate fact which stands before us as a living shame. The very people who preach "race union, race support, race enterprise," are often the first to pass our own mercantile establishments by. The only places where coloured men can prosper in business are where our people are driven out of other people's places of business and actually forced to patronise our own. A certain cigar manufacturer in St. Louis, a first-class business man, putting out the very best classes of cigars, said, a few days ago, that some of the hardest work he ever did was to get a few of our own dealers to handle his goods. If but one-third of the stores and stands that sell cigars and tobacco in St. Louis alone would buy their goods of him he could in a few more years employ one or two dozen more men and women in his factory. A dry goods company in the same city is suffering from the same trouble. Our people will condescend to look in, but more often their purchases are made at a neighbouring Jew store. There are also in that neighbourhood several first-class, up-to-date, clean and tasty-looking coloured restaurants: but twice as many Negroes take their meals at the cheap-John, filthy, fourth-class chop counters run by other people near by. But, after all, my people are doing better in these matters than they did some time past. It was a most pleasant surprise to learn, the other day, that the coloured undertakers in St. Louis do every dollar's worth of business for our people in that line. This information was given by a reliable white undertaker and substantiated by the coloured undertakers. The white man was asked what he thought of it. He said he thought it was a remarkable illustration of the loyalty of the Negro to his own people and that they should be commended for it. And then there are two sides to every question. It is too often true that our people run their business on a low order — noisy, uncleanly, questionable, dive-like concerns — therefore do not deserve the patronage of decent people. Too many of our men do not know anything about business. They don't believe in investing their money in advertising their business in good first-class periodicals. We must not expect everybody to know where we are or what we have to sell unless we advertise. Many of our nickels would find their way to the cash drawer of a coloured man if we just knew where to find the store, restaurant or hotel.

Remarkable Development of Negroes

It is not short of astonishing, indeed, to discover how far the Negro has been able to develop in the forty-odd years since slavery a distinct race spirit and position. It is pretty well known that he has been going into business, that he is acquiring much land, that he has many professional men, that he worships in his own churches and has many schools which he conducts — but in other lines of activity he is also getting a foothold. Just as an illustration: I was surprised at finding so many Negro theatres in the country — theatres not only owned or operated by Negroes, but presenting plays written and acted by Negroes. I saw a fine new Negro theatre in New Orleans; I visited a smaller coloured theatre in Jackson, Miss., and in Chicago the Pekin Theatre is an enterprise wholly conducted by Negroes. Williams and Walker, Negro comedians, have long amused large audiences, both white and coloured. Their latest production, "Bandanna Land," written and produced wholly by Negroes, is not only funny, but clean.

Many other illustrations could be given to show how the Negro is developing in one way or another — but especially along racial lines. The extensive organisation of Negro lodges of Elks and Masons and other secret orders, many of them with clubhouses, might be mentioned. Attention might be called to the almost innumerable insurance societies and companies maintained by Negroes, the largest of which, the True Reformers, of Richmond, has over 50,000 members, and to the growth of Negro newspapers and magazines (there are now over two hundred in the country), but enough has been said, perhaps, to make the point that there has been a real development of a Negro spirit and self-consciousness. Of course these signal successes loom large among the ten million of the country and yet they show the possibilities: there is this hopeful side of Negro conditions in this country as well as the dark and evil aspects of which we hear all too much.

Out of this ferment of racial self-consciousness and readjust-

9. Bert Williams and George Walker were a famous vaudeville team of this period.

ment has grown, as I have shown, the two great Negro parties. Between them and within them lie the destinies of the race in this country, and to no small extent also the destiny of the dominant white race. It is, therefore, of the highest importance for white men to understand the real tendencies of thought and organisation among these ten million Americans. For here is vigour and ability, and whatever may be the white man's attitude toward the Negro, the contempt of mere ignorance of what the Negro is doing is not only short-sighted but positively foolish. Only by a complete understanding can the white man who has assumed the entire responsibility of government in this country meet the crises, like that of the Atlanta riot, which are constantly arising between the races.

CHAPTER XI

THE NEGRO IN POLITICS

THE discussion of the Negro in politics will of necessity deal chiefly with conditions in the South; for it is there, and there only, that the Negro is, at the present time, a great political problem. Negroes in the North are indeed beginning to play a conscious part in politics; but they are only one element among many. They take their place with the "Irish vote," the "German vote," the "Polish vote," the "labour vote," each of which must be courted or placated by the politicians. I have looked into Negro political conditions in several cities, notably Indianapolis and Philadelphia, and I cannot see that they are in any marked way different from the condition of any other class of our population which through ignorance, or fear, or ambition, votes more or less *en masse.* Many Negroes do not vote at all; some are as conscientious and incorruptible as any white citizen; but a large proportion, ignorant and short-sighted, are disfranchised by the use of money in one form or another at every election. One of the broadest observers in Indianapolis said to me:

"The Negro voters are no worse and no better than our foreign voting population."

Mayor Tom Johnson, himself Southern by birth, writes me regarding the Negro vote of Cleveland:

"I do not believe there is any larger percentage of unintelligent or dishonest votes among the coloured voters than among the white voters in the same walks of life."

Negro a National Problem

I wish here to emphasise again the fact that the Negro is not a sectional but a *national* problem. Anything that affects the South favourably or unfavourably reacts upon the whole country. And the same latent race feeling exists in the North that exists in the South (for it is human, not Southern). The North, indeed, as I have shown in previous chapters, confronted with a large influx of Negroes, is coming more and more to understand and sympathise with the heart-breaking problems which beset the South. Nothing short of the patient coöperation of the entire country, North and South, white and black, will ever solve the race question.

In this country, as elsewhere, political thought divides itself into two opposing forces, two great parties or points of view. Whatever their momentary names have been, whether Federalist, Democratic, Whig, Republican, Populist, or Socialist, one of these parties has been an Aristocratic or conservative party, the other a democratic or progressive party. The political struggle in this country (and the world over) has been between the aristocratic idea that a few men (or one man) should control the country and supervise the division of labour and the products of labour and the democratic idea that more people should have a hand in it.

The abolition of slavery in the South was an incident in this struggle. Slavery was not abolished because the North agitated, or because John Brown raided or Mrs. Stowe wrote a book, or for any other sentimental or superficial reason, but because it was undemocratic.

What Slavery Did

This is what slavery did: It enabled a comparatively few men (only about one in ten of the white men of the South was a slave-owner or slave-renter)[1] to control eleven states of the Union, to monopolise learning, to hold all the political offices, to own most of the good land and nearly all of the wealth. Not only did it keep the Negro in slavery, but nine-tenths of the white people (the so-called "poor whites," whom even the Negroes despised) were hardly more than peasants or serfs.[2] It was in many ways a charming aristocracy, but it was doomed from the beginning. If there had been no North, slavery in the South would have disappeared just as inevitably. It was the restless yeast of democracy, spreading abroad upon the earth (in Europe as well as America) that killed slavery and liberated both Negro and poor white men.

1. Actually, almost one-fourth of the southern white families in 1860 owned slaves, although many of these families held only one or two bondmen.
2. This was an exaggeration and a view commonly held during this period. The "typical" Southerner in the ante-bellum era was a yeoman farmer, as

Revolutions such as the Civil War change names: they do not at once change human relationships. Mankind is reconstructed not by proclamations or legislation or military occupation, but by time, growth, education, religion, thought.

When the South got on its feet again after Reconstruction and took account of itself, what did it find? It found 4,000,000 ignorant Negroes changed in name from "slave" to "freeman," but not changed in nature. It found the poor whites still poor whites; and the aristocrats, although they had lost both property and position, were still aristocrats. For values, after all, are not outward, but inward: not material, but spiritual. It was as impossible for the Negro at that time to be less than a slave as it was for the aristocrat to be less than an aristocrat. And this is what so many legal-minded men will not or cannot see.

What happened?

Exactly what might have been predicted. Southern society had been turned wrong side up by force, and it righted itself again by force. The Ku Klux Klan, the Patrollers, the Bloody Shirt movement, were the agencies (violent and cruel indeed, but inevitable) which readjusted the relationships, put the aristocrats on top, the poor whites in the middle, and the Negroes at the bottom. In short, society instinctively reverted to its old human relationships. I once saw a man shot through the body in a street riot. Mortally wounded, he stumbled and rolled over in the dust, but sprung up again as though uninjured and ran a hundred yards before he finally fell dead. Thus the Old South, though mortally wounded, sprung up and ran again.

The Struggle in South Carolina

The political reactions after Reconstruction varied, of course, in the different states, being most violent in states like South Carolina, where the old aristocratic régime was most firmly entrenched, and least violent in North Carolina, which has always been the most democratic of Southern states.

In South Carolina then, for example, the aristocrats in 1875 returned to political supremacy?

General Wade Hampton, who represented all that was highest in the old régime, became governor of the state. A

Frank Lawrence Owsley shows in *Plain Folk of the Old South* (Baton Rouge, 1949).

3. The Democrats, led by Wade Hampton, their candidate for governor in 1876, did not fully regain control until 1877.

similar tendency developed, of course, in the other Southern states, and a notable group of statesmen (and they *were* statesmen) appeared in politics — Hill and Gordon of Georgia, Lamar and George of Mississippi, Butler of South Carolina, Morgan of Alabama, all aristocrats of the old school.[4]

Apparently the ancient order was restored; apparently the wounded man ran as well as ever. But the Old South, after all, had received its mortal wound. There *had* been a revolution; society *had* been overturned. The institution on which it had reared its ancient splendour was gone: for the aristocrat no longer enjoyed the special privilege, the enormous economic advantage of *owning* his labourers. He was reduced to an economic equality with other white men, and even with the Negro, either of whom could *hire* labour as easily and cheaply as he could. And the baronial plantation which had been the mark of his grandeur before the war was now the millstone of his doom.

Special privilege, always the bulwark of aristocracy, being thus removed, the germ of democracy began to work among the poor whites. The disappearance of competitive slave labour made them unexpectedly prosperous; it secured a more equable division of wealth. With prosperity came more book-reading, more schooling, a greater *feeling* of independence. And this feeling animated the poor white with a new sense of freedom and power.

Enter now, when the time was fully ripe for a leader, the rude man of the people.

How often he appears in the pages of history, the sure product of revolutions, bursting upward like some devastating force, not at all silken-handed or subtle-minded, but crude, virile, direct, truthful.

Tillman, the Prophet

So Tillman came in South Carolina.[5] I can see him as he rode to the farmers' fairs and court days in the middle eighties, a sallow-faced, shaggy-haired man with one gleaming, restless, angry eye. He had been long preparing in silence for his task — struggling upward in the poverty-stricken days of the war and through the Reconstruction, without schooling, or chance of schooling, but endowed with a virile-mindedness

4. Benjamin H. Hill, senator in the Confederate Congress 1861-1865, United States representative 1875-1877, and United States senator 1877-1882; John B. Gordon, Confederate general, United States senator 1873-1880, 1891-1897; L. Q. C. Lamar, Confederate soldier and diplomat, United States representative 1857-

which fed eagerly upon certain fermentative books of an inherited library. Lying on his back in the evening on the porch of his farmhouse, he read Carlyle's "French Revolution" and Gibbon's "Rome." He had in him, indeed, the veritable spirit of the revolutionist: in the days of the Patrollers, he, too, had ridden and hunted Negroes. He had seen the aristocracy come again into power; he had heard the whisperings of discontent among the poor whites. And at fairs and on court days in the eighties I hear him screaming his speeches of defiance, raucous, immoderate, denouncing all gentlemen, denouncing government by gentlemen, demanding that government be restored to the "plain people!" On one of the transparencies of those days he himself had printed the words (strange reminder of the Commune!):

"Awake! arise! or be forever fallen."

He spoke not only to the farmers, but he flung defiance at the aristocrats in the heart of the aristocracy. At Charleston, one of the proudest of Southern cities, he said:

"Men of Charleston, I have always heard that you were the most self-idolatrous people that ever lived; but I want to say to you that the sun does not rise in the Cooper and set in the Ashley. It shines all over the state. . . . If the tales that have been told me or the reports which have come to me are one-tenth true, you are the most arrant set of cowards God ever made."

And everywhere he went he closed his speeches with this appeal:

"Organise, organise, organise. With organisation you will become free once more. Without it, you will remain slaves."

Once, upon an historic occasion on the floor of the United States Senate, Tillman paused in the heat of a debate to explain (not to excuse) his fiery utterances.

"I am a rude man," he said, "and don't care."

That is Tillman. They tried to keep him and his followers out of the political conventions; but he would not be kept out, nor kept down. Years later he himself expressed the spirit of revolt in the United States Senate. Zach McGhee tells how he had been making one of his fierce attacks, an ebullition in general against things as they are. A senator arose to snuff him out in the genial senatorial way.

1860, 1873-1877, United States senator 1877-1885, Secretary of the Interior 1885-1888, Associate Justice of the United States Supreme Court 1888-1893; James Z. George, Confederate soldier, United States senator 1881-1897; Matthew C. Butler, Confederate general, United States senator 1877-1895; John T. Morgan,

"I would like to ask, Mr. President, what is before the Senate?"

"*I* am before the Senate," screamed Tillman.

In 1890 Tillman was elected governor of South Carolina: the poor white, at last, was in power.

The same change was going on all over the South. In Mississippi the rise of the people (no longer poor) was represented by Vardaman, in Arkansas by Jeff Davis, and Georgia and Alabama have experienced the same overturn in a more complicated form. It has become a matter of pride to many of the new leaders of the "plain people" that they do not belong to the "old families" or to the "aristocracy." Governor Comer[6] told me that he was a "doodle-blower" — a name applied to the poor white dwellers on the sand hills of Alabama. Governor Swanson[7] of Virginia is proud of the fact that he is the first governor of the state wholly educated in the public schools and colleges. Call these men demagogues if you will, and some of them certainly are open to the charge of appealing to the prejudices and passions of the people, they yet represent a genuine movement for a more democratic government in the South.

The old aristocrats gibe at the new leaders even to the point of bitter hatred (in South Carolina at least one murder has grown out of the hostility of the factions); they see (how acutely!) the blunders of untrained administrators, their pride in their states is rubbed blood-raw by the unblushing crudities of the Tillmans, the Vardamans, the Jeff Davises. Go South and talk with any of these men of the ancient order and you will come away feeling that conditions in the South are without hope.

"High Men" of the Old South

And those old aristocrats had their virtues. One loves to hear the names still applied at Richmond, Montgomery, Macon, and Charleston to the men of the old type, by other men of the old type. How often I have heard the terms a "high man," an "incorruptible man." Beautiful names! For there was a personal honour, a personal devotion to public duties among many of these ante-bellum slave-owners that made them indeed "high men."

When they were in power their reign was usually skilful

Confederate soldier, United States senator 1877-1907.

5. Benjamin R. ("Pitchfork Ben") Tillman, governor of South Carolina 1891-1895, United States senator 1895-1918.

6. Braxton Bragg Comer, governor of Alabama 1907-1911.

and honest: the reign of a beneficent oligarchy. But it was selfish: it reigned for itself — with nine-tenths of the people serfs or slaves. Its luxuries, its culture, its gentleness, like that of all aristocracies, was enjoyed at the fearful cost of poverty, ignorance, and slavery of millions of human beings. It had no sympathy, therefore it perished from off the earth.

The new men of the Tillman type made glaring, even violent mistakes, but for the most part honest mistakes; they saw clearly what they wanted: they wanted more power in the hands of the people, more democracy, and they went crudely at the work of getting it. In spite of the bitterness against Varda-man among some of the best people of Mississippi I heard no one accuse him of corruption in any department of his adminis-tration. On the whole, they said he had directed the business of the state with judgment. And Tillman, in spite of the dire predictions of the aristocrats, did not ruin the state. Quite to the contrary, he performed a notable service in extending popular education, establishing an agricultural college, regulating the liquor traffic (even though the system he established has since degenerated). Never before, indeed, has South Carolina, and the South generally, been more prosperous than it has since these men went into power, never has wealth increased so rapidly, never has education been so general nor the percentage of illiteracy so low. The "highest citizen" may not be so high (if it can be called high) in luxury and culture as he was before the war, but the average citizen is decidedly higher.

Having thus acquired a proper historical perspective, we may now consider the part which the Negro has played in the politics of the South. Where does *he* come in?

Where the Negro Comes In

Though it may seem a sweeping generalisation, it is none the less literally true that up to the present time the Negro's real influence in politics in the South has been almost negligible. He has been an *issue*, but not an *actor* in politics. In the ante-bellum slavery agitation no Negroes appeared; they were an inert lump of humanity possessing no power of inner direction; the leaders on both sides were white men. The Negroes did

7. Claude A. Swanson, United States representative 1893-1906, governor of Virginia 1906-1910, United States senator 1910-1933, and Secretary of the Navy 1933-1939.

not even follow poor old John Brown.   And since the war, as I have shown, the struggle has been between the aristocrats and the poor whites.   They have talked *about* the Negro, but they have not let *him* talk.   Even in Reconstruction times, and I am not forgetting exceptional Negroes like Bruce, Revels, Pinchback,[8] and others, the Negro was in politics by virtue of the power of the North.   As a class, the Negroes were not self-directed but used by Northern carpetbaggers and political Southerners who took most of the offices and nearly all of the stealings.

In short, the Negro in times past has never been in politics in the South in any positive sense.   And that is not in the least surprising.   Coming out of slavery, the Negro had no power of intelligent self-direction, practically no leaders who knew anything.   He was still a slave in everything except name, and slaves have never yet ruled, or helped rule.

The XV Amendment to the Constitution could not really enfranchise the Negro slaves.   Men must enfranchise themselves. And this political equality by decree, not by growth and development, caused many of the woes of Reconstruction.

Two distinct impulses mark the effort of the South to disfranchise the Negro.   The first was the blind revolt of Reconstruction times, in which force and fraud were frankly and openly applied.   The effort to eliminate the Negro brought the white people together in one dominant party and the "Solid South" was born.   For years this method sufficed; but in the meantime the Negro was getting a little education, acquiring self-consciousness, and developing leaders of more or less ability.   It became necessary, therefore, both because the Negro was becoming more restive, less easily controlled by force, and because the awakening white man disliked and feared the basis of fraud on which his elections rested, to establish legal sanction for disfranchisement, to define the political status of the Negro by law.

Now, the truth is that the mass of Southerners have *never believed that the Negro has or should have any political rights.* The South as a whole does not now approve and never has approved of the voting Negro.   A few Negroes vote everywhere, "but not enough," as a Southerner said to me, "to do any hurt."

The South, then, has been placed in the position of *providing by law for something that it did not really believe in.*

8.   Blanche K. Bruce, United States senator from Mississippi 1875-1881; Hiram R. Revels, United States senator from Mississippi 1870-1871; Pinckney B. S. Pinchback, lieutenant governor of Louisiana 1871-1872 and acting governor for a short time during that period.

It was prophesied that when the Negro was disfranchised by law and "eliminated from politics" the South would immediately stop discussing the Negro question and divide politically along new lines. But this has not happened. Though disfranchisement laws have been in force in Mississippi for years there is less division in the white party of that state than ever before.

Why is this so? Because the Negro, through gradual education and the acquisition of property, is becoming more and more a real as well as a potential factor in politics. For he is just beginning to be *really* free. And the South has not yet decided how to deal with a Negro who owns property and is self-respecting and intelligent and who demands rights. The South is suspicious of this new Negro: it dreads him; and the politicians in power are quick to play upon this sentiment in order that the South may remain solid and the present political leadership remain undisturbed.

For the South, however much it may talk of the ignorant masses of Negroes, does not really fear them; it wants to keep them, and keep them ignorant. It loves the ignorant, submissive old Negroes, the "mammies" and "uncles"; it wants Negroes who, as one Southerner put it to me, "will do the dirty work and not fuss about it." It wants Negroes who are really inferior and who *feel* inferior. The Negro that the South fears and dislikes is the educated, property-owning Negro who is beginning to demand rights, to take his place among men as a citizen. This is not an unsupported statement of mine, but has been expressed over and over again by speakers and writers in every part of the South. I have before me a letter from Charles P. Lane, editor of the Huntsville (Alabama) *Daily Tribune*, written to Governor Comer. It was published in the Atlanta *Constitution*. The writer is arguing that the Negro disfranchisement laws in Alabama are too lenient, that they permit too many Negroes to vote. He says:

We thought then (in 1901, when the new Alabama Constitution disfranchising the Negro was under discussion), as we do now, that the menace to peace, the danger to society and white supremacy was not in the illiterate Negro, but in the upper branches of Negro society, the educated, the man who, after ascertaining his political rights, forces the way to assert them,

He continues:

We, the Southern people, entertain no prejudice toward the ignorant per se inoffensive Negro. It is because we know him and for him we entertain a compassion. But our blood boils when the educated Negro asserts himself politically. We regard each assertion as an unfriendly encroachment upon our native superior rights, and a dare-devil menace to our control of the affairs of the state.

In this are we not speaking the truth? Does not every Southern Caucasian "to the manor born" bear witness to this version? Hence we present that the way to dampen racial prejudice, avert the impending horrors, is to emasculate the Negro politically by repealing the XV Amendment of the Constitution of the United States.

I use this statement of Mr. Lane's not because it represents the broadest and freest thought in the South, for it does not, but because it undoubtedly states frankly and clearly the point of view of the *majority* of Southern people. It is the point of view which, talked all over Georgia last year, helped to elect Hoke Smith governor of the state, as it has elected other governors. Hoke Smith's argument was essentially this:

Hoke Smith's Views

The uneducated Negro is a good Negro; "he is contented to occupy the natural status of his race, the position of inferiority." The educated and intelligent Negro, who wants to vote, is a disturbing and threatening influence. We don't want him down here; let him go North.

This feeling regarding the educated Negro, who, as Mr. Lane says, "ascertains his rights and forces his way to assert them," is the basic fact in Southern politics. It is what keeps the white people welded together in a single party; it is what sternly checks revolts and discourages independence.

Keeping this fact in mind, let us look more intimately into Southern conditions.

Following ordinary usage I have spoken of the Solid South. As a matter of fact the South is not solid, nor is there a single party. The very existence of one strong party presupposes another, potentially as strong. In the South to-day there are, as inevitably as human nature, two parties and two political points of view. And one is aristocratic and the other is democratic.

It is noteworthy in the pages of history that parties which were once democratic become in time aristocratic. We are accustomed for example, to look back upon Magna Charta as a mighty instrument of democracy; which it was; but it was not democracy according to our understanding of the word. It merely substituted a baronial oligarchy for the divine-right rule of one man, King John. It did not touch the downtrodden slaves, serfs and peasants of England. And yet that struggle of the barons was of profound moment in history, for it started the spirit of democracy on its way downward, it was the seed from which sprung English constitutionalism, which finally flowered in the American republic.

Tillman, as I have shown, wrung democracy from the old slave-owning oligarchy. He conquered: he established a democracy in South Carolina which included poor whites as well as aristocrats. But Tillman in his fiery pleas for the rights of men no more considered the Negro than the old barons considered the serfs of their day in the struggle against King John. It was and is incomprehensible to him that the Negro "has any rights which the white man is bound to respect."

In short we have in the South the familiar and ancient division of social forces, but instead of two white parties, we now see a white aristocratic party, which seeks to control the government, monopolise learning, and supervise the division of labour and the products of labour, struggling with a democratic party consisting of a few white and many coloured people, which clamours for a part in the government. That, in plain words, is the true situation in the South to-day.

Has the Spirit of Democracy Crossed the Colour Line?

For democracy is like this: once its ferment begins to work in a nation it does not stop until it reaches and animates the uttermost man. Though Tillman's hatred and contempt of the Negro who has aspirations is without bounds, the spirit which he voiced in his wild campaigns does not stop at the colour line. Movements are so much greater than men, often going so much further than men intend. A prophet who stands out for truth as Tillman did cannot, having uttered it, thereafter limit it nor recall it. As I have been travelling about the country, how often I have heard the same animating whisper from the Negroes that Tillman heard in older days among the poor whites:

"We are free; we are free."

Yes, Tillman and Vardaman are right; education, newspapers, books, commercial prosperity, are working in the Negro too; he, too, has the world-old disease of restlessness, ambition, hope. And many a Negro leader and many a Negro organisation — and that is what is causing the turmoil in the South, the fear of the white aristocracy — are voicing the equivalent of Tillman's bold words:

"Awake! arise! or be forever fallen."

Now we may talk all we like about the situation, we may say that the Negro is wrong in entertaining such ambitions, that his hopes can never be gratified, that he is doomed forever to menial and inferior occupations — the plain fact remains (as Tillman himself testifies), that the democratic spirit *has* crossed the colour line irrespective of laws and conventions, that the Negro *is* restless with the ambition to rise, to enjoy all that is best, finest, most complete in this world. How humanly the ancient struggle between aristocracy seeking to maintain its "superiority" and democracy fighting for "equality" is repeating itself! And this struggle in the South is complicated, deeply and variously, by the fact that the lower people are black and of a different race. They wear on their faces the badge of their position.

What is being done about it?

As every student of history is well aware, no aristocracy ever lets go until it is compelled to. How bitterly King John fought his barons; how bitterly the South Carolina gentlemen fought the rude Tillman! Having control of the government, the newspapers, the political parties, the schools, an aristocracy surrounds and fortifies itself with every possible safeguard. It maintains itself at any cost. And that is both human and natural; that is what is happening in the South to-day. Exactly the same conflict occurred before the war when the old slave-owning aristocracy (which everyone now acknowledges to have been wrong) was defending itself and the institution upon which its existence depended. The old slave-owning aristocrats believed that they were made of finer clay than the "poor whites," that their rule was peculiarly beneficent, that if any-

thing should happen to depose them the country would go
to ruin and destruction. It was the old, old conviction, common to kings and oligarchies, that they were possessed of a
divine right, a special and perpetual franchise from God.

The White South Defends Itself

The present white aristocratic party in the South is defending
itself exactly after the manner of all aristocracies.

In the first place, having control of the government it has
entrenched itself with laws. The moment, for example, that
the Negro began to develop any real intelligence and leadership,
the disfranchisement process was instituted. Laws were so
worded that every possible white man be admitted to the
franchise and every possible Negro (regardless of his intelligence) be excluded. These laws now exist in nearly all the
Southern states.[9] Although the XV Amendment to the Federal
Constitution declares that the right to vote shall not be "denied
or abridged . . . on account of race or colour or previous
condition of servitude," the South, in defence of its white
aristocracy, has practically nullified this amendment. Governor Hoke Smith of Georgia, for example, said (June 9, 1906):

> Legislation can be passed which will . . . not interfere with the right
> of any white man to vote, and get rid of 95 per cent. of the Negro voters.

Not only do the enacted laws disfranchise all possible
Negroes, but many other Negroes who have enough property
or education to qualify, are further disfranchised by the
dishonest administration of those laws. For the machinery
of government, being wholly in white hands, the registers and
judges of election have power to keep out any Negro, however
fit he may be. I know personally of many instances in which
educated and well-to-do Negroes have been refused the right to
register where ignorant white men were readily admitted.

The law, after all, in this matter, plays very little figure.
The white majority has determined to control the government
utterly and to give the Negro, whether educated or not, no
political influence. That is the plain truth of the matter.
Listen to Hoke Smith in his campaign pledge of last year:

"I favour, and if elected will urge with all my power, the
elimination of the Negro from politics."

9. Beginning with Mississippi in 1890 and ending with Oklahoma in 1910,
eight southern states introduced literacy and property qualifications and other
ingenious devices into their constitutions in order to disfranchise Negro voters.

Let us also quote the plain-speaking Vardaman in his address of April, 1907, at Poplarville, Miss.:

> How is the white man going to control the government? The way we do it is to pass laws to fit the white man and make the other people (Negroes) come to them. . . . If it is necessary every Negro in the state will be lynched; it will be done to maintain white supremacy. . . . The XV Amendment ought to be wiped out. We all agree on that. Then why don't we do it?

It may be argued that this violent expression does not represent the best sentiment of the South. It does not; and yet Vardaman, Tillman, Jeff Davis, Hoke Smith, and others of the type are *elected*, the *majority* in their states support them. And I am talking here of politics, which deals with majorities. In a following chapter I shall hope to deal with the reconstructive and progressive minority in the South as it expresses itself especially in the more democratic border states like North Carolina.

Thus the spirit of democracy has really escaped among the coloured people and it is running abroad like a prairie fire. Tillman, the prophet, sees it:

"Every man," he says, "who can look before his nose can see that with Negroes constantly going to school, the increasing number of people who can read and write among the coloured race . . . will in time encroach upon our white men."

Demand Repeal of XV Amendment

In order, then, to prevent the Negro getting into politics, the Tillmans, Vardamans, and others declare that the South must strike at the foundation of his political liberty: the XV Amendment must be repealed. In short, the moment the Negro meets one test of citizenship, these political leaders advance a more difficult one: now proposing to take away entirely every hope of ultimate citizenship. In the recent campaign for the United States senatorship in Mississippi, Vardaman and John Sharp Williams were quite in accord on this point, though they disagreed on methods of accomplishing the purpose![10] When the political liberty of the Negro has thus been finally removed, the South, say these men, will again have two parties, and will be able to take the place it should occupy in the counsels of the nation.

Take the next point in the logic of the political leaders.

10. In the Democratic primary of August 1, 1907, Williams was narrowly nominated in a fierce contest with Governor James K. Vardaman.

It is a fact of common knowledge in history that aristocracies cannot long survive when free education is permitted among all classes of people. Education is more potent against oligarchies and aristocracies than dynamite bombs. Every aristocracy that has survived has had to monopolise learning more or less completely — else it went to the wall. It is not surprising that there should have been no effective public-school system in the South before the war where the poor whites could get an education, or that the teaching of Negroes was in many states a crime punishable by law. Education enables the Negro, as Mr. Lane says, to "ascertain his rights and force his way to assert them." Therefore to prevent his ascertaining his rights he must not be educated. The undivided supremacy of the white party, it is clearly discerned, is bound up with Negro ignorance. Therefore we have seen and are now seeing in certain parts of the South continuous agitation against the education of Negroes. That is one reason for the feeling in the South against "Northern philanthropy" which is contributing money to support Negro schools and colleges.

"What the North is sending South is not money," says Vardaman, "but dynamite; this education is ruining our Negroes. They're demanding equality."

A Southern View of Negro Education

When I was in Montgomery, Ala., a letter was published in one of the newspapers from Alexander Troy, a well-known lawyer. It did not express the view of the most thoughtful men of that city, but I am convinced that it represented with directness and force the belief of a large proportion of the white people of Alabama. The letter says:

All the millions which have been spent by the state since the war in Negro education . . . have been worse than wasted. Should anyone ask "Has not Booker Washington's school been of benefit to the Negro?" the so-called philanthropists of the North would say "yes," but a hundred thousand white people of Alabama would say "no." . . . Ask any gentleman from the country what he thinks of the matter, and a very large majority of them will tell you that they never saw a Negro benefited by education, but hundreds ruined. He ceases to be a hewer of wood and a drawer of water. . . .

Exclude the air and a man will die, keep away the moisture and the flower will wither. Stop the appropriations for Negro education, by amendment to the Constitution if necessary, and the school-house in which it is taught will decay.

Not only that, but the Negro will take the place the Creator intended he should take in the economy of the world — a dutiful, faithful, and law-abiding servant.

These are Mr. Troy's words and they found reflection in the discussions of the Alabama legislature then in session. A compulsory education bill had been introduced; the problem was to pass a law that would apply to white people, not to Negroes. In this connection I heard a significant discussion in the state senate. I use the report of it, for accuracy, as given the next morning in the *Advertiser:*

Senator Thomas[11] said . . . he would oppose any bills that would compel Negroes to educate their children, for it had come to his knowledge that Negroes would give the clothing off their backs to send their children to school, while too often the white man, secure in his supremacy, would be indifferent to his duty.

At this point Senator Lusk[12] arose excitedly to his feet and said:

"Does the Senator from Barbour mean to say that the Negro race is more ambitious and has more aspirations than the white race ?"

"The question of the gentleman . . . is an insult to the senate of Alabama," replied Senator Thomas deliberately. "It is an insult to the great Caucasian race, the father of all the arts and sciences, to compare it to that black and kinky race which lived in a state of black and ignorant savagery until the white race seized it and lifted it to its present position."

The result of this feeling against Negro education has shown itself in an actual reduction of Negro schooling in many localities, especially in Louisiana, and little recent progress anywhere else, compared with the rapid educational development among the whites, except through the work of the Negroes themselves, or by Northern initiative.

In cutting off an $8,000 appropriation for Alcorn College (coloured) Governor Vardaman, as a member of the board of trustees, said:

"I am not anxious even to see the Negro turned into a skilled mechanic. God Almighty intended him to till the soil under the direction of the white man and that is what we are going to teach him down there at Alcorn College."

Without arguing the rights or wrongs or necessities of their position, I have thus endeavoured to set down the purposes of the present political leadership in the South.

Economic Cause for White Supremacy

Now the chief object of any aristocracy, the reason why it wishes to monopolise government and learning, is because

11. Elias Perry Thomas of Clayton, Alabama.
12. John Alexander Lusk of Guntersville, Alabama.

it wishes to supervise the division of labour and the products of labour. That is the bottom fact.

In slavery times, of course, the white man supervised labour absolutely and took *all* the profits. In some cases to-day, by a system of peonage, he still controls the labourer and takes all the profits. But as the Negro has grown in education and property he not only wishes to supervise his own labour, but demands a larger share in the returns of labour. He is no longer willing to be an abject "hewer of wood and a drawer of water" as he was in slavery times; he has an ambition to own his own farm, do his own business, employ his own professional men, and so on. He will not "keep his place" as a servant. And that is the basis of all the trouble.

Many of the utterances of white political leaders resolve themselves into a statement of this position.

At the American Bankers' Association last fall Governor Swanson of Virginia said:

"At last the offices, the business houses, and the financial institutions are all in the hands of intelligent Anglo-Saxons, and with God's help and our own good right hand we will hold him (the Negro) where he is."

In other words, the white man will by force hold all political, business and financial positions; he will be boss, and the Negro must do the menial work; he must be a servant.

Hoke Smith says in his speech (the italics are mine):

"Those Negroes who are contented to occupy the natural status of their race, the position of inferiority, *all competition being eliminated between the whites and the blacks*, will be treated with greater kindness."

In other words, if the Negro will be contented to keep himself inferior and not compete with the white man, everything will be all right. And thus, curiously enough, while Hoke Smith in his campaign was thundering against railroad corporations for destroying competition, while he was glorifying the principle of "free and unrestricted trade," he was advocating the formation of a monopoly of all white men by the elimination of the competition of all coloured men.

Indeed, we find sporadic attempts to pass laws to compel the Negro to engage only in certain sorts of menial work. In Texas not long ago a bill was introduced in the legislature "to confine coloured labour to the farm whenever it was found in city and town communities to be competing with white labour." In the last session of the Arkansas legislature Senator McKnight introduced a bill providing that Negroes be forbidden "from waiting on white persons in hotels, restaurants, or becoming barbers, or porters on trains, and to prevent any white man from working for any Negro."

In a number of towns respectable, educated, and prosperous Negro doctors, grocers, and others have been forcibly driven out. I visited Monroe, La., where two Negro doctors had been forced to leave town because they were taking the practice of white physicians. In the same town a Negro grocer was burned out, because he was encroaching on the trade of white grocers.

Neither of the laws above referred to, of course, was passed; and the instances of violence I have given are sporadic and unusual. For the South has not followed the dominant political leaders to the extremes of their logic. Human nature never, finally, goes to extremes: it is forever compromising, never wholly logical. While perhaps a large proportion of Southerners would agree perfectly with Hoke Smith or Tillman in his *theory* of a complete supremacy of all white men in all respects, as a matter of fact nearly every white Southerner is encouraging some practical exception which quite overturns the theory. Tens of thousands of white Southerners swear by Booker T. Washington, and though doubtful about Negro education, the South is expending millions of dollars every year on coloured schools. Vardaman, declaiming violently against Negro colleges, has actually, in specific instances, given them help and encouragement. I told how he had cut off an $8,000 appropriation from Alcorn College because he did not believe in Negro education: but he turned around and gave Alcorn College $14,000 for a new lighting system, *because he had come in personal contact with the Negro president of Alcorn College, and liked him.*

And though the politicians may talk about complete Negro disfranchisement, the Negro has nowhere been completely disfranchised: a few Negroes vote in every part of the South.

I once heard a Southerner argue for an hour against the participation of the Negro in politics, and then ten minutes

COLONEL JAMES LEWIS
United States Receiver at New Orleans

Photograph by G. V. Buck
W. T. VERNON
Register of the United States Treasury

RALPH W. TYLER
An auditor of the Government at Washington

J. POPE BROWN
of Pulaski County, Georgia

EX-GOVERNOR JAMES K. VARDAMAN
of Mississippi

Photograph by Harris-Ewing

Copyright, 1906, by Hallen Studios

SENATOR JEFF DAVIS
of Arkansas

GOVERNOR HOKE SMITH
of Georgia

Photograph by F. B. Johnston

SENATOR B. R. TILLMAN
of South Carolina

EX-GOVERNOR W. J. NORTHEN
of Georgia

later tell me with pride of a certain Negro banker in his city whom we both knew.

"Dr. ——'s all right," he said. "He's a sensible Negro. I went with him myself when he registered. He ought to vote."

So personal relationships, the solving touch of human nature, play havoc with political theories and generalities. Mankind develops not by rules but by exceptions to rules. While the white aristocracy has indeed succeeded in controlling local government in the South almost completely, it has not been able to dominate the federal political organisations, which include many Negroes. And though often opposing education for the Negro, the aristocracy has not, after all, monopolised education; and the Negro, in spite of Jim Crow laws and occasional violence, has actually been pushing ahead, getting a foothold in landownership, entering the professions, even competing in some lines of business with white men. So democracy, though black, is encroaching in the world-old way on aristocracy; how far Negroes can go toward real democratic citizenship in the various lines — industrial, political, social — no man knows. We can see the fight; we do not know how the spoils of war will finally be divided.

CHAPTER XII

THE BLACK MAN'S SILENT POWER

HOW THE DOMINANCE OF THE IDEA OF THE NEGRO STIFLES
FREEDOM OF THOUGHT AND SPEECH IN SOUTHERN POLITICS

A T PRESENT the point of view of a large proportion of Southern white people on the Negro question is adequately expressed by such men as Tillman, Jeff Davis, and Hoke Smith. They are the political leaders. Their policies are, in general, the policies adopted; they are the men elected to office. Even in the border states, where the coloured population is not so dense as in the black belt, the attitude of the politicians is much the same as it is in the black belt. So far as the Negro question is concerned, Governor Swanson of Virginia stands on practically the same platform as Tillman and Hoke Smith — though he has not found it necessary to express his views as vigorously. And the position of the black-belt states in regard to the disfranchisement of the Negro and the extension of " Jim Crow" laws is being accepted by the border state of Maryland and the Western state of Oklahoma.

But there also exists, and particularly in Virginia, North Carolina, Tennessee, and Georgia, a vigorous minority point of view, which I have referred to in a former chapter as the "broadest and freest thought of the South." Although it has not yet attained political position, it is a party of ideas, force, convictions, with a definite constructive programme. To this constructive point of view I have been able, thus far, to refer only incidentally.

In the present chapter I wish to consider some of the effects upon Southern life of the domination of the Negro as a political issue, and the result of the continued supremacy of leaders like Tillman.

In the next chapter, under the title "The New Southern

Statesmanship," I shall outline the programme and recount the activities of the new Southern leaders.

The Most Sinister Form of Negro Domination

Travelling in the South one hears much of the "threat of Negro domination," by which is generally meant political control by Negro voters or the election of Negro officeholders. But there already exists a far more real and sinister form of Negro domination. For the Negro still dominates the *thought* of the South. For over eighty years, until quite recently, few great or serious issues have occupied the attention of the South save those growing out of slavery and the Negro problem. Though the very existence of our nation is due largely to the courage, wisdom, and political genius of Southern statesmanship — to Washington, Jefferson, Marshall, Patrick Henry, and their compatriots — the South, since the enunciation of the Monroe doctrine in 1823, has played practically no constructive part in national affairs. As Professor Mitchell[1] of Richmond well points out, the great, vitalising influences which swept over the entire civilised world during the first half of the nineteenth century, the liberalising, nationalising, industrialising influences, left the South untouched. For it was chained in common slavery with the Negro. Instead of expanding with the new thought, it clung to slavery in opposition to the liberal tendency of the age, it insisted upon states' rights in opposition to nationality, it contented itself with agriculture alone, instead of embracing the rising industrialism. "It was an instance," as Professor Mitchell says, "of arrested development."

Dr. John E. White of Atlanta has ably expressed the ethical result upon a people of confining their thought to a single selfish interest:

"As long as we struggled for that which was good for everybody everywhere," he says, "we moved with Providence and the South led the van. There were great human concerns in the building up of the Republic. The whole world was interested in it. It was a work ennobling to a people — the inspiration of a great national usefulness. The disaster began when the South began to think only for and of itself — began to have only one problem."

[1]. Samuel Chiles Mitchell, professor of history at Richmond College and later president of the University of South Carolina and of Delaware College.

Thus the South, owing to the presence of the Negro, dropped behind in the progress of the world. And while the new and vitalising world influences are now spreading abroad throughout the South, manifesting themselves in factories, mines, mills, better schools, and more railroads, the old, ugly Negro problem still shackles political thought and cripples freedom of action. In other words, the South is being rapidly industrialised, but not so rapidly liberalised and nationalised, though these developments are certainly following.

Exploiting Negro Prejudice

The cause of this dominance of thought by the Negro lies chiefly with a certain group of politicians whose interest it is to maintain their party control and to keep the South solid. And they do this by harping perpetually on the Negro problem. I observed, wherever I went in the South and found busy and prosperous industries, that the Negro problem was little discussed. One manufacturer in New Orleans said to me, when I asked him about the Negro question:

"Why, I'm so busy I never think about it."

And that is the attitude of the progressive, constructive Southerner: he is impatient with the talk about the Negro and the Negro problem. He wants to forget it.

But there remains a body of men in the South who, not prosperous in other industries, still make the Negro a sort of industry: they live by exploiting Negro prejudice. They prevent the expression of new ideas and force a great people to confine its political genius to a worn-out issue.

Roosevelt Democrats Down South

Talking with all classes of white men in the South, I was amazed to discover how many of them had ceased to be Democrats (in the party sense) at all, and were followers in their beliefs of Roosevelt and the Republican party. Many of them told me that they wished they could break away and express themselves openly and freely, but they did not dare. A considerable number have ventured to vote the Republican ticket in national elections (especially on the free-silver issue), but few indeed have had the courage to declare their independence in state or local affairs. For the instant a rift appears in the harmony of the white party (and that is a better name for it than Democratic) the leaders talk Negro, and the would-be independents are driven back into the fold. Over and over again leaders with new issues have endeavoured to get a hearing. A number of years ago the Populist movement spread widely throughout the South. Tom Watson of Georgia, Kolb[2] of Alabama, Butler[3] of North Carolina, led revolts against the old Democratic party. By fusion with the Republicans the Populists carried North Carolina. But the old political leaders immediately raised the Negro issue, declared that the Populists were encouraging the Negro vote, and defeated the insurgents, driving most of their leaders into political obscurity. Now, I am not arguing that Populism was an ideal movement, nor that its leaders were ideal men; I am merely trying to show the cost of independence in the South. A number of years ago Emory Speer, of Georgia, now Federal Judge, ran for Congress on an independent ticket. His platform was "The Union and the Constitution, a free ballot and a fair count." The inevitable Negro issue was raised against him, it was insisted that there must be no division among white people lest the Negro secure the balance of political power, and Speer was finally defeated.[4] He became a Republican and has since had no influence in state politics.

Upon this point an able Southern writer, Professor Edwin Mims of Trinity College, N. C., has said:

"The independents in the South have to face the same state of affairs that the independents of the North did in the '80's — all the better traditions connected with one party, and most of the respectable people belonging to the same party. Just as George William Curtis and his followers were accused of being Democrats in disguise and of being traitors to the 'grand old party' that had saved the Union and freed the slaves, and deserters to a party of Copperheads, so the Southern independent is said to be a Republican in disguise, and is told of the awful crimes of the Reconstruction era. When all other arguments have failed, there is the inevitable appeal to the threatened domination of an inferior race which is not now even a remote possibility."

2. Reuben F. Kolb, Farmers' Alliance leader and unsuccessful candidate for governor of Alabama in 1890, 1892, and 1894.

3. Marion Butler, agrarian spokesman and fusionist leader, United States senator 1895-1901.

As a result of this domination of a worn-out issue, political contests in the South have ordinarily concerned themselves not with stimulating public questions, but with the personal qualifications of the candidates. The South has not dared to face real problems lest the white party be split and the Negro voter somehow slip into influence. A campaign was fought last year in Mississippi. Of course the candidates all belonged to the white party; all therefore subscribed to identically the same platform — which had been prepared by the party leaders — so that the only issue was the personality of the candidates. Let me quote from the Mississippi correspondent of the New Orleans *Times-Democrat*, April 29, 1907:

The only "issue" . . . is the personality of the candidate himself. The voter may take the speeches of each candidate and analyse them from start to finish, and he will fail to find where there is any difference of opinion between the candidates on any of the live questions of the day which are likely to affect Mississippi. He must, therefore, turn from the speeches to the candidate himself for an "issue" and must take his choice of the several candidates as men, and decide which of them will do most good to the state and be the safest man to entrust with the helm.

Negro Holds Democratic Party Together

I am speaking here, of course, of the Negro as a dominant issue, the essential element which holds the Democratic party together and without which other policies could not be carried or candidates elected. Vigorous divisions on other issues have taken place locally within the lines of the Democratic party, especially during the last two or three years. The railroad and trust questions have been prominently before the people in most of the Southern states. During his long campaign for governor Hoke Smith talked railroads and railroad influence in politics constantly, but in order to be elected he raised the Negro question and talked it vigorously, especially in all of his country addresses. It is also highly significant that the South should have taken so strong a lead in the prohibition movement, although even this question has been more or less connected with the Negro problem, the argument being that the South must forbid the liquor traffic because of its influence on the Negro. No states in the Union, indeed, have been more radical in dealing with the trust

4. Speer was elected as an Independent Democrat in 1878 and re-elected as an Independent in 1880, serving in Congress from 1879 to 1883.

question than Texas and Arkansas; and Alabama, Georgia, and North Carolina have been the scenes of some of the hottest fights in the country on the railroad question. All this goes to show that, once freed from the incubus of the Negro on Southern thought, the South would instantly become a great factor in national questions. And being almost exclusively American in its population, with few rich men and ideals of life not yet so subservient to the dollar as those of the North, it would become a powerful factor in the progressive and constructive movements of the country. The influence of a single bold man like Tillman in the Senate has been notable. In the future the country has much to look for from the idealism of Southern statesmanship.

Stifling Free Speech

But the unfortunate result of the dominance of the single idea of the Negro upon politics has been to benumb the South intellectually; to stifle free thought and free speech. Let a man advance a new issue and if the party leaders do not favour it they have only to cry out "Negro," twisting the issue so as to emphasise its Negro side (and every question in the South has a Negro side), and the independent thinker is crushed. I once talked with the editor of a newspaper in the South who said to me, "such and such is my belief."

"But," I said, "you take just the opposite position in your paper."

"Yes — but I can't talk out; it would kill my business."

This timorousness has touched not only politics, but has reached the schools and the churches — and still shackles the freest speech. George W. Cable, the novelist, was practically forced to leave the South because he advocated the "continual and diligent elevation of that lower man which human society is constantly precipitating," because he advocated justice for the Negro.

Professor Andrew Sledd was compelled to resign from Emory College in Georgia because he published an article in the *Atlantic Monthly* taking a point of view not supported by the majority in Southern sentiment![5] Professor John Spencer Bassett was saved from a forced resignation from Trinity

5. Andrew Sledd, "The Negro: Another view," *Atlantic Monthly,* XC (July, 1902), pp. 65-73.

College in North Carolina for a similar offence after a lively fight in the Board of Trustees which left Trinity with the reputation of being one of the freest institutions in the South.[6]

The situation in the South has made people afraid of the truth. Political oratory, particularly, often gets away entirely from the wholesome and regenerative world of actual facts. I quoted in the last chapter from a speech of Governor Swanson of Virginia, in which he said: "The business houses and financial institutions are in the hands of intelligent Anglo-Saxons, and with God's help and our own good right hand we will hold him (the Negro) where he is."

Negro's Progress in Richmond

What a curious thing oratory is! Right in Governor Swanson's own city of Richmond there are four banks owned and operated by Negroes; one of the Negro bankers sat in the convention to which Governor Swanson was at that moment speaking. There is a Negro insurance company, "The True Reformers," in which I saw eighty Negro clerks and stenographers at work. It has a surplus of $300,000, with a business in thirty states. Negroes also own and operate in Richmond four clothing stores, five drug stores, many grocery stores (some very small, of course), two hotels, four livery stables, five printing establishments, eight fraternal insurance companies, seven meat markets, fifty eating-places, and many other sorts of business enterprises, small, of course, but growing rapidly. In Richmond also, there are ten Negro lawyers, fifteen physicians, three dentists, two photographers, eighty-five school teachers, forty-six Negro churches.

Southerners Who See the Danger

When I make the assertion regarding "free speech" and the fear of truth in the South, I am making no statement which has not been far more forcibly put by thoughtful and fearless Southerners who see and dread this sinister tendency.

The late Chancellor Hill,[7] of the University of Georgia, spoke of the "deadly paralysis of intellect caused by the enforced uniformity of thought within the lines of one party." He said: "Before the war the South was in opposition to the rest of

6. The Bassett case developed from the publication of an article, "Stirring Up the Fires of Race Antipathy," in the October, 1903, number of the *South Atlantic Quarterly,* in which Professor Bassett asserted that Booker T. Washington was "the greatest man, save General Lee, born in the South in a hundred

civilisation on the question of slavery. It defended itself: its thinking, its political science, even its religion was not directed toward a search for truth, but it was concentrated on the defence of a civil and political order of things. These conditions made impossible a vigorous intellectual life."

William Preston Few, dean of Trinity College, North Carolina, writes (*South Atlantic Quarterly*, January, 1905):

"This prevalent lack of first hand thinking and of courage to speak out has brought about an unfortunate scarcity of intellectual honesty."

An excellent illustration of this condition grew out of the statement of Dr. Edwin A. Alderman, president of the University of Virginia, at a dinner a year or so ago, in which he compared the recent political leadership of the South somewhat unfavourably with the statesmanship of the Old South. Upon hearing of this remark Senator Bailey of Texas angrily resigned from the alumni committee of the University. Chancellor Hill said, concerning the incident:

"The question whether Dr. Alderman was right or wrong becomes insignificant beside the larger question whether Senator Bailey was right or wrong in his method of dealing with a difference of opinion. And this leads to the question: Have we freedom of opinion in the South? Must every man who thinks above a whisper do so at the peril of his reputation and his influence, or at the deadlier risk of having an injury inflicted upon the institution which he represents?"

In giving so much space to the words and position of Vardaman, Tillman, Hoke Smith, and others, I have not yet sufficiently emphasised the work and influence of the thoughtful and constructive men of the South. But it must be borne in mind that I am writing of politics, of majorities: and politicians of the Tillman type are still the political forces in the South. They are in control: they are elected. Yet there is the growing class of new statesmen whose work I shall recount in the next chapter.

Whites Disfranchised as Well as Blacks

But the limitation of intellectual freedom has not been the only result of the political dominance of the Negro issue. **It**

years." Bassett's colleagues at Trinity rallied to his support during the subsequent furor and the trustees refused to accept the professor's resignation.

7. Walter B. Hill, chancellor of the University of Georgia and a leader of the educational reform movement in Georgia prior to his death in 1905.

is curious to observe that when one class of men in any society is forced downward politically, another is forced up: for so mankind keeps its balances and averages. A significant phase of the movement in the South to eliminate the Negro is the sure return to government by a white aristocracy. For disfranchisement of the Negro has also served to disfranchise a very large proportion of the white people as well. In every Southern state where Negro disfranchisement has been forced, the white vote also has been steadily dwindling. To-day in Alabama not half the white males of voting age are qualified voters. In Mississippi the proportion is still lower.

In the last Presidential election the state of Mississippi was carried by Parker with a total vote of only 58,383, out of a total of 349,177 citizens (both white and coloured) of voting age. Only one-third of the white men voted. It has been found, indeed, in several counties in Mississippi, that while the number of white eligibles has been decreasing, the number of Negroes on the registration lists has been increasing. In the city of Jackson, Miss., last year, 1,200 voters were registered out of a population of 32,000 people.

To show the dwindling process, take the single county of Tallapoosa in Alabama. The last census shows 4,203 whites and 2,056 blacks of voting age, 6,259 in all. After the adoption of the new constitution disfranchising the Negro in 1901, the total registration was 4,008. Last fall, although the important question of prohibition had arisen and an especial effort was made to get voters out, an investigation showed there were only 1,700 qualified voters in the country.

This astonishing condition is due primarily to the fact that there is no vital party division on new issues in the South; but it is also due to the franchise tests, which, having been made severe to keep the Negro out, operate also to disfranchise hundreds of thousands of poor and ignorant white men. I spent much time talking with white workingmen, both in the cities and in the country. I asked them why so many workingmen and farmers did not vote. Here is one comprehensive reply of a labour leader:

"What's the use? We have to pay two dollars a year poll-tax, and pay it nearly a year before election. And why vote? There are no real issues at stake. An election is merely

---

8. Joseph W. Bailey, member of the United States House of Representatives 1891-1901, and of the United States Senate 1901-1913.

a personal quarrel in the clique of men who control the Democratic party. Why should we pay two dollars a year and go to the bother of satisfying the personal ambition of some man we are not interested in?"

A White Oligarchy

So the white vote is dwindling; the political power is being gathered into the hands of fewer and fewer men. And there is actually springing up a large class of non-voting white men not unlike the powerless "poor whites" of ante-bellum times. The white politicians, indeed, in some places do not encourage the poorer white men to qualify, for the fewer voters, the more certain their control.

Of course the chief fights in Mississippi and elsewhere are not at the elections, but in the Democratic (white) primaries; but this fact only accentuates the point I wish to make: the limitation of political independence of action. Such conditions are deeply concerning the thoughtful men of the South; but while they think, few dare to brave political extinction by speaking out. One would think that the Republican party, which ostensibly stands for the opposition in the South, would cry out about conditions. But it does not. The fact is, the Republican party, as now constituted in the South, is even a more restricted white oligarchy than the Democratic party. In nearly all parts of the South, indeed, it is a close corporation which controls or seeks to control all the federal offices. Speak out? Of course not. It, too, is attempting to eliminate the Negro (in some places it calls itself "lily white"), and it works not inharmoniously with the Democratic politicians. For the Republican machine in the South really has no quarrel with the Democratic machine; it takes the federal offices which the Democrats cannot get, and the Democrats take local offices which the Republicans know they cannot get.

The South a Weapon in National Conventions

The Republican Presidents at Washington have, unfortunately, played into the hands of the Southern office-holding machine. Why? Partly because Republicans are few in the South and partly because a solid Republican delegation from the South, easily handled and controlled and favouring the administration, is a powerful weapon in national conventions. McKinley played almost absolutely into the hands of this Southern Republican machine, and Hanna operated it. Indeed, McKinley's nomination was probably due to the skill with which Hanna marshaled this solid phalanx of Southern delegates. Roosevelt has made a number of first-class appointments outside of the machine, even appointing a few Democrats of the high type of Judge Jones of Alabama.

Over and over in this book I have spoken of the Negro as a national, not a Southern issue; and in politics this is peculiarly true. Though having few Republicans, the South, through its office-holding Republican delegations, has largely influenced the choice of more than one Republican president. The "Solid South" is as useful to the Republican party as to the Democratic party. Why the certainty expressed by Republican politicians of the nomination of Taft? Because the national organisation felt sure it could control the Southern delegations. It counted on the "Solid South."

Thus in a very real sense the government of this entire nation turns upon the despised black man — whether he votes or not!

The Negro's Political Power in the North

In another way the Southern attitude toward the Negro affects the nation. Owing to disfranchisement and "Jim Crow" laws, thousands of Negroes have moved northward and settled in the great cities, until to-day Negro voters, though they may not (as has been claimed) hold the balance of power, yet wield a great influence in the politics of at least four states — Indiana, Ohio, New Jersey, and Rhode Island — and are also considerable factors in the political destiny of Illinois, Pennsylvania, New York, and Delaware. The potential influence of the Negro voter in the North is excellently illustrated in the recent campaign for the Republican nomination to the Presidency, especially in the fight in Ohio between Foraker and Taft and in the eagerness displayed by Taft to placate the Negro vote.

In still another way the Negro affects the entire nation. Through its attitude of exclusion the South exercises an influence on national legislation out of all proportion to its voting population. Though nearly all Negroes are disfranchised, as well as a large number of white voters, all these disfranchised voters are counted in the allotment of Congressmen to Southern states.

Out of this has grown a curious condition. In 1904 Alabama, Arkansas, Georgia, and Mississippi, which have thirty-five members in Congress, cast 413,516 votes, while Massachusetts alone, with only fourteen Congressmen, cast 445,098 votes.

Here, for example, is the record of South Carolina:

Total population of voting age, both white and coloured (1900) . .	283,325
Total white voting population	130,375
Total actual vote in 1902 for Congressmen	32,185
Total Democratic vote which elected seven Congressmen	29,343

Thus in South Carolina in 1902 an average of about 4,600 voters voted at the election for each Congressman (in 1904, a Presidential year, the average was about 8,100) while in New York State over 40,000 votes are cast in each Congressional district and in Pennsylvania about 38,000.

Now, I am not here criticising this condition; I am merely endeavouring to set down the facts as I find them. My purpose is to illustrate the profound and far-reaching effects of the Negro issue upon the nation. And is it not curious, when all is said, to observe how this rejected black man, whom the South has attempted to eliminate utterly from politics, has been for years changing and warping the entire government of this nation in the most fundamental ways! Did he not cause a civil war, the results of which still curse the country? And though excluded in large measure from the polls, does he not in reality cast his mighty vote for Presidents, Congressmen, Governors?

Often, looking out across the South, it appears to the observer that the Negro has a more far-reaching and real influence on our national life for being excluded from the polls than he would have if he were frankly and justly admitted to the franchise on the same basis as white men.

All the real thinkers and statesmen of the South have looked and longed for the hour when the South, free of this dominance of an ugly issue, should again take its great place in national affairs. In 1875, at the close of Reconstruction, Senator Lamar of Mississippi predicted in a speech at Jackson that the South, having eliminated the Negro from politics, would now divide on new economic issues and become politically healthy. But that has not happened; less division on real issues probably exists in Mississippi to-day than in 1875. Why? Is it not possible that the manner of the elimination of the Negro from politics is wrong? Has it occurred to leaders and statesmen that Negroes who are qualified can be eliminated *into* politics; that the present method in reality makes the Negro a more dangerous political factor than he would be if he were allowed to vote regularly and quietly?

Southerners Who Are Speaking Out

In spite of the domination of both parties in the South by narrowing groups of leaders there are not wanting men to fight for a new alignment. On the Republican side one of these men is Joseph C. Manning, of Alexander City, Ala., who publishes a paper called the *Southern American*. He has shown how white men are being disfranchised as well as Negroes, how the South is controlled by a "Bourbon oligarchy" in the Democratic party and a "federal-for-revenue" Republican party — as he calls them. His paper appears every week with his denunciations in big letters, urging the Republican party to reform and become a party of truth and progress. He says:

THE RALLYING CRY

The great body of the people of the white South, the masses of the white people of Alabama, are to-day suppressed by the strategy of a political autocracy dominating under the guise and pretence of a democracy.

Why not throw off the yoke and get in the fight?

Rise up above this petty delegate getting, patronage manipulating, state chairman squabbling, until this small politics shall become lost in the great and the supreme issue.

Stop this "lily-white" nonsense. Quit being sidetracked by this Bourbon wail of Negro. Recognise this vital force of the immovable truth that an injustice to one American citizen will react upon all. You can't have one law for the white man and another for the Negro in our form of government. You know that those who have talked the most of suppressing blacks have really suppressed you, white Republicans, and the most of the Southern whites.

The outcry of Negro and social equality and the like is the very essence of political moonshine.

A number of men inside the Democratic party are not afraid to speak out. Ex-Congressman Fleming[9] of Georgia said in a notable address at Athens, Ga.:

9. William H. Fleming, member of the United States House of Representatives 1897-1903.

"Those whose stock in trade is 'hating the nigger' may easily gain some temporary advantage for themselves in our white primaries, where it requires no courage, either physical or moral, to strike those who have no power to strike back — not even with a paper ballot. But these men will achieve nothing permanent for the good of the state or of the nation by stirring up race passion and prejudice. Injustice and persecution will not solve any of the problems of the ages. God did not so ordain his universe.

" Justly proud of our race, we refuse to amalgamate with the Negro, but the Negro is an American citizen, and is protected as such by guarantees of the Constitution that are as irrepealable almost as the Bill of Rights itself. Nor, if such a thing as repealing these guarantees were possible, would it be wise for the South. Suppose we admit the oft-reiterated proposition that no two races so distinct as the Caucasian and the Negro can live together on terms of perfect equality; yet it is equally true that without some access to the ballot, present or prospective, some participation in the government, no inferior race in an elective republic could long protect itself against reduction to slavery in many of its substantial forms — and God knows the South wants no more of that curse."

Men of the type of Mr. Fleming are far in the minority in the South; they are so few as yet as to count, politically speaking, for little or nothing. But the fact that they are there, that they are not afraid to speak out, even though it ruins them politically, is significant and hopeful.

Ante-bellum Aggression

Now it is this way with a party having only one issue: when attacked, it can only become more and more violent and vociferous upon that issue. And this is what we discover in the South: an increasing bitterness of leaders like Tillman and Vardaman, for they know that their own existence and that of the party which they represent depends upon keeping the Negro issue prominent. The very fact that they are violent is significant: it shows that they recognise powerful and growing new elements in the South, which, though not yet apparent politically, are getting hold of the people.

In other words, the present group of autocratic leaders is seeking at any length to defend itself. And its work is not only defensive, it is also offensive. It must be. The institution of slavery might have lasted many years longer if the Southern leaders had been content with the slave territory they already held. But they were not so content. They tried to extend slavery to the new territories of the Union, and it was this aggression that was the chief immediate cause of the Civil War. It was the struggle over Missouri and Kansas,[10] and the policy of the country regarding the new West, whether it should be admitted slave or free, which precipitated hostilities.

"Continual aggression," John Hay once said, "is the necessity of a false position." The ante-bellum Southern leaders saw that they must either extend their institution or else face its ultimate extinction.

At the present time we have a repetition of the ante-bellum aggression. As it happened then, we have speakers like Tillman and others coming North urging the validity of the Southern treatment of the Negro. Writers like Thomas Dixon rekindle old fires of hatred. At the same moment that Tillman is abusing the North for its interest in Southern education, he himself is speaking from Northern platforms to make sentiment for the Southern position. So we have the extension of disfranchisement and "Jim Crow" laws to the new Western state of Oklahoma and the agitation for disfranchisement in Maryland. So we have the advancing demand by Southerners in Congress for the repeal of the XV Amendment. And just recently Congressman Heflin[11] of Alabama has introduced a bill seeking to provide for "Jim Crow" distinctions upon the street-cars of Washington. How all this recalls the efforts of the ante-bellum Southern Congressmen to force the United States Government to take the Southern position on the slavery question!

Fighting to Put the Negro Down

I have recently read some of the voluminous discussions upon the subject of slavery which took place before the Civil War, and I have been astonished to find the arguments of the

10. Baker probably meant the struggle over Kansas and Nebraska and the bitterness resulting from the repeal of the Missouri Compromise.

11. James Thomas ("Cotton Tom") Heflin, United States representative

Southern political leaders of to-day almost identical in substance (though changed somewhat in form) with the reasoning of the old slave-owning class.   One hears the same arguments regarding the physiological and ethnological inferiority of all coloured men to all white men: the argument that "one drop of Negro blood makes a Negro," and even that the Negro is not a human being at all, but a beast.

I have before me a book recently published by a Bible house (of all places!) in St. Louis and widely circulated in the South. It is entitled "Is the Negro a Beast?" and it goes on to prove by Biblical quotation that he has no soul![12] Being a beast, it becomes a small matter to kill him.

One also hears the argument now, as in slavery times, of the divine right of the white man to rule the Negro.   "God intended the white man to rule," says Vardaman, "and the Negro to be a humble servant."   And finally there is the frank argument of physical force; that the white man, being strong, will and must rule the Negro.

Hoke Smith to-day is supporting much the same position that Robert Toombs held before the war.   Of course Hoke Smith has receded from the belief in the chattel slavery of the Negro for which Toombs contended; but in many other respects he evidently believes that the Negro should be reduced (as Ex-Congressman Fleming of Georgia says in the quotation given above) "to slavery in many of its substantial forms."   In order to validate its position and keep its place (and make the Negro keep his) the white aristocracy has been forced to defend the doctrine of all monarchies and aristocracies — the inequality of men in all respects.   Hoke Smith states the fundamental assumption thus plainly in his address (June 9, 1906):

"I believe the wise course is to plant ourselves squarely upon the proposition in Georgia that the Negro is in no respect the equal of the white man, and that he cannot in the future in this state occupy a position of equality."

Both the South and the North Undemocratic

Thus I have attempted to present the political situation in the South and the reasoning which underlies it.   It possesses a large significance for the entire country.

1904-1920, United States senator 1920-1931.

12. Charles Carroll, "*The Negro a Beast*": or, "*In the Image of God*" (St. Louis, 1900).

Here is the fact: the war and the emancipation proclamation did not make the South completely democratic; it merely cut away one bulwark of aristocracy — slavery. The South is still dominated by the aristocratic idea, and more or less frankly so. The South has admitted only grudgingly, and not yet fully, the "poor white" man to democratic political fellowship. There are, as I have shown, hundreds of thousands of disfranchised white Americans in the South. Moreover many white leaders look askance on the new Italian immigrants, though they, too, are white men. The extreme point of view in regard to the foreigner was expressed in a speech by the Hon. Jeff Truly, candidate for governor of Mississippi, at Magnolia in that state on March 18, 1907:

"I am opposed to any inferior race. The Italian immigration scheme does not settle the labour question; Italians are a threat and a danger to our racial, industrial, and commercial supremacy. Mississippi needs no such immigration. Leave your lands to your own children. As governor of the state, I promise that not one dollar of the state shall be spent for the immigration of any such."

As for the Negro, of course, the South has never believed in a democracy which really includes him.

But neither does the North. When we get right down to it, the controlling white men in the North do not believe in an inclusive democracy much more than the South. I have talked with many Northerners who go South, and it is astonishing to see how quickly most of them adopt the Southern point of view. For it is the doctrine which many of them, down in their hearts, really believe.

In reality the North also has an aristocratic government, an oligarchy based upon wealth and property, which dominates politics and governs the country more or less completely. Roosevelt has been fighting some of the more boisterous aspects of the rule of this oligarchy — and has showed the country how powerful it is!

The Underman Fighting All Over the World

It is curious, indeed, when one's attention is awakened to the facts, how strong the parallel is between the South and the

North. I mean here a parallel not in laws or even in customs, but in spirit, in the living reality which lies down deep under institutions, which is, after all, the only thing that really counts.

The cause of all the trouble in the North is similar to what it is in the South: the underman will not keep his place. He is restless, ambitious, he wants civil, political, and industrial equality. Thus we see the growth of labour organisations, and the spread of populists and socialists, who demand new rights and a greater share in the products of labour. They will not, as Hoke Smith says of the Negroes, "content themselves with the place of inferiority." The essential feature of the history of the last five years in this country, and it will go down in history as the beginning of great things, has been the vague, crudely powerful effort of the underman (half his strength wasted because he is blind) to limit in some degree the power of this moneyed aristocracy. Such is the meaning of the demand for trust and railroad legislation, such the significance of the insurance investigation, such the effort to curb the power of men like Rockefeller, Harriman, Morgan.

So the North, in spirit, also disfranchises its lower class. It does it by the purchase at elections in one form or another of its "poor whites" and its Negroes. What else is the meaning of Tammany Hall and the boss and machine system in other cities? Tammany Hall is our method of disfranchisement: it is our cunning machine for nullifying the fourteenth and fifteenth amendments. While the South is disfranchising by legislation, the North is doing it by cash.

The Question We Are Coming To

I have spoken of the lack of free speech in the South; but that is not peculiar to the South. Though there is undoubtedly a far greater intellectual freedom to-day in the North than in the South, yet the North has disciplined more than one professor for his utterances on the trust or railroad questions. South or North, it is dangerous to attack the entrenched privilege of those in control.

We criticise the frankness of Vardaman in advocating different standards of justice for white men and Negroes, but do we not have the same custom in the North? How extremely difficult it is sometimes to get a rich criminal into jail in the North!

In short, we are coming again face to face in this country with the same tremendous (even revolutionary) question which presents itself in every crisis of the world's history:

"What is democracy? What does democracy include? Does democracy really include Negroes as well as white men? Does it include Russian Jews, Italians, Japanese? Does it include Rockefeller and the Slavonian street-sweeper? And Tillman and the Negro farmhand?"

CHAPTER XIII

THE NEW SOUTHERN STATESMANSHIP

Democracy is the progress of all through all, under the leadership of the best and the wisest."—*Mazzini*.

IN FORMER chapters I have had much to tell that was unpleasant and perhaps discouraging; but it had to be told, for it is there, and must be honestly met and reckoned with.

But the chief pleasure of the present task has been the opportunity it has given me to meet the working idealists of the South, and to see the courageous and unselfish way in which they are meeting the obstacles which confront them. If any man would brighten his faith in human nature, if he would attain a deeper and truer grasp upon the best things of life, let him attend one of the educational rallies of Virginia, North Carolina, Tennessee, Georgia, or Texas, and hear the talks of Dr. S. C. Mitchell, President Alderman, J. Y. Joyner, P. P. Claxton, Chancellor Barrow, President Houston,[2] and others; or let him spend a few days at Hampton with Dr. Frissell, or at Tuskegee with Dr. Washington, or at Calhoun with Miss Thorne.[3] Coming away from a meeting one night at Tuskegee after there had been speaking in the chapel by both white and coloured men, I could not help saying to myself:

"The Negro problem is not unsolvable; it is being solved, here and now, as fast as any human problem can be solved."

Men may be found straining their vision to see some distant and complex solution to the question (have we not heard talk of deportation, extermination, amalgamation, segregation, and the like?) when the real solution is under their very eyes, going forward naturally and simply.

It is this quiet, constructive movement among the white people in the South which I wish to consider here.

1. David C. Barrow, chancellor of the University of Georgia.
2. David F. Houston, president of the University of Texas, later a member of Wilson's cabinet.

In a former chapter I showed how the Negroes of the country are divided into two parties or points of view, the greater led by Booker T. Washington, the lesser by W. E. B. DuBois. Washington's party is the party of the opportunist and optimist, which deals with the world as it is: it is a constructive, practical, cheerful party. It emphasises duties rather than rights. Dr. DuBois's party, on the other hand, represents the critical point of view. It is idealistic and pessimistic: a party of agitation, emphasising rights rather than duties.

But these two points of view are by no means peculiar to Negroes: they divide all human thought; and the action and reaction between them is the mode of human progress.

Division of White Leadership in the South

White leadership in the South, then, is divided along similar lines with Negro leadership — a party of rights and a party of duties. But with this wide difference: among the Negroes as I showed, the party of agitation and criticism led by DuBois is far inferior both numerically and in influence to the party of opportunity and duties led by Washington. For the Negroes have been forced to concede the futility of trying to progress by political action and legislation, by rights specified but not earned. Washington's preaching has been:
"Stop thinking about your rights and get down to work. Get yourself right and the world will be all right."

But among the white people of the South the party of agitation and the emphasis of rights rather than duties is still far in the ascendency. Led by such men as Tillman, Vardaman, Jeff Davis, Hoke Smith, and others, it controls, for the present, the policies of the entire South. It has much to say of the rights of the white man, very little about his duties. It is, indeed, doing for the whites by agitation and legislation (often a kind of force) exactly what Dr. DuBois would like to do for the Negro, if he could.

"Agitate, object, fight," say both Tillman and DuBois.

"Work," says Washington.

Now, the same logic of circumstances which produced Booker T. Washington and his significant movement among the Negroes has produced a group of new and highly able

3. Charlotte R. Thorne, former teacher at Hampton Institute, operated a school for Negroes at Calhoun in south Alabama.

white leaders. These new leaders saw that agitation (while most necessary in its place) would not, after all, build up the South; they saw that although the sort of leader typified by Tillman and Vardaman was passing laws and winning elections, he was not, after all, getting anywhere; that race feeling was growing more bitter, often to the injury of Southern prosperty; that progress is not built upon stump speeches. The answer to all this was plain enough.

"Let us stop talking, forget the race problem, and get to work. It does not matter where we take hold, but let us go to work."

And the doctrine of work in the South has become a great propaganda, almost, indeed, a passion. It has found expression in a remarkable growth of industrial activities, cotton-mills, coal-mines, iron and steel industries; in new methods of farming; in spreading railroads. But more than all else, perhaps, it has developed a new enthusiasm for education, not only for education of the old classical sort, but for industrial and agricultural education — the training of workers. All this, indeed, represents the rebound from years of agitation in which the Negro has been "cussed and discussed," as one Southerner put it to me, beyond the limit of endurance. Wherever I went in the South among the new industrial and educational leaders I found an active distaste for the discussion of the Negro problem. These men were too busy with fine new enterprises to be bothered with ancient and unprofitable issues.

New Prescriptions for Solving the Negro Problem

When I asked Professor Dillard[4] of New Orleans how he thought the Negro question should be treated, he replied:

"With silence."

"My prescription," says President Alderman in his address on "Southern Idealism," "is 'silence and slow time,' faith in the South, and wise training for both white and black."

Edgar Gardner Murphy of Alabama, himself one of the new leaders, has thus outlined the position of the rising Southern leadership:

"The South is growing weary of extremists and of sen-

4. James H. Dillard, professor at Tulane University, member of the Southern Education Board, and, from 1908, director of the Jeanes Fund.

sational problem-solvers. . . . Our coming leadership will have a sense of proportion which will involve a steady refusal to be stampeded by antique nightmares and ethnological melodrama. It will possess an increasing passion for getting hold of the real things in a real world. And it will . . . deal with one task at a time. It will subordinate paper schemes of distant amelioration to duties that will help right now."

Emphasis here is laid upon "real things in a real world" and "duties that will help right now"; and that is the voice everywhere of the new statesmanship.

But let us be clear upon one point at the start. The platforms of these parties are matters of emphasis. One emphasises rights; the other emphasises duties. I have no doubt that Booker T. Washington believes as firmly in the rights of the Negro as any leader of his race; he has merely ceased to emphasise these rights by agitation until his people have gained more education and more property, until by honest achievement they are prepared to exercise their rights with intelligence.

In the same way, the views of many of the new Southern white leaders of whom I shall speak in this article have not radically changed, so far as the Negro is concerned; some of them, I have found, do not differ from Tillman upon essential points; but, like Washington, they have decided not to emphasise controversial matters, and go to work and develop the South, and the people of the South, for the good of the whole country. If the test has to come in the long run between white men and coloured men, as it will have to come and is coming all the time, they want it to be an honest test of efficiency. The fittest here, too, will survive (there is no escaping the great law!), but these new thinkers wish the test of fitness to be, not mere physical force, not mere brute power, whether expressed in lynching or politics, but the higher test of real capacity. They have supreme confidence that the white man is superior on his merits in any contest; and Washington, on his side, is willing to (indeed, he must) take up the gauntlet thus thrown down.

The condition in the South may be likened to a battle in which the contestants, weary of profitless and wordy warfare, are turning homeward to gather up new ammunition. Each

Photograph by Hitchler

JAMES H. DILLARD
of New Orleans, President Jeanes Fund Board.

Photograph by Pach Bros.

EDWIN A. ALDERMAN
President of the University of Virginia.

A. M. SOULE
President Georgia State College of Agriculture.

Photograph by The Elliotts

D. F. HOUSTON
President of the University of Texas.

Photograph by Pach Bros.

GEORGE FOSTER PEABODY
of New York, member of the Southern Education and Jeanes Fund Boards.

Photograph by Knaffl & Bro.

P. P. CLAXTON
of the University of Tennessee, leader of the educational campaign in Tennessee.

S. C. MITCHELL
of Richmond College; President of the Coöperative Education Association of Virginia.

JUDGE EMORY SPEER
of Georgia. After two terms in Congress he
was appointed to the Federal bench.

EDGAR GARDNER MURPHY
of Alabama, member Southern Education Board;
author "Problems of the Present South."

DR. H. B. FRISSELL
Principal Hampton Institute and member of
Southern Education and Jeanes Fund Boards.

R. C. OGDEN
of New York, President of the Southern Education Board.

J. Y. JOYNER
Superintendent of Public Instruction of North
Carolina.

side is passionately getting education, acquiring land, developing wealth and industry, preparing for the struggles of the future. And it is a fine and wholesome tendency. In a large sense, indeed, this movement typifies the progressive thought of the entire country for it means a sincere attempt to change the plane of battle (for battle there must be) from one of crude, primitive force, whether physical, political, or, indeed, industrial, to one of intellectual efficiency or usefulness to society.

And these working idealists of both races understand one another better than most people think. Dr. Mitchell and President Alderman understand Booker T. Washington, and he understands them. This is not saying that they agree. But agreement upon every abstract principle is not necessary where both parties are hard at work at practical, definite, and immediate tasks.

Self-Criticism in the South

The new Southern statesmanship began (as all new movements begin) with self-criticism. Henry W. Grady, a real statesman, by criticising the old order of things, announced the beginning of the "New South" — an active, working, hopeful South.

He saw the faults of the old exclusive agricultural life and the danger of low-class, uneducated labour, and he urged industrial development and a better school system. R. H. Edmonds of Baltimore, through the *Manufacturers' Record*, and many other able business leaders have done much to bring about the new industrial order: the day of new railroads, cotton-mills, and coal-mines; the day of cities.

But it is in the educational field that the development of the new statesmanship has been most remarkable. Although it was unfortunate in one way that so much of the political leadership of the South should have fallen to men of the type of Vardaman, Jeff Davis, and Heflin, it is hightly fortunate in another way. For it has driven the broadest and ablest minds in the South to seek expression in other lines of activity, in industry and in the church, but particularly in educational leadership. It is not without profound significance that the great American, General Lee, turned his attention and gave his highest energies after Appomattox, not to politics, but to education. The South to-day has a group of schoolmen who are leaders of extraordinary force and courage. The ministry has also attained an influence in the South which it does not possess in most parts of the North. The influence of Bishop Galloway[5] of Mississippi, Dr. John E. White and Dr. C. B. Wilmer of Atlanta, and many others has been notable.

For many years after the war the South was passive with exhaustion. Young men, who were not afraid, had to grow up to the task of reconstruction. And no one who has not traced the history of the South since the war can form any conception of the magnitude of that task. It was essentially the building of a new civilisation. The leaders were compelled not only to face abject poverty, but they have had to deal constantly with the problem of a labouring class just released from slavery. At every turn, in politics, in industry, in education, they were confronted with the Negro and the problem of what to do with him. Where one school-house would do in the North, they were compelled to build two school-houses, one for white children, one for black. It took from twenty-five to forty years of hard work after the war before the valuation of wealth in the South had again reached the figures of 1860. The valuations in the year 1890 for several of the states were less than in 1860. South Carolina in 1900 — forty years after the beginning of the war — had only just caught up with the record of 1860. Since 1890, however, the increase everywhere has been swift and sure.

Courage and Vision of New Leaders

Well, it required courage and vision in the earlier days to go before a poverty-stricken people, who had not yet enough means for living comfortably, and to demand of them that they build up and support two systems of education in the South. And yet that was exactly the task of the educational pioneers. Statesmanship, as I have said, begins with self-criticism. While the mere politician is flattering his followers and confirming them in their errors, the true statesman is criticising them and spurring them to new beliefs and stronger

5. Bishop Charles B. Galloway of the Methodist Episcopal Church, South.

activities. While the politician is pleading rights, the statesman also dares to emphasise duties. While the politicians
in the South (not all, but many of them) have been harping
on race prejudice and getting themselves elected to office by
reviving ancient hatred, these new statesmen have been facing
courageously forward, telling the people boldly of the conditions of illiteracy which surround them, and demanding
that schools be built and every child, white and black, be
educated. In many cases they have had to overcome a
settled prejudice against education, especially education of
Negroes; and after that was overcome they have had to build
up a sense of social responsibility for universal education
before they could count on getting the money they needed for
their work.

After the war the North, in one form or another, poured
much money into the South for teaching the Negroes; lesser
sums, like those coming from the Peabody fund, were contributed toward white schools. But in the long run there can
be no real education which is not self-education; outside
influences may help (or indeed hurt), but until a state — like
a man — is inspired with a desire for education and a willingness to make sacrifices to get it, the people will not become
enlightened.

In the middle eighties the fire of this inspiration began
to blaze up in many parts of the South. Various combustible
elements were present: a sense of the appalling condition of
illiteracy existing in the South; a pride and independence
of character which was hurt by the gifts of money from the
North; a feeling that the Negroes in some instances were
getting better educational opportunities than the white children; and, finally, the splendid idealism of young men who
saw clearly that the only sure foundation for democracy is
universal education.

Inspiration of Democracy in North Carolina

Not unnaturally the movement found its earliest expression
in North Carolina, which has been the most instinctively
democratic of Southern states. From the beginning of the
country North Carolina, with its population of Scotch-

Presbyterians and Quakers, has been inspired with a peculiar spirit of independence. When I was in Charlotte I went to see the monument which commemorates the Mecklenburg Declaration of Independence: the work of a group of stout-hearted citizens who decided, before the country at large was ready for it, to declare their independence of British rule. North Carolina was among the last of the Southern states to secede from the Union, and its treatment of its Negroes all along has been singularly liberal. For example, in several Southern states little or no provision is made for the Negro defective classes, but at Raleigh I visited a large asylum for Negro deaf, dumb, and blind which is conducted according to the most improved methods. And to-day North Carolina is freer politically, the state is nearer a new and healthy party alignment, than any other Southern state except Tennessee and possibly Kentucky.

Such a soil was fertile for new ideas and new movements. In 1889 two young men, Charles D. McIver and Edwin A. Alderman, now president of the University of Virginia, began a series of educational campaigns under the supervision of the state. They spoke in every county, rousing the people to build better school-houses and to send legislators to Raleigh who should be more liberal in educational appropriations. In many cases their rallies were comparable with the most enthusiastic political meetings — only no one was asking to be elected to office, and the only object was public service. As Alderman has said:

"It was an effort to move the centre of gravity from the court-house to the school-house."

And it really moved; the state took fire and has been afire ever since. Governor Aycock made the educational movement a part of his campaign; Governor Glenn[6] has been hardly less enthusiastic; and the development of the school system has been little short of amazing. When I was in Raleigh last spring J. Y. Joyner, State Superintendent of Schools, who was also one of the pioneer campaigners, told me that a new school-house was being built for every day in the year, and new school libraries established at the same rate. Between 1900 and 1906 the total amount of money expended for schools in North Carolina more than doubled, and while the school

6. Robert B. Glenn, governor of North Carolina 1905-1909.

population in the same years had increased only 6 per cent., the daily attendance had increased 28 per cent.

North Carolina Compared with Massachusetts

To give a graphic idea of the progress in education, I can do no better than to show the increase in public expenditures since 1872:

1872 Total school expenditures	. . . .	$ 42,856
1880 Total school expenditures	. . . . . .	349,831
1890 Total school expenditures	. . . . . .	787,145
1900 Total school expenditures	. . . . . .	1,091,610
1906 Total school expenditures	. . . . . .	2,291,053

I have looked into the statistics and I find that North Carolina spends more per hundred dollars of taxable property for school purposes than Massachusetts, which is perhaps the leading American state in educational expenditures. In 1906 North Carolina raised $.40 on every one hundred dollars, while Massachusetts raised $.387. But this does not mean, of course, that North Carolina has reached the standard of Massachusetts; it only shows how the people, though not rich, have been willing to tax themselves. And they have only just begun; the rate of illiteracy of the state, as in all the South, is still excessive among both white and coloured people. According to the last census, North Carolina has more illiterate white people than any other state in the Union, a condition due, of course, to its large population of mountaineers. While the progress already made is notable the leaders still have a stupendous task before them. At the present time, although taxing itself more per hundred dollars' worth of property than Massachusetts, North Carolina pays only $2.63 each year for the education of each child, whereas Massachusetts expends $24.89 — nearly ten times as much.

I do not wish to over-emphasise the work in North Carolina; I am merely using conditions there as a convenient illustration of what is going on in greater or less degree all over the South. One of the group of early enthusiasts in North Carolina was P. P. Claxton, who is now in charge of the educational campaign in Tennessee. With President Dabney,[7] formerly of the University of Tennessee and State Superintendent Mynders,[8]

7. Charles W. Dabney, a leading member of the Southern Education Board, went from the presidency of the University of Tennessee to the presidency of the University of Cincinnati.
8. Seymour A. Mynders.

Mr. Claxton has conducted a state-wide campaign for education. Every available occasion has been utilised: picnics, court-days, Decoration Days: and often the audiences have been larger and more enthusiastic than political rallies. Indeed, the meetings have been carried on much like a political campaign. At one time over one hundred speakers were in the field. Every county in the state was stumped, and in two years it was estimated that over half of the entire population of the state actually attended the meetings. Labour unions and women's clubs were stirred to activity, resolutions were passed, politicians were called upon to declare themselves, and teachers' organisations were formed. The result was most notable. In 1902 the state expended $1,800,000 for educational purposes; in 1908 — six years later — the total will exceed $4,000,000.

A similar campaign has been going on in Virginia, under the auspices of the Coöperative Educational Association, in which the leaders have been Dr. S. C. Mitchell, Professor Bruce Payne, President Alderman, and others. In this work Ex-Governor Montague[9] has also been a force for good, both while he was governor and since, and Governor Swanson at present is actively interested. Local leagues were formed in every part of the state to the number of 324. Negroes have also organised along the same line and now have ten local associations in five counties.

How the South Is Taxing Itself

One of the most striking features of the movement has been the development of the system of local taxation for school purposes — which is a long step in the direction of democracy. In the past the people have looked more or less to some outside source for help — to state or national funds, or the private gifts of philanthropists, or they have depended upon private schools — but now they are voting to take the burden themselves. In other words, with the building up of a popular school system, supported by local taxation, education in the South is becoming, for the first time, democratic. It would be difficult to overestimate the importance of this movement in stimulating the local pride and self-reliance of the people, or in inspiring each community with educational enthusiasm.

9. Andrew Jackson Montague, governor of Virginia 1902-1906, United States representative 1913-1937.

Another development of profound influence has been going on in the South. As I have already pointed out, the so-called "Northern philanthropist" has long been interested in Southern education, especially Negro education. For years his activities awakened, and indeed still awaken, a good deal of hostility in some parts of the South. Many Southerners have felt that the Northerners, however good their intentions, did not understand Southern conditions, and that some of the money was expended in a way that did not help the cause of progress in the South.

South and North Work Together

But both the Northerners (whatever their mistakes in method may have been) and the new Southern leaders were intensely and sincerely interested in the same thing: namely, better education and better conditions in the South. It was natural that these two groups of earnest and reasonable men should finally come together in a spirit of coöperation; and this is, indeed, what has happened. Out of a series of quiet conferences held in the South grew what has been called the "Ogden movement" and the Southern Education Board![10] This organisation was made up of three different classes of men: first, a group of the Southern leaders of whom I have spoken — Mitchell, Alderman, Dabney, Curry, Houston, Hill, McIver, Claxton, Edgar Gardner Murphy, Sydney J. Bowie, and Henry E. Fries; second, Southern men who, living in the North, were yet deeply interested in the progress of the South — men like Walter H. Page, George Foster Peabody, and Frank R. Chambers; and, finally, the Northerners — Robert C. Ogden, who was president of the board, William H. Baldwin, H. H. Hanna, Dr. Wallace Buttrick, Albert Shaw, and Dr. G. S. Dickerman.

One of the inspirers of the movement, also a member of the board, was Dr. H. B. Frissell, who followed General Armstrong as principal of Hampton Institute.

Each year conferences have been held in the South, a feature of which has been the "Ogden Special" — a special train from the North bringing Northern citizens to Southern institutions and encouraging a more intimate acquaintanceship on

10. The Ogden Movement began at a meeting in Capon Springs, West Virginia, in 1898. The Southern Education Board was created in 1901 to function

both sides. No one influence has been more potent than this in developing a spirit of nationalisation in the Southern educational movement.

So far in this chapter I have had very little to say about the Negro, and especially Negro education. It is important to know the view of the new leadership on this question. I have shown in previous articles that the majority view in the South was more or less hostile to the education of the Negro, or, at least, to his education beyond the bare rudiments.

The new leaders have recognised this feeling, and while without exception they believe that the Negro must be educated and most of them have said so openly, the general policy has been to emphasise white education and unite the people on that.

"In education," one of the leaders said to me, "it does n't matter much where we begin. If we can arouse the spirit of the school, the people are going to see that it is as important to the state to have a trained Negro as it is to have a trained white man."

One of the troubles in the South, one of the reasons for the prejudice against education, and particularly Negro education, has arisen from the fact that what has been called education was not really education at all. In the first place many of the schools have been so poor and the teachers so inefficient that the "education" acquired was next to worthless. There was not enough of it, nor was it of a kind to give the Negro any real hold upon life, and it often hurt him far more than it helped. Much of the prejudice in the South against Negro education is unquestionably due to the wretched school system, which in many places has not really educated anybody. But, deeper than all this, the old conception in the South of a school was for a long time the old aristocratic conception — what some one has called "useless culture" — of educating a class of men, not to work, but to despise work. That idea of education has wrought much evil, especially among the Negroes. It has taught both white and coloured men, not the doctrine of service, which is necessary to democracy, but it has given them a desire for artificial superiority, which is the characteristic of aristocracies. It has made the Negro "uppish" and "bumptious"; it has caused some white men to argue their

---

as the executive committee of the Conference for Southern Education, of which Robert C. Ogden was president.

superiority when they had no basis of accomplishment or usefulness to make them really superior.

The Inspiration of Hampton Institute

But when the idea of education began to be democratic, when men began to think more of their duties than of their rights, a wholly new sort of school appeared; and it appeared first among the Negroes. The country has not yet begun to realise the debt of gratitude which it owes to the promoters of Hampton Institute — to the genius of General Armstrong, its founder and to the organising ability of Dr. H. B. Frissell who followed him. These men will be more highly honoured a hundred years from now than they are to-day, for Americans will then appreciate more fully their service to the democracy.

The "Hampton idea" is the teaching of work — of service, of humility, of duties to God and to man. It is in the highest sense the democratic idea in education. And it has come, as most great movements have come, from the needs and the struggles of those who are downtrodden and outcast. And how wonderfully the idea has spread! Out of Hampton sprung Tuskegee and Calhoun and Kowaliga and scores of other Negro schools, until to-day nearly all Negro institutions for higher training in the South have industrial or agricultural departments.

The best Southern white people were and are friendly to schools of this new type. They thought at first that Hampton and Tuskegee were going to train servants in the old personal sense of servants who become only cooks, butlers, and farmers, and many still have that aristocratic conception of service. But the "Hampton idea" of servants is a much greater one, for it is the democratic idea of training men who will serve their own people and thereby serve the country. Men who graduate from Hampton and Tuskegee become leaders of their race. They buy and cultivate land, they set up business establishments — in short, they become producers and state-builders in the largest sense.

New World Idea of Education

The idea of Hampton is the new world idea of education, and white people in the South (and in the North as well) are now applying it everywhere in their educational movements. Agricultural and industrial schools for white boys and girls are spreading throughout the South: schools to teach work, just as Hampton teaches it. Only last year the state of Georgia provided for eleven new agricultural schools in various parts of the state, and there is already talk in the South, as in the North, of agricultural training in high schools. These men, white and black, who are educated for democratic service will in time become masters of the state.

The new leaders, then, of whom I have spoken, do not oppose Negro education: they favour it and will go forward steadily with the task of bring it about. So far, the Negro public schools have felt little of the new impulse; in some states and localities, as I have shown in other chapters, the Negro schools have actually retrograded, where the white schools have been improving rapidly. But that is the continuing influence of the old leadership; the new men have not yet come fully into their own.

I could quote indefinitely from the real statesmen of the South regarding Negro education, but I have too little space. Senator Lamar of Mississippi once said:

"The problem of race, in a large part, is a problem of illiteracy. Most of the evils which have grown up out of the problem have arisen from a condition of ignorance, prejudice and superstition. Remove these and the simpler elements of the question will come into play. . . . I will go with those who will go furthest in this matter."

No higher note has been struck in educational ideals than in the Declaration of Principles adopted last winter (1907) at the meeting of the Southern Educational Association at Lexington, Ky., an exclusively Southern gathering of white men and women. Their resolutions, which for lack of space cannot be here printed in full, should be read by every man and woman in the country who is interested in the future of democratic institutions. I copy here only a few of the declarations:

1. All children, regardless of race, creed, sex, or the social station or economic condition of their parents, have equal right to, and should have equal opportunity for, such education as will develop to the fullest possible degree all that

is best in their individual natures, and fit them for the duties of life and citizenship in the age and community in which they live.

2. To secure this right and provide this opportunity to all children is the first and highest duty of the modern democratic state, and the highest economic wisdom of an industrial age and community. Without universal education of the best and highest type, there can be no real democracy, either political or social; nor can agriculture, manufactures, or commerce ever attain their highest development.

3. Education in all grades and in all legitimate directions, being for the public good, the public should bear the burden of it. The most just taxes levied by the state, or with the authority of the state, by any smaller political division, are those levied for the support of education. No expenditures can possibly produce greater returns and none should be more liberal.

The New South on Negro Education

Concerning Negro education, I am publishing the resolutions in full, because they voice the present thought of the best leadership in the South:

1. We endorse the accepted policy of the states of the South in providing educational facilities for the youth of the Negro race, believing that whatever the ultimate solution of this grievous problem may be, education must be an important factor in that solution.

2. We believe that the education of the Negro in the elementary branches of education should be made thorough, and should include specific instruction in hygiene and home sanitation, for the better protection of both races.

3. We believe that in the secondary education of Negro youth emphasis should be placed upon agriculture and the industrial occupations, including nurse training, domestic science, and home economics.

4. We believe that for practical, economical and psychological reasons Negro teachers should be provided for Negro schools.

5. We advise instruction in normal schools and normal institutions by white teachers, whenever possible, and closer supervision of courses of study and methods of teaching in Negro normal schools by the State Department of Education.

6. We recommend that in urban and rural Negro schools there should be closer and more thorough supervision, not only by city and county superintendents, but also by directors of music, drawing, manual training, and other special topics.

7. We urge upon school authorities everywhere the importance of adequate buildings, comfortable seating, and sanitary accommodations for Negro youth.

8. We deplore the isolation of many Negro schools, established through motives of philanthropy, from the life and the sympathies of the communities in which they are located. We recommend the supervision of all such schools by the state, and urge that their work and their methods be adjusted to the civilisation in which they exist, in order that the maximum good of the race and of the community may be thereby attained.

9. On account of economic and psychological differences in the two races, we believe that there should be a difference in courses of study and methods of

teaching, and that there should be such an adjustment of school curricula as shall meet the evident needs of Negro youth.

10. We insist upon such an equitable distribution of the school funds that all the youth of the Negro race shall have at least an opportunity to receive the elementary education provided by the state, and in the administration of state laws, and in the execution of this educational policy, we urge patience, toleration, and justice.

(Signed) G. R. GLENN, P. P. CLAXTON, J. H. PHILLIPS,
C. B. GIBSON, R. N. ROARK, J. H. VAN SICKLE,
Committee.

In this connection also let me call attention to the reports of J. Y. Joyner, Superintendent of Education, and Charles L. Coon of North Carolina, for a broad view of Negro education.

I have already shown how the South and the North came together in educational relationships in the Southern Education Board. I have pointed it out as a tendency toward nationalisation in educational interests. But the Southern Education Board, while it contained both Northern and Southern white men, was primarily interested in white education and contained no Negro members. At the time the board was organised, an active interest in the Negro would have defeated, in part at least, its declared purpose.

The South, the North, and the Negro at Last Work Together

Since that time another highly significant movement has arisen. In 1907 Miss Jeanes, a wealthy Quakeress of Philadelphia, gave $1,000,000 for the encouragement of Negro primary education. She placed it in the hands of Dr. H. B. Frissell of Hampton and Dr. Booker T. Washington of Tuskegee. In the organisation of the board for the control of this fund and its work, a further step forward in nationalisation and, indeed, in the direction of democracy, was made. It marks a new development in the coöperation of all the forces for good in the solution of this difficult national problem. The membership of the board includes not only Southern and Northern white men, but also several leading Negroes. The president and general director is a Southern white man, coming of an old family, James H. Dillard, dean of Tulane University of New Orleans. It will be of interest to publish here a full list of the members, because they represent, in more ways than one, the new leadership not only in the South, but in the nation:

Southern white men:

James H. Dillard, President,
David C. Barrow, chancellor University of Georgia.
Belton Gilreath, manufacturer and mine-owner, Alabama.
Dr. S. C. Mitchell, of Richmond College, Richmond, Va.

Northern white men:

Robert C. Ogden, of New York.
Andrew Carnegie, of New York.
Talcott Williams, of Philadelphia.
George McAneny, president of the City Club of New York.
William H. Taft, of Ohio.

To these must be added:

Dr. H. B. Frissell, of Hampton Institute, a Northerner, whose work and residence has long been in the South.
George Foster Peabody, treasurer, a Georgian, trustee of the University of Georgia, who resides in the North.
Walter H. Page, the editor of the *World's Work*, a North Carolinian who has long lived in the North.

Negro membership:

Booker T. Washington.
Bishop Abraham Grant, of Kan.
R. R. Moton, of Hampton Institute, secretary of the board.
J. C. Napier, a banker of Nashville, Tenn.
R. L. Smith, a farmer of Paris, Tex.

In a true sense the Southern Education Board and the Jeanes Fund Board represent organisations of working idealists. Such coöperation as this, between reasonable, broad-minded, and unselfish men of the entire country, is, at the present moment, the real solution of our problems. It is the solution of the Negro problem — all the solution there ever will be. For there is no finality in human endeavour: there is only activity; and when that activity is informed with the truth and inspired with faith and courage, it is not otherwise than success, for it is the best that human nature at any given time can do.

In making this statement, I do not, of course wish to infer that conditions are as good as can be expected, and that nothing remains to be done. As a matter of fact, the struggle is just beginning; as I have shown in previous chapters, all the forces of entrenched prejudice and ignorance are against the movement, the political leaders who still dominate the South are as hostile as they dare to be. The task is, indeed, too big for the South alone, or the North alone, or the white man alone: it will require all the strength and courage the nation possesses.

Universities Feel the New Impulse

Besides the campaign for better common schools, the educational revival has also renewed and revivified all the higher institutions of learning in the South. The state universities, especially, have been making extraordinary progress. I shall not soon forget my visit to the University of Georgia, at Athens, nor the impression I received while there of strong men at work, not merely erecting buildings of mortar and brick, but establishing a new sort of university system, which shall unify and direct to one common end all of the educational activities of the state: beginning with the common school and reaching upward to the university itself; including the agricultural and industrial schools, and even the Negro college of agriculture. The University of Georgia is one of the oldest state colleges in America, and the ambition of its leaders is to make it one of the greatest. Mr. Hodgson[11] drove me around the campus, which has recently been extended until it contains nearly 1,000 acres. He showed me where the new buildings are to be, the drives and the bridges. Much of it is yet a vision of the future, but it is the sort of vision that comes true. I spent a day with President Soule[12] of the Agricultural College, on his special educational train, which covered a considerable part of the state of Georgia, stopping at scores of towns where the speakers appeared before great audiences of farmers and made practical addresses on cotton and corn and cattle-raising, and on education generally. And everywhere the practical work of these public educators was greeted with enthusiasm.

I heard from Professor Stewart[13] of his work in organising rural high schools, in encouraging local taxation, and in bringing the work of the public schools into closer correlation with that of the university.

Seeing the educational work of states like Georgia, North Carolina, Virginia, and others, one cannot but feel that the

11. Harry Hodgson, Athens manufacturer and supporter of educational reform in the South.
12. Andrew M. Soule, president of the Georgia State College of Agriculture

time is coming shortly when the North will be going South for new ideas and new inspiration in education.

In a brief review like this, I have been able, of course, to give only the barest outline of a very great work, and I have mentioned only a few among hundreds of leaders; the work I have described is only illustrative of what is going on in greater or less degree everywhere in the South.

Many important developments have come from these campaigns for education. The actual building of new schoolhouses and the expenditure of more money for the struggle with illiteracy is only one of many results. For the crusade for education, supplemented by the new industrial impulse in the South, has awakened a new spirit of self-help. The success with which the public was aroused in the educational campaign has inspired leaders in all lines of activity with new courage and faith. It is a spirit of youthfulness which is not afraid to attempt anything.

Much printers' ink has been expended in trying to account for the spread of the anti-saloon movement throughout the South. But there is nothing strange about it: it is, indeed, only another manifestation of the new Southern spirit, the desire to get things right in the South. And this movement will further stir men's minds, develop self-criticism, and reveal to the people their power of concerted action whether the politicians are with them or not. It is, indeed, significant that the women of the South, perhaps for the first time, have become a powerful influence in public affairs. Their organisations have helped, in some instances led, in both the educational and the anti-saloon movement. No leaders in the Virginia educational movement have been more useful than Mrs. L. R. Dashiell and Mrs. B. B. Munford of Richmond.

Practically all the progress of the South, both industrial and educational, has been made by non-political movements and non-political leaders — often in opposition to the political leaders. Indeed, nearly every one of the hopeful movements of the South has had to capture some entrenched stronghold of the old political captains. In several states, for example, the school systems a few years ago were crippled by political domination and nepotism. Superintendents, principals, and

and Mechanic Arts in Athens.

13. Professor Joseph S. Stewart of the University of Georgia was a pioneer in the development of high school education in the South.

teachers were frequently appointed not for their ability, but because they were good members of the party or because they were related to politicians.

New Statesmen Against Old Politicians

In Alabama I found prominent men attacking the fee system of payment of lesser magistrates. The evil in this system lies in the encouragement it gives to trivial litigation and the arrest of citizens for petty offences. Let me give a single example. A Negro had another Negro arrested for "'sault and battery." Both appeared in court. The accused Negro was tried, and finally sent to the chain-gang. The justice suggested to the convicted man that if he wanted satisfaction he should turn around and have his accuser arrested; which he did, promptly accusing him of "'busive language." Another trial was held; and in the end both Negroes found themselves side by side in the chain-gang; the magistrate, the constable, the sheriff, had all drawn liberal fees, and the private contractor who hired the chain-gang, and who also "stood in" with the politicians, had obtained another cheap labourer for his work. It is a vicious circle, which has enabled the politicians and their backers to profit at every turn from the weakness and evil of both Negro and low-class white man.

In attacking the fee system and the old, evil chain-gang system as the new leaders are doing in many parts of the South, in closing the saloons (always a bulwark of low politics), in building up a new school system free from selfish control, the new leaders are striking squarely at the roots of the old political aristocracy, undermining it and cutting it away. It is sure to fall; and in its place the South will rear a splendid new leadership of constructive ability and unselfish patriotism. There will be a division on matters of vital concern, and a turning from ancient and worn-out issues to new interests and activities. When that time comes the whole nation will again profit by the genius of Southern statesmanship and we shall again have Southern Presidents.

Already the old type of politician sees the handwriting of fate. He knows not which way to turn. At one moment he harps more fiercely and bitterly than ever before on the issue which has maintained him so long in power, the Negro; and at the next moment he seizes frantically on some one of the new issues — education, prohibition, anti-railroad — hoping thereby to maintain himself and his old party control. But he cannot do it; every force in the South is already making for new things, for more democracy, for more nationalisation.

CHAPTER XIV

WHAT TO DO ABOUT THE NEGRO — A FEW CONCLUSIONS

THE deeper one delves into the problem of race, the humbler he becomes concerning his own views. Studying a black man, he discovers that he must study human nature. The best he can do, then, is to present his latest and clearest thought, knowing that newer light and deeper knowledge may modify his conclusions. It is out of such expressions of individual thought (no one man has or can have all the truth) and the kindly discussion which follows it (and why should n't it be kindly?) that arises finally that power of social action which we call public opinion. Together — not otherwise — we may approach the truth.

The world to-day is just beginning to meet new phases of the problem of race difference. Improved transportation and communication are yearly making the earth smaller. As Americans we are being brought every year into closer contact with black and yellow people. We are already disturbed not only by a Negro race problem, but on our Pacific coast and in Hawaii we have a Japanese and Chinese problem. In the Philippine Islands we have a tangle of race problems in comparison with which our Southern situation seems simple. Other nations are facing complexities equally various and difficult. England's problems in both South Africa and India are largely racial. The great issue in Australia, where Chinese labour has become a political question, is expressed in the campaign slogan: "A white Australia."

What Is the Race Problem?

Essentially, then, what is the race problem?

The race problem is the problem of living with human beings who are not like us, whether they are, in our estimation, our "superiors" or "inferiors," whether they have kinky hair or pigtails, whether they are slant-eyed, hook-nosed, or thick-lipped.   In its essence it is the same problem, magnified, which besets every neighbourhood, even every family.

In our own country we have 10,000,000 Negroes distributed among 75,000,000 white people.   They did not come here to invade us, or because they wanted to come.   We brought them by force, and at a fearful and cruel sacrifice of life.   We brought them, not to do them good, but selfishly, that they might be compelled to do the hard work and let us live lazily, eat richly, sleep softly.   We treated them as beasts of burden. I say "we," for the North owned slaves, too, at first, and emancipated them (by selling them to the South) because it did not pay to keep them.   Nor was the anti-slavery senti-ment peculiar to the North; voices were raised against the institution of slavery by many Southern statesmen from Jefferson down — men who knew by familiar observation of the evil of slavery, especially for the white man.

Differences Between Southern and Northern Attitudes Toward the Race Problem

But differences are apparent in the outlook of the South and North which must be pointed out before we can arrive at any general conclusions.   By understanding the reasons for race feeling we shall be the better able to judge of the remedies proposed.

In the first place, the South is still clouded with bitter mem-ories of the war, and especially of the Reconstruction period. The North cannot understand how deep and real this feeling is, how it has been warped into the souls of even the third generation.   The North, victorious, forgot; but the South, broken and defeated, remembered.   Until I had been a good while in the South and talked with many people I had no idea what a social cataclysm like the Civil War really meant to those who are defeated, how long it echoes in the hearts of men and women.   The Negro has indeed suffered — suffered on his way upward; but the white man, with his higher culti-vation, his keener sensibilities, his memories of a departed glory, has suffered far more.   I have tried, as I have listened to the stories of struggle which only the South knows, to put myself in the place of these Anglo-Saxon men and women, and I think I can understand a little at least of what it must have meant to meet defeat, loss of relatives and friends, grinding poverty, the chaos of reconstruction—and after all that to have, always at elbow-touch, the unconscious cause of all their trouble, the millions of inert, largely helpless Negroes who, imbued with a sharp sense of their rights, are attaining only slowly a corresponding appreciation of their duties and responsibilities.

The ruin of the war left the South poor, and it has provided itself slowly with educational advantages. It is a long step behind the North in the average of education among white people not less than coloured. But more than all else, perhaps, the South is in the throes of vast economic changes. It is in the transition stage between the old wasteful, semi-feudal civilisation and the sharp new city and industrial life. It is suffering the common pains of readjustment; and, being hurt, it is not wholly conscious of the real reason.

For example, many of the troubles between the races attributed to the perversity of the Negro are often only the common difficulties which arise out of the relationship of employer and employee. In other words, difficulties in the South are often attributed to the race problem which in the North we know as the labour problem. For the South even yet has not fully established itself on the wage system. Payment of Negroes in the country is still often a matter of old clothes, baskets from the white man's kitchen or store, with occasionally a little money, which is often looked upon as an indulgence rather than a right. No race ever yet has sprung directly from slavery into the freedom of a full-fledged wage system, no matter what the laws were. It is not insignificant of progress that the "basket habit" is coming to be looked upon as thievery, organised charity in the cities is taking the place of indiscriminate personal gifts, wages are more regularly paid and measure more accurately the value of the service rendered.

But the relationships between the races still smack in no small degree, especially in matters of social contact (which are always the last to change), of the old feudal character; they are personal and sentimental. They express themselves in the personal liking for the old "mammies," in the personal contempt for the "smart Negro."

A large part of the South still believes that the Negro was created to serve the white man, and for no other purpose. This is especially the belief in the conservative country districts.

"If these Negroes become doctors and merchants or buy their own farms," a Southern woman said to me as a clinching argument against Negro education, "what shall we do for servants?"

Another reason for the feeling in the South against the Negro is that the South has never had any other labouring class of people (to speak of) with which to compare the Negro. All the employers have been white; most of the workers have been black. The North, on the other hand, has had a constant procession of ignorant working people of various sorts. The North is familar with the progress of alien people, wherein the workingman of to-day becomes the employer of to-morrow — which has not happened in the South.

Confusion of Labour and Race Problems

An illustration of the confusion between the race problem and the labour problem is presented in certain Southern neighbourhoods by the influx of European immigrants. Because the Italian does the work of the Negro, a tendency exists to treat him like a Negro. In Louisiana on the sugar plantations Italian white women sometimes work under Negro foremen and no objection is made. A movement is actually under way in Mississippi to keep the children of Italian immigrants out of the white schools. In not a few instances white workmen have been held in peonage like Negroes; several such cases are now pending in the courts. Here is a dispatch showing how new Italian immigrants were treated in one part of Mississippi — only the Italians, unlike the Negroes, have an active government behind them:

MOBILE, ALA., October 3. — The Italian Government has taken notice of the situation at Sumrall, Miss., where the native whites are endeavouring to keep Italian children out of the schools and where a leader of the Italians was taken to the woods and whipped.

The Italian Consul at New Orleans, Count G. Morroni, reached Mobile this afternoon and began an investigation of the situation. He to-day heard the story of Frank Seaglioni, the leader of the Italian colony at Sumrall, who was a few days ago decoyed from his home at night with a bogus message from New Orleans and unmercifully whipped by a mob of white men.

A decided tendency also exists to charge up to the Negro, because he is a Negro, all the crimes which are commonly committed by any ignorant, neglected, poverty-stricken people. Only last summer we had in New York what the newspaper reporters called a "crime wave." The crime in that case was what is designated in the South as the "usual crime" (offences against women) for which Negroes are lynched. But in New York not a Negro was implicated.

I was struck while in Philadelphia by a presentment of a grand jury in Judge Kinsey's court upon the subject of a "crime wave" which read thus:

In closing our duties as jurymen, we wish to call to the attention of this court the large proportion of cases presented to us for action wherein the offences were charged to either persons of foreign birth or those of the coloured race, and we feel that some measures should be taken to the end that our city should be relieved of both the burden of the undesirable alien and the irresponsible coloured person.

Here, it will be seen, the "undesirable alien" and "irresponsible coloured person" are classed together, although it is significant of the greater prejudice against the coloured man that the newspaper report of the action of the grand jury should be headed "Negro Crime Abnormal," without referring to the alien at all. When I inquired at the prosecutor's office about the presentment, I was told:

"Oh, the dagoes are just as bad as the Negroes."

And both are bad, not because they are Negroes or Italians, but because they are ignorant, neglected, poverty-stricken.

Thus in the dust and confusion of the vast readjustments now going on in the South, the discomfort of which both races feel but neither quite understands, we have the white man blindly blaming the Negro and the Negro blindly hating the white. When they both understand that many of the troubles they are having are only the common gall-spots of the new industrial harness there will be a better living together.

I do not wish to imply, of course, that an industrial age or the wage system furnishes an ideal condition for race relationships; for in the North the Negro's struggle for survival in the competitive field is accompanied, as I have shown elsewhere, by the severest suffering. The condition of Negroes in Indianapolis, New York, and Philadelphia is in some ways worse than it is anywhere in the South. But, say what we will, the wage system is one step upward from the old feudalism. The Negro is treated less like a slave and more like a man in the North. It is for this reason that Negroes, no matter what their difficulties of making a living in the North, rarely wish to go back to the South. And as the South develops industrially it will approximate more nearly to Northern conditions. In Southern cities to-day, because of industrial development, the Negro is treated more like a man than he is in the country; and this is one reason why Negroes crowd into the cities and can rarely be persuaded to go back into the country — unless they can own their own land.

But the South is rapidly shaking off the remnants of the old feudalism. Development of mines and forests, the extension of manufacturing, the introduction of European immigrants, the inflow of white Northerners, better schools, more railroads and telephones, are all helping to bring the South up to the economic standard of the North. There will be a further break-up of baronial tenant farming, the plantation store will disappear, the ruinous credit system will be abolished, and there will be a widespread appearance of independent farm-owners, both white and black. This will all tend to remove the personal and sentimental attitude of the old Southern life; the Negro will of necessity be judged more and more as a man, not as a slave or dependent. In short, the country, South and North, will become economically more homogeneous.

But even when the South reaches the industrial development of the North the Negro problem will not be solved; it is certainly not solved in New York or Philadelphia, where industrial development has reached its highest form. The prejudice in those cities, as I have shown, has been growing more intense as Negro population increased. What, then, will happen?

Two Elements in Every Race Problem

Two elements appear in every race problem: the first, race prejudice — the repulsion of the unlike; second, economic or competitive jealousy. Both operate, for example, in the case of the Irishman or Italian, but with the Negro and Chinaman race prejudice is greater because the difference is greater.

The difficulty of the Negro in this country is the colour of his skin, the symbol of his difference. In China the difficulty of the white trader is his whiteness, his difference. Race lines, in short, are drawn by white men, not because the other race is inferior (the Japanese and Chinese are in many ways our superiors), nor because of criminality (certain classes of foreigners are more criminal in our large cities than the Negroes), nor because of laziness, but because of discernible physical differences — black skin, almond eyes, pigtails, hook noses, a peculiar bodily odour, or small stature. That dislike of a different people is more or less instinctive in all men.

A tendency has existed on the part of Northern students who have no first-hand knowledge of the masses of Negroes to underestimate the force of race repulsion; on the other hand, the Southern student who is confronted with the Negroes themselves is likely to overestimate racial repulsion and under-estimate economic competition as a cause of the difficulty. The profoundest question, indeed, is to decide how much of the so-called problem is due to race repulsion and how much to economic competition.

This leads us to the most sinister phase of the race problem. As I have shown, we have the two elements of conflict: instinc-tive race repulsion and competitive jealousy. What is easier for the race in power, the white race in this country (the yellow race in Asia) than to play upon race instinct in order to serve selfish ends? How shrewdly the labour union, whether in San Francisco or Atlanta, seizes upon that race hatred to keep the black or yellow man out of the union and thereby control all the work for its members! Race prejudice played upon becomes a tool in clinching the power of the labour monopoly.

How the politician in the South excites race hatred in order that he may be elected to office! Vardaman governed because he could make men hate one another more bitterly than his opponent. The Rev. Thomas Dixon has appealed in his books and plays to the same passion.

In several places in this country Negroes have been driven out by mobs — not because they were criminal, or because they were bad citizens, but because they were going into the grocery and drug business, they were becoming doctors, dentists, and the like, and taking away the trade of their white competitors. So the stores and restaurants of highly efficient Japanese were wrecked in San Francisco.

What is easier or cruder to use as a weapon for crushing a rival than the instinctive dislike of man for man? And that usage is not peculiar to the white man. In Africa the black man wastes no time with the different-looking white man; he kills him, if he dares, on the spot. And how ably the Chinaman has employed the instinctive hatred of his countrymen for "foreign devils" in order to fight American trade and traders! We hate the Chinaman and drive him out, and he hates us and drives us out.

Chief Danger of Race Prejudice

And this is one of the dangers of the race problem in this country — the fostering of such an instinct to make money or to get political office. Such a basis of personal prosperity is all the more dangerous because the white man is in undisputed power in this country; the Negro has no great navy behind him; he is like a child in the house of a harsh parent. All that stands between him and destruction is the ethical sense of the white man. Will the white man's sense of justice and virtue be robust enough to cause him to withhold the hand of unlimited power? Will he see, as Booker T. Washington says, that if he keeps the Negro in the gutter he must stay there with him? The white man and his civilisation, not alone the Negro, will rise or fall by that ethical test.

The Negro, on his part, as I have shown repeatedly in former chapters, employs the same methods as the white man, for Negro nature is not different from human nature. He argues: "The white man hates you; hate him. Trade with Negro storekeepers; employ Negro doctors; don't go to white dentists and lawyers."

Out of this condition proceed two tendencies. The first is the natural result of mutual fear and suspicion, and that is, a rapid flying apart of the races. All through my former chapters I have been showing how the Negroes are being segregated. So are the Chinese segregated, and the blacks in South Africa, and certain classes in India. Parts of the South are growing blacker. Negroes crowd into "coloured quarters" in the cities. More and more they are becoming a people wholly apart — separate in their churches, separate in their schools, separate in cars, conveyances, hotels, restaurants, with separate professional men. In short, we discover tendencies in this country toward the development of a caste system.

Now, one of the most striking facts in our recent history is the progress of the former slave. And this finds its world parallel in the progress of people whom the vainglorious Anglo-Saxon once despised: the Japanese, Chinese, and East Indians. In forty years the Negro has advanced a distance that would have been surprising in almost any race. In the bare accomplishments — area of land owned, crops raised, professional men supported, business enterprises conducted, books and poetry written, music composed, pictures painted — the slaves of forty years ago have made the most astonishing progress. This leads to the second tendency, which proceeds slowly out of the growing conviction that hatred and suspicion and fear as motives in either national or individual progress will not work; that there must be some other way for different people to work side by side in peace and justice. And thus we discover a tendency toward a friendly living together under the new relationship, in which the Negro is not a slave or a dependent, but a man and a citizen. Booker T. Washington preaches the gospel of this new life. And gradually as race prejudice becomes inconvenient, threatens financial adversity, ruffles the smooth current of comfortable daily existence, the impulse grows to set it aside. Men don't keep on fighting when it is no longer profitable to fight.

And thus, side by side, these two impulses exist — the one pointing toward the development of a hard caste system which would ultimately petrify our civilisation as it has petrified that of India; and the other looking to a reasonable, kindly, and honourable working together of the races.

What Are the Remedies for the Evil Conditions?

So much for conditions; what of remedies?

I have heard the most extraordinary remedies proposed. Serious men actually talk of the deportation of the entire

Negro population to Africa, not stopping to inquire whether we have any right to deport them, or calculating the economic revolution and bankruptcy which the deportation of the entire labouring class would cause in the South, without stopping to think that even if we could find a spot in the world for 10,000,000 Negroes, and they all wanted to go, that all the ships flying the American flag, if constantly employed, could probably not transport the natural increase of the Negro population, let alone the 10,000,000 present inhabitants. I have heard talk of segregation in reservations, like the Indians — segregation out of existence! I have even heard unspeakable talk of the wholesale extinction of the race by preventing the breeding of children! All quack remedies and based upon hatred, not upon justice.

There is no sudden or cut-and-dried solution of the Negro problem, or of any other problem. Men are forever demanding formulæ which will enable them to progress without effort. They seek to do quickly by medication what can only be accomplished by deliberate hygiene. A problem that has been growing for two hundred and fifty years in America, and for thousands of years before that in Africa, warping the very lives of the people concerned, changing their currents of thought as well as their conduct, cannot be solved in forty years. Why expect it?

And yet there are definite things that can be done which, while working no immediate miracles, will set our faces to the light and keep us trudging toward the true goal.

Down at the bottom — it will seem trite, but it is eternally true — the cause of the race "problem" and most other social problems is simply lack of understanding and sympathy between man and man. And the remedy is equally simple — a gradual substitution of understanding and sympathy for blind repulsion and hatred.

Consider, for example, the Atlanta riot. Increasing misunderstanding and hatred caused a dreadful explosion and bloodshed. What happened? Instantly the wisest white men in Atlanta invited the wisest coloured men to meet them. They got together: general explanations followed. They found that there had been error on both sides; they found that there were reasonable human beings on both sides.

One of the leading white men said: "I did not know there were any such broad-minded Negroes in the South." In other words, they tried to understand and sympathise with one another. Over and over again men will be found hating Negroes, or Chinamen, or "dagoes," and yet liking some individual Negro, or Chinaman, or "dago." When they get acquainted they see that the Negro or Chinaman is a human being like themselves, full of faults, but not devoid of good qualities.

As a fundamental proposition, then, it will be found that the solution of the Negro problem lies in treating the Negro more and more as a human being like ourselves. Treating the Negro as a human being, we must judge him, not by his colour, or by any other outward symbol, but upon his worth as a man. Nothing that fails of that full honesty and fairness of judgment in the smallest particular will suffice. We disgrace and injure ourselves more than we do the Negro when we are not willing to admit virtue or learning or power in another human being because his face happens to be yellow or black.

Of the soundness of this fundamental standard of judgment there can be no doubt; the difficulty lies in applying it practically to society as it is to-day. In the suggestions which I offer here I am trying to do two things: to outline the present programme, and to keep open a clear view to the future goal.

Shall the Negro Vote?

Let us approach, then, without fear the first of the three groups of problems — political, industrial, and social — which confront us.

Shall the Negro vote?

Thousands of Negroes in this country are fully as well equipped, fully as patriotic, as the average white citizen. Moreover, they are as much concerned in the real welfare of the country. The principle that our forefathers fought for, "taxation only with representation," is as true to-day as it ever was.

On the other hand, the vast majority of Negroes (and many foreigners and "poor whites") are still densely ignorant, and have little or no appreciation of the duties of citizenship.   It seems right that they should be required to wait before being allowed to vote until they are prepared.   A wise parent hedges his son about with restrictions;   he does not authorise his signature at the bank or allow him to run a locomotive;   and until he is twenty-one years old he is disfranchised and has no part in the government.   But the parent restricts his son because it seems the wisest course for him, for the family, and for the state that he should grow to manhood before he is burdened with grave responsibilities.   So the state limits suffrage; and rightly limits it, so long as it accompanies that limitation with a   determined   policy   of   education.   But the suffrage law is so executed in the South to-day as to keep many capable Negroes from the exercise of their rights, to prevent recognition of honest merit, and it is executed unjustly as between white men   and   coloured.   It is no condonement of the Southern position to say that the North also disfranchises a large part of the Negro vote by bribery, which it does;   it is only saying that the North is also wrong.

As for the agitation for the repeal of the Fifteenth Amendment to the Federal Constitution, which gives the right of suffrage to the coloured man, it must be met by every lover of justice and democracy with a face of adamant.   If there were only one Negro in the country capable of citizenship, the way for him must, at least, be kept open.   No doubt full suffrage was given to the mass of Negroes before they were prepared for it, while yet they were slaves in everything except bodily   shackles,   and   the   result   during   the   Reconstruction period was disastrous.   But the principle of a free franchise — fortunately, as I believe, for this country—has been forever established.   If the white man is not willing to meet the Negro in any contest whatsoever without plugging the dice, then he is not the superior but the inferior of the Negro.

What Shall Be the Industrial Relation of the Races?

So much for the political relationships of the races.   How about the industrial relationships?

The same test of inherent worth must here also apply, and the question will not be settled until it does apply.   A carpenter must be asked, not "What colour are you?" but "How cunningly and efficiently can you build a house?" Of all absurdities, the judgment of the skill of a surgeon by the kink of his hair will certainly one day be looked upon as the most absurd.   The same observation applies broadly to the attempt to confine a whole people, regardless of their capabilities, to menial occupations because they are dark-coloured.   No, the place of the Negro is the place he can fill most efficiently and the longer we attempt to draw artificial lines the longer we shall delay the solution of the race problem.   On the other hand, the Negro must not clamour for places he cannot yet fill.

"The trouble with the Negro," says Booker T. Washington, "is that he is all the time trying to get recognition, whereas what he should do is to get something to recognise."

Negroes as a class are to-day far inferior in education, intelligence, and efficiency to the white people as a class.   Here and there an able Negro will develop superior abilities; but the mass of Negroes for years to come must find their activities mostly in physical and more or less menial labour.   Like any race, they must first prove themselves in these simple lines of work before they can expect larger opportunities.

There must always be men like Dr. DuBois who agitate for rights ; their service is an important one, but at the present time it would seem that the thing most needed was the teaching of such men as Dr. Washington, emphasising duties and responsibilities, urging the Negro to prepare himself for his rights.

Social Contact

We come now, having considered the political and industrial relationships of the races, to the most difficult and perplexing of all the phases of the Negro question — that of social contact. Political and industrial relationships are more or less outward, but social contact turns upon the delicate and deep questions of home life, personal inclinations, and of privileges rather than rights.   It is always in the relationships of oldest developments, like those that cling around the home, that human nature is slowest to change.   Indeed, much of the complexity of the Negro problem has arisen from a confusion in people's minds between rights and privileges

Everyone recalls the excitement caused — it became almost a national issue — when President Roosevelt invited Booker T. Washington to luncheon at the White House. Well, that feeling is deep in the South, as deep almost as human nature. Many Northern people who go South to live come to share it; indeed, it is the gravest question in ethics to decide at what point natural instincts should be curbed.

Social contact is a privilege, not a right; it is not a subject for legislation or for any other sort of force. "Social questions," as Colonel Watterson[1] of Kentucky says, "create their own laws and settle themselves. They cannot be forced." All such relationships will work themselves out gradually, naturally, quietly, in the long course of the years: and the less they are talked about the better.

Jim Crow Laws

As for the Jim Crow laws in the South, many of them, at least, are at present necessary to avoid the danger of clashes between the ignorant of both race. They are the inevitable scaffolding of progress. As a matter of fact, the Negro has profited in one way by such laws. For the white man has thus driven the Negroes together, forced ability to find its outlet in racial leadership, and by his severity produced a spirit of self-reliance which would not otherwise have existed. Dr. Frissell of Hampton is always talking to his students of the "advantages of disadvantages."

As for laws against the intermarriage of the races, they do not prevent what they are designed to prevent: the mixing of white and coloured blood. In many parts of the South, despite the existence of such laws, miscegenation, though decreasing rapidly, still continues. On the other hand, in the North, where Negroes and whites may marry, there is actually very little marriage and practically no concubinage. The solution of this question, too, lies far more in education than in law. As a matter of fact, the more education both races receive, the less the amalgamation. In the South, as in the North, the present tendency of the educated and prosperous

1. Henry Watterson, colorful and long-time editor of the Louisville *Courier-Journal*.

Negroes is to build up a society of their own, entirely apart
from and independent of white people. As I have shown in
a former chapter, a white woman in the North who marries
a Negro is declassed — ostracised by both races. The danger
of amalgamation lies with ignorant and vicious people, black
or white, not with educated and sensitive people.

As in the case of the Jim Crow laws, separate schools in the
South are necessary, and in one way I believe them to be of
great advantage to the Negroes themselves. In Northern
cities like Indianapolis and New York, where there are no
separation laws of any kind, separate schools have appeared,
naturally and quietly, in districts where the Negro population
is dense. That the pupils in each should be treated with exact
justice in the matter of expenditures by the state is axiomatic.
And the Negro boy should have the same unbounded opportunity for any sort of education he is capable of using as the
white boy; nothing less will suffice.

One influence at present growing rapidly will have its profound effect on the separation laws. Though a tendency
exists toward local segregation of Negroes to which I have
already referred, there is also a counter-tendency toward a
scattering of Negroes throughout the entire country. The
white population in the South, now 20,000,000 against 9,000,000
Negroes, is increasing much more rapidly than the Negro
population. The death-rate of Negroes is exceedingly high;
and the sharper the conditions of competition with white
workers, the greater will probably be the limitation of increase
of the more inefficient Negro population.

As for the predictions of "amalgamation," "a mongrel
people," "black domination," and other bogies of prophecy,
we must not, as I see it, give them any weight whatsoever. We
cannot regulate our short lives by the fear of something far
in the future which will probably never happen at all. All
we can do is to be right at this moment and let the future take
care of itself; it will anyway. There is no other sane method
of procedure. Much as we may desire it, the future arrangement of this universe is not in our hands. As to the matter
of "superiority" or "inferiority," it is not a subject of argument
at all; nor can we keep or attain "superiority" by laws or
colour lines, or in any other way, except by being superior,

If we are right, absolutely right, in the eternal principles, we can rest in peace that the matter of our superiority will take care of itself.

The Real Solution of the Negro Problem

I remember asking a wise Southern man I met what, in his opinion, was the chief factor in the solution of the Negro problem.

"Time," he said, "and patience."

But time must be occupied with discipline and education — more and more education, not less education, education that will teach first of all the dignity of service not only for Negroes but for white men. The white man, South and North, needs it quite as much as the coloured man. And this is exactly the programme of the new Southern statesmanship of which I spoke in a former chapter. These wise Southerners have resolved to forget the discouragements and complexities of the Negro problem, forget even their disagreements, and go to work on present problems: the development of education and industry.

Whether we like it or not the whole nation (indeed, the whole world) is tied by unbreakable bonds to its Negroes, its Chinamen, its slum-dwellers, its thieves, its murderers, its prostitutes. We cannot elevate ourselves by driving them back either with hatred or violence or neglect; but only by bringing them forward: by service.

For good comes to men, not as they work alone, but as they work together with that sympathy and understanding which is the only true Democracy. The Great Teacher never preached the flat equality of men, social or otherwise. He gave mankind a working principle by means of which, being so different, some white, some black, some yellow, some old, some young, some men, some women, some accomplished, some stupid — mankind could, after all, live together in harmony and develop itself to the utmost possibility. And that principle was the Golden Rule. It is the least sentimental, the most profoundly practical teaching known to men.

INDEX

A

Alcorn College, 248.
Alderman, President Edwin A., 259, 271, 273, 278.
Amalgamation of Races, 153, 164, 171.
Amos, Moses, 42.
Atlanta, colour line in, 27.
 riot, 3.
Atlanta University, 40, 49, 54, 92, 170.

B

Barrow, Chancellor D. C., 271, 287.
Bassett, Professor John Spencer, 257.
Black Belt, 67.
Boston, race prejudice in, 118.
 prosperous Negroes in, 119.
Bowie, Sydney J., 281.
Boycott by Negroes, 34.
Bradley, Rev. H. S., quoted, 56.
Brittain, M. L., quoted, 37.
Brown, J. Pope, 68.
Broyles, Judge, 18, 45.
Bulkley, William L., quoted, 131, 142.
"Bumptiousness," 125.
Buttrick, Dr. Wallace, 281.

C

Cable, George W., 141.
Cable, George W., the novelist, 257.
Carnegie, Andrew, 35, 287.
Chain-gang, 50, 96, 98, 290.
Chambers, Frank R., 281.
Charities, attitude toward Negroes, 35, 114, 138.
Churches, Negro, 89, 168.
Civil Service, Negroes in, 146.
"Clansman, The," 4.
Clark University, 12.
Clark, Walter, President Mississippi Cotton Association, quoted, 104.
Claxton, P. P., 271, 279.

Cocaine, use of by Negroes, 46, 89, 104.
Colour line, drawn by Negroes, 226.
Concubinage, a case of, 48.
Convicts, Negro, make profits for Georgia, 50.
Cooper, W. G., report on Atlanta riot, 15.
Cotton mill workers, 53, 70.
Courts and the Negro, 45, 96, 141, 185, 205.
Credit system, influence on Negro, 105.
Crime against women, 5, 128, 296.
 as incentive to riot, 3, 4, 46, 183, 193, 204.
 condoned to keep Negro on farms, 98.
 juvenile, 51, 141.
"Crossing the Line" 161.
Cunningham, Acting Governor, 199.
Currie, J. H., District Attorney, quoted, 167.

D

Danville, Ill., lynching, 212.
Davis, Jefferson, way with Negroes, 103, 275.
Davis, Senator Jeff, 112, 238, 252.
Death rate among Negroes, 115.
Dickerman, Dr. G. S., 281.
Dillard, Professor James H., 273, 286.
Dixon, Rev. Thomas, 111, 266, 298.
DuBois, Dr. W. E. B., 100, 156, 158, 173, 222, 272, 304.

E

Edmonds, R. H., 275.
Education, 65, 139.
 Booker T. Washington on, 221.
 in South, 271, 273.
 Negro, 282.
 "New South" on Negro, 285.

Revised December, 1967

harper ☩ torchbooks

HUMANITIES AND SOCIAL SCIENCES

American Studies: General

LOUIS D. BRANDEIS: Other People's Money, and How the Bankers Use It. ‡ Ed. with an Intro. by Richard M. Abrams   TB/3081

THOMAS C. COCHRAN: The Inner Revolution. Essays on the Social Sciences in History   TB/1140

HENRY STEELE COMMAGER, Ed.: The Struggle for Racial Equality   TB/1300

EDWARD S. CORWIN: American Constitutional History. Essays edited by Alpheus T. Mason and Gerald Garvey △   TB/1136

CARL N. DEGLER, Ed.: Pivotal Interpretations of American History   Vol. I TB/1240; Vol. II TB/1241

A. HUNTER DUPREE: Science in the Federal Government: A History of Policies and Activities to 1940   TB/573

A. S. EISENSTADT, Ed.: The Craft of American History: Recent Essays in American Historical Writing
                        Vol. I TB/1255; Vol. II TB/1256

CHARLOTTE P. GILMAN: Women and Economics: A Study of the Economic Relation between Men and Women as a Factor in Social Evolution. ‡ Ed. with an Introduction by Carl N. Degler   TB/3073

OSCAR HANDLIN, Ed.: This Was America: As Recorded by European Travelers in the Eighteenth, Nineteenth and Twentieth Centuries. Illus.   TB/1119

MARCUS LEE HANSEN: The Atlantic Migration: 1607-1860. Edited by Arthur M. Schlesinger   TB/1052

MARCUS LEE HANSEN: The Immigrant in American History.   TB/1120

JOHN HIGHAM, Ed.: The Reconstruction of American History △   TB/1068

ROBERT H. JACKSON: The Supreme Court in the American System of Government   TB/1106

JOHN F. KENNEDY: A Nation of Immigrants. △ Illus.
                                                 TB/1118

LEONARD W. LEVY, Ed.: American Constitutional Law: Historical Essays   TB/1285

LEONARD W. LEVY, Ed.: Judicial Review and the Supreme Court   TB/1296

LEONARD W. LEVY: The Law of the Commonwealth and Chief Justice Shaw   TB/1309

HENRY F. MAY: Protestant Churches and Industrial America. New Intro. by the Author   TB/1334

RALPH BARTON PERRY: Puritanism and Democracy
                                                 TB/1138

ARNOLD ROSE: The Negro in America   TB/3048

MAURICE R. STEIN: The Eclipse of Community. An Interpretation of American Studies   TB/1128

W. LLOYD WARNER and Associates: Democracy in Jonesville: A Study in Quality and Inequality ¶ TB/1129

W. LLOYD WARNER: Social Class in America: The Evaluation of Status   TB/1013

American Studies: Colonial

BERNARD BAILYN, Ed.: Apologia of Robert Keayne: Self-Portrait of a Puritan Merchant   TB/1201

BERNARD BAILYN: The New England Merchants in the Seventeenth Century   TB/1149

JOSEPH CHARLES: The Origins of the American Party System   TB/1049

HENRY STEELE COMMAGER & ELMO GIORDANETTI, Eds.: Was America a Mistake? An Eighteenth Century Controversy   TB/1329

CHARLES GIBSON: Spain in America †   TB/3077

LAWRENCE HENRY GIPSON: The Coming of the Revolution: 1763-1775. † Illus.   TB/3007

LEONARD W. LEVY: Freedom of Speech and Press in Early American History: Legacy of Suppression TB/1109

PERRY MILLER: Errand Into the Wilderness   TB/1139

PERRY MILLER & T. H. JOHNSON, Eds.: The Puritans: A Sourcebook of Their Writings
                        Vol. I TB/1093; Vol. II TB/1094

EDMUND S. MORGAN, Ed.: The Diary of Michael Wigglesworth, 1653-1657: The Conscience of a Puritan
                                                 TB/1228

EDMUND S. MORGAN: The Puritan Family: Religion and Domestic Relations in Seventeenth-Century New England   TB/1227

RICHARD B. MORRIS: Government and Labor in Early America   TB/1244

KENNETH B. MURDOCK: Literature and Theology in Colonial New England   TB/99

WALLACE NOTESTEIN: The English People on the Eve of Colonization: 1603-1630. † Illus.   TB/3006

JOHN P. ROCHE: Origins of American Political Thought: Selected Readings   TB/1301

JOHN SMITH: Captain John Smith's America: Selections from His Writings. Ed. with Intro. by John Lankford   TB/3078

LOUIS B. WRIGHT: The Cultural Life of the American Colonies: 1607-1763. † Illus.   TB/3005

American Studies: From the Revolution to 1860

JOHN R. ALDEN: The American Revolution: 1775-1783. † Illus.   TB/3011

MAX BELOFF, Ed.: The Debate on the American Revolution, 1761-1783: A Sourcebook △   TB/1225

RAY A. BILLINGTON: The Far Western Frontier: 1830-1860. † Illus.   TB/3012

EDMUND BURKE: On the American Revolution: Selected Speeches and Letters. ‡ Edited by Elliott Robert Barkan   TB/3068

WHITNEY R. CROSS: The Burned-Over District: The Social and Intellectual History of Enthusiastic Religion in Western New York, 1800-1850 △   TB/1242

GEORGE DANGERFIELD: The Awakening of American Nationalism: 1815-1828. † Illus.   TB/3061

---

† The New American Nation Series, edited by Henry Steele Commager and Richard B. Morris.
‡ American Perspectives series, edited by Bernard Wishy and William E. Leuchtenburg.
* The Rise of Modern Europe series, edited by William L. Langer.
** History of Europe series, edited by J. H. Plumb.
¶ Researches in the Social, Cultural and Behavioral Sciences, edited by Benjamin Nelson.
§ The Library of Religion and Culture, edited by Benjamin Nelson.
Σ Harper Modern Science Series, edited by James R. Newman.
○ Not for sale in Canada.
△ Not for sale in the U. K.

CLEMENT EATON: The Freedom-of-Thought Struggle in the Old South. *Revised and Enlarged. Illus.* TB/1150
CLEMENT EATON: The Growth of Southern Civilization: 1790-1860. † *Illus.* TB/3040
LOUIS FILLER: The Crusade Against Slavery: 1830-1860. † *Illus.* TB/3029
DIXON RYAN FOX: The Decline of Aristocracy in the Politics of New York: 1801-1840. ‡ *Edited by Robert V. Remini* TB/3064
WILLIAM W. FREEHLING, Ed.: The Nullification Era: *A Documentary Record* ‡ TB/3079
FELIX GILBERT: The Beginnings of American Foreign Policy: *To the Farewell Address* TB/1200
FRANCIS GRIERSON: The Valley of Shadows: *The Coming of the Civil War in Lincoln's Midwest: A Contemporary Account* TB/1246
FRANCIS J. GRUND: Aristocracy in America: *Social Class in the Formative Years of the New Nation* TB/1001
ALEXANDER HAMILTON: The Reports of Alexander Hamilton. ‡ *Edited by Jacob E. Cooke* TB/3060
THOMAS JEFFERSON: Notes on the State of Virginia. ‡ *Edited by Thomas P. Abernethy* TB/3052
JAMES MADISON: The Forging of American Federalism: *Selected Writings of James Madison. Edited by Saul K. Padover* TB/1226
BERNARD MAYO: Myths and Men: *Patrick Henry, George Washington, Thomas Jefferson* TB/1108
JOHN C. MILLER: Alexander Hamilton and the Growth of the New Nation TB/3057
RICHARD B. MORRIS, Ed.: The Era of the American Revolution TB/1180
R. B. NYE: The Cultural Life of the New Nation: 1776-1801. † *Illus.* TB/3026
JAMES PARTON: The Presidency of Andrew Jackson. *From Vol. III of the Life of Andrew Jackson. ‡ Ed. with an Intro. by Robert V. Remini* TB/3080
FRANCIS S. PHILBRICK: The Rise of the West, 1754-1830. † *Illus.* TB/3067
TIMOTHY L. SMITH: Revivalism and Social Reform: *American Protestantism on the Eve of the Civil War* TB/1229
ALBION W. TOURGÉE: A Fool's Errand. ‡ *Ed. by George Fredrickson* TB/3074
A. F. TYLER: Freedom's Ferment: *Phases of American Social History from the Revolution to the Outbreak of the Civil War. 31 illus.* TB/1074
GLYNDON G. VAN DEUSEN: The Jacksonian Era: 1828-1848. † *Illus.* TB/3028
LOUIS B. WRIGHT: Culture on the Moving Frontier TB/1053

American Studies: The Civil War to 1900

W. R. BROCK: An American Crisis: Congress and Reconstruction, 1865-67 º △ TB/1283
THOMAS C. COCHRAN & WILLIAM MILLER: The Age of Enterprise: *A Social History of Industrial America* TB/1054
W. A. DUNNING: Essays on the Civil War and Reconstruction. *Introduction by David Donald* TB/1181
W. A. DUNNING: Reconstruction, Political and Economic: 1865-1877 TB/1073
HAROLD U. FAULKNER: Politics, Reform and Expansion: 1890-1900. † *Illus.* TB/3020
HELEN HUNT JACKSON: A Century of Dishonor: *The Early Crusade for Indian Reform. ‡ Edited by Andrew F. Rolle* TB/3063
ALBERT D. KIRWAN: Revolt of the Rednecks: *Mississippi Politics, 1876-1925* TB/1199
ROBERT GREEN MC CLOSKEY: American Conservatism in the Age of Enterprise: 1865-1910 TB/1137
ARTHUR MANN: Yankee Reformers in the Urban Age: *Social Reform in Boston, 1880-1900* TB/1247
WHITELAW REID: After the War: *A Tour of the Southern States, 1865-1866. ‡ Edited by C. Vann Woodward* TB/3066

CHARLES H. SHINN: Mining Camps: *A Study in American Frontier Government. ‡ Edited by Rodman W. Paul* TB/3062
VERNON LANE WHARTON: The Negro in Mississippi: 1865-1890 TB/1178

American Studies: 1900 to the Present

RAY STANNARD BAKER: Following the Color Line: *American Negro Citizenship in Progressive Era. ‡ Illus. Edited by Dewey W. Grantham, Jr.* TB/3053
RANDOLPH S. BOURNE: War and the Intellectuals: *Collected Essays, 1915-1919. ‡ Edited by Carl Resek* TB/3043
A. RUSSELL BUCHANAN: The United States and World War II. † *Illus.* Vol. I TB/3044; Vol. II TB/3045
ABRAHAM CAHAN: The Rise of David Levinsky: *a documentary novel of social mobility in early twentieth century America. Intro. by John Higham* TB/1028
THOMAS C. COCHRAN: The American Business System: *A Historical Perspective, 1900-1955* TB/1080
FOSTER RHEA DULLES: America's Rise to World Power: 1898-1954. † *Illus.* TB/3021
JOHN D. HICKS: Republican Ascendancy: 1921-1933. † *Illus.* TB/3041
SIDNEY HOOK: Reason, Social Myths, and Democracy TB/1237
ROBERT HUNTER: Poverty: *Social Conscience in the Progressive Era. ‡ Edited by Peter d'A. Jones* TB/3065
WILLIAM L. LANGER & S. EVERETT GLEASON: The Challenge to Isolation: *The World Crisis of 1937-1940 and American Foreign Policy* Vol. I TB/3054; Vol. II TB/3055
WILLIAM E. LEUCHTENBURG: Franklin D. Roosevelt and the New Deal: 1932-1940. † *Illus.* TB/3025
ARTHUR S. LINK: Woodrow Wilson and the Progressive Era: 1910-1917. † *Illus.* TB/3023
GEORGE E. MOWRY: The Era of Theodore Roosevelt and the Birth of Modern America: 1900-1912. † *Illus.* TB/3022
RUSSEL B. NYE: Midwestern Progressive Politics: *A Historical Study of Its Origins and Development, 1870-1958* TB/1202
WILLIAM PRESTON, JR.: Aliens and Dissenters: *Federal Suppression of Radicals, 1903-1933* TB/1287
WALTER RAUSCHENBUSCH: Christianity and the Social Crisis. ‡ *Edited by Robert D. Cross* TB/3059
JACOB RIIS: The Making of an American. ‡ *Edited by Roy Lubove* TB/3070
PHILIP SELZNICK: TVA and the Grass Roots: *A Study in the Sociology of Formal Organization* TB/1230
IDA M. TARBELL: The History of the Standard Oil Company: *Briefer Version. ‡ Edited by David M. Chalmers* TB/3071
GEORGE B. TINDALL, Ed.: A Populist Reader ‡ TB/3069
TWELVE SOUTHERNERS: I'll Take My Stand: *The South and the Agrarian Tradition. Intro. by Louis D. Rubin, Jr., Biographical Essays by Virginia Rock* TB/1072

Anthropology

JACQUES BARZUN: Race: *A Study in Superstition. Revised Edition* TB/1172
JOSEPH B. CASAGRANDE, Ed.: In the Company of Man: *Twenty Portraits of Anthropological Informants. Illus.* TB/3047
W. E. LE GROS CLARK: The Antecedents of Man: *Intro. to Evolution of the Primates. º △ Illus.* TB/559
CORA DU BOIS: The People of Alor. *New Preface by the author. Illus.* Vol. I TB/1042; Vol. II TB/1043
RAYMOND FIRTH, Ed.: Man and Culture: *An Evaluation of the Work of Bronislaw Malinowski* ¶ º △ TB/1133
DAVID LANDY: Tropical Childhood: *Cultural Transmission and Learning in a Puerto Rican Village* ¶ TB/1235

L. S. B. LEAKEY: Adam's Ancestors: *The Evolution of Man and His Culture.* △ *Illus.* TB/1019

EDWARD BURNETT TYLOR: Religion in Primitive Culture. Part II of "Primitive Culture." § *Intro. by Paul Radin* TB/34

W. LLOYD WARNER: A Black Civilization: *A Study of an Australian Tribe.* ¶ *Illus.* TB/3056

Art and Art History

WALTER LOWRIE: Art in the Early Church. *Revised Edition. 452 illus.* TB/124

EMILE MÂLE: The Gothic Image: *Religious Art in France of the Thirteenth Century.* § △ *190 illus.* TB/44

MILLARD MEISS: Painting in Florence and Siena after the Black Death: *The Arts, Religion and Society in the Mid-Fourteenth Century. 169 illus.* TB/1148

ERICH NEUMANN: The Archetypal World of Henry Moore. △ *107 illus.* TB/2020

DORA & ERWIN PANOFSKY : Pandora's Box: *The Changing Aspects of a Mythical Symbol. Revised Edition. Illus.* TB/2021

ERWIN PANOFSKY: Studies in Iconology: *Humanistic Themes in the Art of the Renaissance.* △ *180 illustrations* TB/1077

ALEXANDRE PIANKOFF: The Shrines of Tut-Ankh-Amon. *Edited by N. Rambova. 117 illus.* TB/2011

JEAN SEZNEC: The Survival of the Pagan Gods: *The Mythological Tradition and Its Place in Renaissance Humanism and Art. 108 illustrations* TB/2004

OTTO VON SIMSON: The Gothic Cathedral: *Origins of Gothic Architecture and the Medieval Concept of Order.* △ *58 illus.* TB/2018

HEINRICH ZIMMER: Myth and Symbols in Indian Art and Civilization. *70 illustrations* TB/2005

Business, Economics & Economic History

REINHARD BENDIX: Work and Authority in Industry: *Ideologies of Management in the Course of Industrialization* TB/3035

GILBERT BURCK & EDITORS OF FORTUNE: The Computer Age: *And Its Potential for Management* TB/1179

THOMAS C. COCHRAN: The American Business System: *A Historical Perspective, 1900-1955* TB/1080

THOMAS C. COCHRAN: The Inner Revolution: *Essays on the Social Sciences in History* △ TB/1140

THOMAS C. COCHRAN & WILLIAM MILLER: The Age of Enterprise: *A Social History of Industrial America* TB/1054

ROBERT DAHL & CHARLES E. LINDBLOM: Politics, Economics, and Welfare: *Planning and Politico-Economic Systems Resolved into Basic Social Processes* TB/3037

PETER F. DRUCKER: The New Society: *The Anatomy of Industrial Order* △ TB/1082

EDITORS OF FORTUNE: America in the Sixties: *The Economy and the Society* TB/1015

ROBERT L. HEILBRONER: The Great Ascent: *The Struggle for Economic Development in Our Time* TB/3030

ROBERT L. HEILBRONER: The Limits of American Capitalism TB/1305

FRANK H. KNIGHT: The Economic Organization TB/1214

FRANK H. KNIGHT: Risk, Uncertainty and Profit TB/1215

ABBA P. LERNER: Everybody's Business: *Current Assumptions in Economics and Public Policy* TB/3051

ROBERT GREEN MC CLOSKEY: American Conservatism in the Age of Enterprise, 1865-1910 △ TB/1137

PAUL MANTOUX: The Industrial Revolution in the Eighteenth Century: *The Beginnings of the Modern Factory System in England* o △ TB/1079

WILLIAM MILLER, Ed.: Men in Business: *Essays on the Historical Role of the Entrepreneur* TB/1081

RICHARD B. MORRIS: Government and Labor in Early America △ TB/1244

HERBERT SIMON: The Shape of Automation: *For Men and Management* TB/1245

PERRIN STRYKER: The Character of the Executive: *Eleven Studies in Managerial Qualities* TB/1041

Education

JACQUES BARZUN: The House of Intellect △ TB/1051

RICHARD M. JONES, Ed.: Contemporary Educational Psychology: *Selected Readings* TB/1292

CLARK KERR: The Uses of the University TB/1264

JOHN U. NEF: Cultural Foundations of Industrial Civilization △ TB/1024

Historiography & Philosophy of History

JACOB BURCKHARDT: On History and Historians. △ *Introduction by H. R. Trevor-Roper* TB/1216

WILHELM DILTHEY: Pattern and Meaning in History: *Thoughts on History and Society.* o △ *Edited with an Introduction by H. P. Rickman* TB/1075

J. H. HEXTER: Reappraisals in History: *New Views on History & Society in Early Modern Europe* △ TB/1100

H. STUART HUGHES: History as Art and as Science: *Twin Vistas on the Past* TB/1207

RAYMOND KLIBANSKY & H. J. PATON, Eds.: Philosophy and History: *The Ernst Cassirer Festschrift. Illus.* TB/1115

ARNALDO MOMIGLIANO: Studies in Historiography o △ TB/1283

GEORGE H. NADEL, Ed.: Studies in the Philosophy of History: *Selected Essays from History and Theory* TB/1208

JOSE ORTEGA Y GASSET: The Modern Theme. *Introduction by Jose Ferrater Mora* TB/1038

KARL R. POPPER: The Open Society and Its Enemies △
Vol. I: *The Spell of Plato* TB/1101
Vol. II: *The High Tide of Prophecy: Hegel, Marx and the Aftermath* TB/1102

KARL R. POPPER: The Poverty of Historicism o △ TB/1126

G. J. RENIER: History: *Its Purpose and Method* △ TB/1209

W. H. WALSH: Philosophy of History: *An Introduction* △ TB/1020

History: General

WOLFGANG FRANKE: China and the West. *Trans by R. A. Wilson* TB/1326

L. CARRINGTON GOODRICH: A Short History of the Chinese People. △ *Illus.* TB/3015

DAN N. JACOBS & HANS H. BAERWALD: Chinese Communism: *Selected Documents* TB/3031

BERNARD LEWIS: The Arabs in History △ TB/1029

BERNARD LEWIS: The Middle East and the West o △ TB/1274

History: Ancient

A. ANDREWES: The Greek Tyrants △ TB/1103

ADOLF ERMAN, Ed. The Ancient Egyptians: *A Sourcebook of Their Writings. New material and Introduction by William Kelly Simpson* TB/1233

MICHAEL GRANT: Ancient History o △ TB/1190

SAMUEL NOAH KRAMER: Sumerian Mythology TB/1055

NAPHTALI LEWIS & MEYER REINHOLD, Eds.: Roman Civilization. *Sourcebook I: The Republic* TB/1231

NAPHTALI LEWIS & MEYER REINHOLD, Eds.: Roman Civilization. *Sourcebook II: The Empire* TB/1232

History: Medieval

P. BOISSONNADE: Life and Work in Medieval Europe: *The Evolution of the Medieval Economy, the 5th to the 15th Century.* o △ *Preface by Lynn White, Jr.* TB/1141

HELEN CAM: England before Elizabeth △ TB/1026

NORMAN COHN: The Pursuit of the Millennium: *Revolutionary Messianism in Medieval and Reformation Europe* △ TB/1037

3

G. G. COULTON: Medieval Village, Manor, and Monastery
TB/1022
CHRISTOPHER DAWSON, Ed.: Mission to Asia: *Narratives and Letters of the Franciscan Missionaries in Mongolia and China in the 13th and 14th Centuries* △
TB/315
HEINRICH FICHTENAU: The Carolingian Empire: *The Age of Charlemagne* △ TB/1142
GALBERT OF BRUGES: The Murder of Charles the Good. *Trans. with Intro. by James Bruce Ross* TB/1311
F. L. GANSHOF: Feudalism △ TB/1058
DENO GEANAKOPLOS: Byzantine East and Latin West: *Two Worlds of Christendom in the Middle Ages and Renaissance* TB/1265
EDWARD GIBBON: The Triumph of Christendom in the Roman Empire (*Chaps. XV-XX of "Decline and Fall,"* J. B. Bury edition). § △ Illus. TB/46
W. O. HASSALL, Ed.: Medieval England: *As Viewed by Contemporaries* △ TB/1205
DENYS HAY: Europe: The Emergence of an Idea TB/1275
DENYS HAY: The Medieval Centuries ° △ TB/1192
J. M. HUSSEY: The Byzantine World △ TB/1057
ROBERT LATOUCHE: The Birth of Western Economy: *Economic Aspects of the Dark Ages.* ° △ *Intro. by Philip Grierson* TB/1290
FERDINAND LOT: The End of the Ancient World and the Beginnings of the Middle Ages. *Introduction by Glanville Downey* TB/1044
ACHILLE LUCHAIRE: Social France at the Time of Philip Augustus. *New Intro. by John W. Baldwin* TB/1314
MARSILIUS OF PADUA: The Defender of the Peace. *Trans. with Intro. by Alan Gewirth* TB/1310
G. MOLLAT: The Popes at Avignon: 1305-1378 △ TB/308
CHARLES PETIT-DUTAILLIS: The Feudal Monarchy in France and England: *From the Tenth to the Thirteenth Century* ° △ TB/1165
HENRI PIRENNE: Early Democracies in the Low Countries: *Urban Society and Political Conflict in the Middle Ages and the Renaissance. Introduction by John H. Mundy* TB/1110
STEVEN RUNCIMAN: A History of the Crusades. △
Volume I: *The First Crusade and the Foundation of the Kingdom of Jerusalem. Illus.* TB/1143
Volume II: *The Kingdom of Jerusalem and the Frankish East, 1100-1187. Illus.* TB/1243
Volume III: *The Kingdom of Acre and the Later Crusades* TB/1298
SULPICIUS SEVERUS et al.: The Western Fathers: *Being the Lives of Martin of Tours, Ambrose, Augustine of Hippo, Honoratus of Arles and Germanus of Auxerre.* △ *Edited and trans. by F. O. Hoare* TB/309
J. M. WALLACE-HADRILL: The Barbarian West: *The Early Middle Ages, A.D. 400-1000* △ TB/1061

History: Renaissance & Reformation

JACOB BURCKHARDT: The Civilization of the Renaissance in Italy. △ *Intro. by Benjamin Nelson & Charles Trinkaus. Illus.* Vol. I TB/40; Vol. II TB/41
JOHN CALVIN & JACOPO SADOLETO: A Reformation Debate. *Edited by John C. Olin* TB/1239
ERNST CASSIRER: The Individual and the Cosmos in Renaissance Philosophy. △ *Translated with an Introduction by Mario Domandi* TB/1097
FEDERICO CHABOD: Machiavelli and the Renaissance △
TB/1193
EDWARD P. CHEYNEY: The Dawn of a New Era, 1250-1453. * Illus. TB/3002
G. CONSTANT: The Reformation in England: *The English Schism, Henry VIII, 1509-1547* △ TB/314
R. TREVOR DAVIES: The Golden Century of Spain, 1501-1621 ° △ TB/1194
G. R. ELTON: Reformation Europe, 1517-1559 ** ° △
TB/1270

DESIDERIUS ERASMUS: Christian Humanism and the Reformation: *Selected Writings. Edited and translated by John C. Olin* TB/1166
WALLACE K. FERGUSON et al.: Facets of the Renaissance
TB/1098
WALLACE K. FERGUSON et al.: The Renaissance: *Six Essays. Illus.* TB/1084
JOHN NEVILLE FIGGIS: The Divine Right of Kings. *Introduction by G. R. Elton* TB/1191
JOHN NEVILLE FIGGIS: Political Thought from Gerson to Grotius: 1414-1625: *Seven Studies. Introduction by Garrett Mattingly* TB/1032
MYRON P. GILMORE: The World of Humanism, 1453-1517. * Illus. TB/3003
FRANCESCO GUICCIARDINI: Maxims and Reflections of a Renaissance Statesman (*Ricordi*). *Trans. by Mario Domandi. Intro. by Nicolai Rubinstein* TB/1160
J. H. HEXTER: More's Utopia: *The Biography of an Idea. New Epilogue by the Author* TB/1195
HAJO HOLBORN: Ulrich von Hutten and the German Reformation TB/1238
JOHAN HUIZINGA: Erasmus and the Age of Reformation. △ *Illus.* TB/19
JOEL HURSTFIELD: The Elizabethan Nation △ TB/1312
JOEL HURSTFIELD, Ed.: The Reformation Crisis △ TB/1267
ULRICH VON HUTTEN et al.: On the Eve of the Reformation: *"Letters of Obscure Men." Introduction by Hajo Holborn* TB/1124
PAUL O. KRISTELLER: Renaissance Thought: *The Classic, Scholastic, and Humanist Strains* TB/1048
PAUL O. KRISTELLER: Renaissance Thought II: *Papers on Humanism and the Arts* TB/1163
NICCOLÒ MACHIAVELLI: History of Florence and of the Affairs of Italy: *from the earliest times to the death of Lorenzo the Magnificent.* △ *Introduction by Felix Gilbert* TB/1027
ALFRED VON MARTIN: Sociology of the Renaissance. *Introduction by Wallace K. Ferguson* TB/1099
GARRETT MATTINGLY et al.: Renaissance Profiles. △ *Edited by J. H. Plumb* TB/1162
MILLARD MEISS: Painting in Florence and Siena after the Black Death: *The Arts, Religion and Society in the Mid-Fourteenth Century.* △ *169 illus.* TB/1148
J. E. NEALE: The Age of Catherine de Medici ° △ TB/1085
ERWIN PANOFSKY: Studies in Iconology: *Humanistic Themes in the Art of the Renaissance.* △ *180 illustrations* TB/1077
J. H. PARRY: The Establishment of the European Hegemony: 1415-1715: *Trade and Exploration in the Age of the Renaissance* △ TB/1045
BUONACCORSO PITTI & GREGORIO DATI: Two Memoirs of Renaissance Florence: *The Diaries of Buonaccorso Pitti and Gregorio Dati. Ed. with an Intro. by Gene Brucker. Trans. by Julia Martines* TB/1333
J. H. PLUMB: The Italian Renaissance: *A Concise Survey of Its History and Culture* △ TB/1161
A. F. POLLARD: Henry VIII. ° △ *Introduction by A. G. Dickens* TB/1249
A. F. POLLARD: Wolsey. ° △ *Introduction by A. G. Dickens*
TB/1248
CECIL ROTH: The Jews in the Renaissance. *Illus.* TB/834
A. L. ROWSE: The Expansion of Elizabethan England. ° △ *Illus.* TB/1220
GORDON RUPP: Luther's Progress to the Diet of Worms ° △
TB/120
FERDINAND SCHEVILL: The Medici. *Illus.* TB/1010
FERDINAND SCHEVILL: Medieval and Renaissance Florence. *Illus.* Volume I: *Medieval Florence* TB/1090
Volume II: *The Coming of Humanism and the Age of the Medici* TB/1091
R. H. TAWNEY: The Agrarian Problem in the Sixteenth Century. *New Intro. by Lawrence Stone* TB/1315
G. M. TREVELYAN: England in the Age of Wycliffe, 1368-1520 ° △ TB/1112

History: Modern European

H. R. TREVOR-ROPER: Historical Essays ° △ TB/1269
ELIZABETH WISKEMANN: Europe of the Dictators, 1919-1945 ** ° △ TB/1273
JOHN B. WOLF: The Emergence of the Great Powers, 1685-1715. * Illus. TB/3010
JOHN B. WOLF: France: 1814-1919: The Rise of a Liberal-Democratic Society TB/3019

Intellectual History & History of Ideas

HERSCHEL BAKER: The Image of Man: A Study of the Idea of Human Dignity in Classical Antiquity, the Middle Ages, and the Renaissance TB/1047
R. R. BOLGAR: The Classical Heritage and Its Beneficiaries: From the Carolingian Age to the End of the Renaissance △ TB/1125
RANDOLPH S. BOURNE: War and the Intellectuals: Collected Essays, 1915-1919. △ ‡ Edited by Carl Resek TB/3043
J. BRONOWSKI & BRUCE MAZLISH: The Western Intellectual Tradition: From Leonardo to Hegel △ TB/3001
ERNST CASSIRER: The Individual and the Cosmos in Renaissance Philosophy. △ Translated with an Introduction by Mario Domandi TB/1097
NORMAN COHN: The Pursuit of the Millennium: Revolutionary Messianism in Medieval and Reformation Europe △ TB/1037
C. C. GILLISPIE: Genesis and Geology: The Decades before Darwin § TB/51
G. RACHEL LEVY: Religious Conceptions of the Stone Age and Their Influence upon European Thought. △ Illus. Introduction by Henri Frankfort TB/106
ARTHUR O. LOVEJOY: The Great Chain of Being: A Study of the History of an Idea TB/1009
FRANK E. MANUEL: The Prophets of Paris: Turgot, Condorcet, Saint-Simon, Fourier, and Comte △ TB/1218
PERRY MILLER & T. H. JOHNSON, Editors: The Puritans: A Sourcebook of Their Writings
    Vol. I TB/1093; Vol. II TB/1094
RALPH BARTON PERRY: The Thought and Character of William James: Briefer Version TB/1156
GEORG SIMMEL et al.: Essays on Sociology, Philosophy, and Aesthetics. ¶ Edited by Kurt H. Wolff TB/1234
BRUNO SNELL: The Discovery of the Mind: The Greek Origins of European Thought △ TB/1018
PAGET TOYNBEE: Dante Alighieri: His Life and Works. Edited with Intro. by Charles S. Singleton △ TB/1206
W. WARREN WAGAR, Ed.: European Intellectual History since Darwin and Marx TB/1297
PHILIP P. WIENER: Evolution and the Founders of Pragmatism. △ Foreword by John Dewey TB/1212
BASIL WILLEY: Nineteenth Century Studies: Coleridge to Matthew Arnold ° △ TB/1261
BASIL WILLEY: More Nineteenth Century Studies: A Group of Honest Doubters ° △ TB/1262

Law

EDWARD S. CORWIN: American Constitutional History: Essays edited by Alpheus T. Mason & Gerald Garvey TB/1136
ROBERT H. JACKSON: The Supreme Court in the American System of Government TB/1106
LEONARD W. LEVY, Ed.: American Constitutional Law: Historical Essays TB/1285
LEONARD W. LEVY: Freedom of Speech and Press in Early American History: Legacy of Suppression TB/1109
LEONARD W. LEVY, Ed.: Judicial Review and the Supreme Court TB/1296
LEONARD W. LEVY: The Law of the Commonwealth and Chief Justice Shaw TB/1309
RICHARD B. MORRIS: Fair Trial: Fourteen Who Stood Accused, from Anne Hutchinson to Alger Hiss. New Preface by the Author. TB/1335

Literature, Poetry, The Novel & Criticism

JAMES BAIRD: Ishmael: The Art of Melville in the Contexts of International Primitivism TB/1023
JACQUES BARZUN: The House of Intellect △ TB/1051
W. J. BATE: From Classic to Romantic: Premises of Taste in Eighteenth Century England TB/1036
RACHEL BESPALOFF: On the Iliad TB/2006
JAMES BOSWELL: The Life of Dr. Johnson & The Journal of a Tour to the Hebrides with Samuel Johnson LL.D.: Selections. ° △ Edited by F. V. Morley. Illus. by Ernest Shepard TB/1254
ERNST R. CURTIUS: European Literature and the Latin Middle Ages △ TB/2015
ADOLF ERMAN, Ed.: The Ancient Egyptians: A Sourcebook of Their Writings. New Material and Introduction by William Kelly Simpson TB/1233
ALFRED HARBAGE: As They Liked It: A Study of Shakespeare's Moral Artistry TB/1035
STANLEY R. HOPPER, Ed : Spiritual Problems in Contemporary Literature § TB/21
A. R. HUMPHREYS: The Augustan World: Society, Thought and Letters in 18th Century England ° △ TB/1105
ARNOLD KETTLE: An Introduction to the English Novel. △
    Volume I: Defoe to George Eliot TB/1011
    Volume II: Henry James to the Present TB/1012
RICHMOND LATTIMORE: The Poetry of Greek Tragedy △ TB/1257
J. B. LEISHMAN: The Monarch of Wit: An Analytical and Comparative Study of the Poetry of John Donne ° △ TB/1258
J. B. LEISHMAN: Themes and Variations in Shakespeare's Sonnets ° △ TB/1259
ROGER SHERMAN LOOMIS: The Development of Arthurian Romance △ TB/1167
JOHN STUART MILL: On Bentham and Coleridge. △ Introduction by F. R. Leavis TB/1070
KENNETH B. MURDOCK: Literature and Theology in Colonial New England TB/99
SAMUEL PEPYS: The Diary of Samuel Pepys. ° Edited by O. F. Morshead. Illus. by Ernest Shepard TB/1007
ST.-JOHN PERSE: Seamarks TB/2002
V. DE S. PINTO: Crisis in English Poetry, 1880-1940 ° TB/1260
ROBERT PREYER, Ed.: Victorian Literature TB/1302
GEORGE SANTAYANA: Interpretations of Poetry and Religion § TB/9
C. K. STEAD: The New Poetic: Yeats to Eliot △ TB/1263
HEINRICH STRAUMANN: American Literature in the Twentieth Century. △ Third Edition, Revised TB/1168
PAGET TOYNBEE: Dante Alighieri: His Life and Works. Edited with Intro. by Charles S. Singleton TB/1206
DOROTHY VAN GHENT: The English Novel: Form and Function TB/1050
BASIL WILLEY: Nineteenth Century Studies: Coleridge to Matthew Arnold △ TB/1261
BASIL WILLEY: More Nineteenth Century Studies: A Group of Honest Doubters ° △ TB/1262
RAYMOND WILLIAMS: Culture and Society, 1780-1950 ° △ TB/1252
RAYMOND WILLIAMS: The Long Revolution. ° △ Revised Edition TB/1253
MORTON DAUWEN ZABEL, Editor: Literary Opinion in America Vol. I TB/3013; Vol. II TB/3014

Myth, Symbol & Folklore

MIRCEA ELIADE: Cosmos and History: The Myth of the Eternal Return § △ TB/2050
MIRCEA ELIADE: Rites and Symbols of Initiation: The Mysteries of Birth and Rebirth § △ TB/1236
THEODOR H. GASTER: Thespis: Ritual, Myth and Drama in the Ancient Near East △ TB/1281

GERHART B. LADNER: The Idea of Reform: Its Impact on Christian Thought and Action in the Age of the Fathers   TB/149

ARTHUR DARBY NOCK: Early Gentile Christianity and Its Hellenistic Background   TB/111

ARTHUR DARBY NOCK: St. Paul o △   TB/104

ORIGEN: On First Principles. △ Edited by G. W. Butterworth. Introduction by Henri de Lubac   TB/311

JAMES PARKES: The Conflict of the Church and the Synagogue: The Jews and Early Christianity   TB/821

SULPICIUS SEVERUS et al.: The Western Fathers: Being the Lives of Martin of Tours, Ambrose, Augustine of Hippo, Honoratus of Arles and Germanus of Auxerre. △ Edited and translated by F. R. Hoare   TB/309

JOHANNES WEISS: Earliest Christianity: A History of the Period A.D. 30-150. Introduction and Bibliography by Frederick C. Grant   Volume I   TB/53
                                            Volume II TB/54

Christianity: The Middle Ages and The Reformation

ANSELM OF CANTERBURY: Truth, Freedom and Evil: Three Philosophical Dialogues. Ed., trans., and Intro. by Jasper Hopkins & Herbert Richardson   TB/317

JOHN CALVIN & JACOPO SADOLETO: A Reformation Debate. Edited by John C. Olin   TB/1239

G. CONSTANT: The Reformation in England: The English Schism, Henry VIII, 1509-1547 △   TB/314

CHRISTOPHER DAWSON, Ed.: Mission to Asia: Narratives and Letters of the Franciscan Missionaries in Mongolia and China in the 13th and 14th Centuries △
                                                 TB/315

JOHANNES ECKHART: Meister Eckhart: A Modern Translation by R. B. Blakney   TB/8

DESIDERIUS ERASMUS: Christian Humanism and the Reformation: Selected Writings. Edited and translated by John C. Olin   TB/1166

ÉTIENNE GILSON: Dante and Philosophy △   TB/1089

WILLIAM HALLER: The Rise of Puritanism △   TB/22

HAJO HOLBORN: Ulrich von Hutten and the German Reformation   TB/1238

JOHAN HUIZINGA: Erasmus and the Age of Reformation. △ Illus.   TB/19

A. C. MC GIFFERT: Protestant Thought Before Kant △ Preface by Jaroslav Pelikan   TB/93

JOHN T. MC NEILL: Makers of the Christian Tradition: From Alfred the Great to Schleiermacher △   TB/121

G. MOLLAT: The Popes at Avignon, 1305-1378 △   TB/308

GORDON RUPP: Luther's Progress to the Diet of Worms o △   TB/120

Christianity: The Protestant Tradition

KARL BARTH: Church Dogmatics: A Selection △   TB/95

KARL BARTH: Dogmatics in Outline △   TB/56

KARL BARTH: The Word of God and the Word of Man
                                                 TB/13

RUDOLF BULTMANN et al: Translating Theology into the Modern Age: Historical, Systematic and Pastoral Reflections on Theology and the Church in the Contemporary Situation. Volume 2 of Journal for Theology and the Church, edited by Robert W. Funk in association with Gerhard Ebeling   TB/252

WHITNEY R. CROSS: The Burned-Over District: The Social and Intellectual History of Enthusiastic Religion in Western New York, 1800-1850 △   TB/1242

NELS F. S. FERRÉ: Swedish Contributions to Modern Theology. New Preface by the Author. Additional chapter by William A. Johnson   TB/147

ERNST KÄSEMANN, et al.: Distinctive Protestant and Catholic Themes Reconsidered. Volume 3 of Journal for Theology and the Church, edited by Robert W. Funk in association with Gerhard Ebeling   TB/253

SOREN KIERKEGAARD: On Authority and Revelation: The Book on Adler. Translated by Walter Lowrie. Intro. by Frederick Sontag   TB/139

SOREN KIERKEGAARD: Crisis in the Life of an Actress and Other Essays on Drama. △ Trans. with Intro. by Stephen D. Crites   TB/145

SOREN KIERKEGAARD: Edifying Discourses. Edited with an Introduction by Paul Holmer   TB/32

SOREN KIERKEGAARD: The Journals of Kierkegaard. o △ Ed. with Intro. by Alexander Dru   TB/52

SOREN KIERKEGAARD: The Point of View for My Work as an Author: A Report to History. § Preface by Benjamin Nelson   TB/88

SOREN KIERKEGAARD: The Present Age. § △ Translated and edited by Alexander Dru. Introduction by Walter Kaufmann   TB/94

SOREN KIERKEGAARD: Purity of Heart △   TB/4

SOREN KIERKEGAARD: Repetition: An Essay in Experimental Psychology. △ Translated with Introduction & Notes by Walter Lowrie   TB/117

SOREN KIERKEGAARD: Works of Love: Some Christian Reflections in the Form of Discourses △   TB/122

WALTER LOWRIE: Kierkegaard: A Life   Vol. I   TB/89
                                        Vol. II TB/90

JOHN MACQUARRIE: The Scope of Demythologizing: Bultmann and His Critics △   TB/134

PERRY MILLER & T. H. JOHNSON, Editors: The Puritans: A Sourcebook of Their Writings   Vol. I   TB/1093
                                          Vol. II TB/1094

WOLFHART PANNENBERG, et al.: History and Hermeneutic. Volume 4 of Journal for Theology and the Church, edited by Robert W. Funk in association with Gerhard Ebeling   TB/254

JAMES M. ROBINSON et al.: The Bultmann School of Biblical Interpretation: New Directions? Volume 1 of Journal for Theology and the Church, edited by Robert W. Funk in association with Gerhard Ebeling
                                                 TB/251

F. SCHLEIERMACHER: The Christian Faith. △ Introduction by Richard R. Niebuhr   Vol. I   TB/108
                                          Vol. II TB/109

F. SCHLEIERMACHER: On Religion: Speeches to Its Cultured Despisers. Intro. by Rudolf Otto   TB/36

TIMOTHY L. SMITH: Revivalism and Social Reform: American Protestantism on the Eve of the Civil War
                                                 TB/1229

PAUL TILLICH: Dynamics of Faith △   TB/42

PAUL TILLICH: Morality and Beyond △   TB/142

EVELYN UNDERHILL: Worship △   TB/10

Christianity: The Roman and Eastern Traditions

DOM CUTHBERT BUTLER: Western Mysticism: The Teaching of Augustine, Gregory and Bernard on Contemplation and the Contemplative Life § o △   TB/312

A. ROBERT CAPONIGRI, Ed.: Modern Catholic Thinkers I: God and Man △   TB/306

A. ROBERT CAPONIGRI, Ed.: Modern Catholic Thinkers II: The Church and the Political Order△   TB/307

THOMAS CORBISHLEY, S.J.: Roman Catholicism △   TB/112

CHRISTOPHER DAWSON: The Historic Reality of Christian Culture   TB/305

G. P. FEDOTOV: The Russian Religious Mind: Kievan Christianity, the 10th to the 13th centuries TB/370

ÉTIENNE GILSON: The Spirit of Thomism   TB/313

GABRIEL MARCEL: Being and Having: An Existential Diary. △ Introduction by James Collins   TB/310

GABRIEL MARCEL: Homo Viator: Introduction to a Metaphysic of Hope   TB/397

FRANCIS DE SALES: Introduction to the Devout Life. Trans. by John K. Ryan   TB/316

GUSTAVE WEIGEL, S. J.: Catholic Theology in Dialogue
                                                 TB/301

10

12